WHEN THE SPIDER DANCED

WHEN THE FOLK DANCE

WHEN THE SPIDER DANCED
Notes from an African village

Alexander Alland, Jr.
Columbia University

WAVELAND

PRESS, INC.

Prospect Heights, Illinois

For information about this book, write or call:
Waveland Press, Inc.
P.O. Box 400
Prospect Heights, Illinois 60070
(708) 634-0081

For Tchina Kofi, Afua Morofyé, Ajoa Badu,
Kofi Apo, Kwamé Apo, and all the
other members of my Abron family and friends.

For their children and grandchildren.
And in memory of Kwasi (Tan) Daté.

ISBN 0-88133-553-3

Printed in the United States of America

7 6 5 4 3 2 1

Contents

Acknowledgments

The research on which this book is based was supported by the Yale University program in African studies; Yale University Department of Anthropology, summer 1960; and the National Institute of Mental Health, fall, winter, and spring 1961–62. Part of the material appears in my Yale doctoral dissertation *Health and Disease in an African Society,* 1963. The dissertation was supervised by Professor William Davenport, whose guidance and patience are gratefully acknowledged.

I made three trips to the Abron. These occurred in the summer of 1960, from November to April of 1961–62, and for ten days in March of 1973. My wife, Sonia, joined me in the field for four weeks in March of 1962. During that time, she gathered important material, particularly on women's behavior. She has also helped with the revising of this manuscript.

I wish to thank Ms. Marilyn Paul and Mr. Steven Greenberg, who accompanied me on my last trip to Diassenpa, in 1973. Several of Ms. Paul's photographs appear as illustrations in this work.

I also wish to thank Ms. Maureen Mahon and Ms. Elizabeth Knappman, my editors at Anchor Press/Doubleday, for their encouragement, help, and advice.

The names of individuals referred to in a negative light have been changed. This includes "Dupont," the French trader. All humans are complicated, and if I have emphasized only the weaker side of some, it has been to make a point about the Abron or the setting in which they find themselves.

Introduction

It is no accident that Lévi-Strauss begins *Tristes Tropiques* with a denial of the joys of travel. Few anthropologists are travelers. Our identification is with people, not places.

Some anthropologists move in space to conquer time. The search for the primitive is the search for our own beginnings. Yet there is no time machine. Too often, the societies we study represent exploited remnants of once independent cultures. No living contemporary society, even that recently discovered tribe in the Philippines, can stand in for our own primordial condition. Every society in the world has been touched, even if indirectly, by the spread of Eastern or Western civilization. This process began centuries ago, long before Europe embarked on its age of discovery. The movement outward began with the rise of great trading nations in the Middle East and Asia and continued with the perpetual expansion and contraction of Asian, African, and European empires down to our own time. The New World, relatively isolated before the Spanish conquest, was nonetheless affected by the rise of its own civilizations in the valleys of Mexico and in the highlands of Guatemala and Peru. When the Spanish conquistadors came, they started a wave of disease and commercial exploitation that rocked the foundations of every society in the New World.

The task of anthropologists is to study, and gather information on the extent and variety of, human behavior. Our mandate is to seek generalizations about the human condition. Although we are employed primarily by universities, more and more anthropologists are beginning to work for government agencies.

Most of us see anthropology as a means of documenting the richness of our species' creative capacities. Each time a way of life disappears, the repertoire of human experience is diminished. We are witnesses to that diminution, and our books are the guardians of variety. On a more subjective level, field work challenges our personal values. After living in another culture, we never see things the same way again. In this respect, its effect is comparable to that of psychoanalysis.

When work begins, anthropologists are ignorant of even the most basic rules of behavior. Socially, we are infants who must grow like Alice to satisfy the time limits of research, the foundation that has granted its financial support, and the people we study. They, in turn, cannot believe that our heads can be so thick, our ability to learn language so limited, and our physical skill so lacking.

Looking back, I remember an Abron woman spinning thread. In one hand, she holds an amorphous, loose ball of raw cotton. She pulls and twists at it as the beginning of a coherent thread forms. This is deftly attached to the top of a thin stick weighted at the bottom with a ball of clay. The point of the stick protrudes through the clay, forming a top. The woman spins the top with her free hand and somehow a thread forms around the spindle. As the top spins, she pulls more fiber away from the ball, twisting it with her fingers, letting it wind onto the top. No motion is lost. The thread is even and continuous. The action is mysterious to my own muscular system.

The thread becomes a spider web in my mind. The woman becomes a spider. How can I know a spider? The spider does not learn to spin. This woman was once a little girl. Her mother spent many hours spinning while she watched, until, one day, she tried to spin as her mother did. At first it was difficult. Her mother did not correct her, but let her try again, watch again, try again, until she could do it herself. The movements became natural, and a skill formed that would not be lost until old age took the deftness out of her fingers.

Why does a woman coming back from the water hole with a full basin have leafy branches in the water? Is she going to cook them? I follow her home. She takes the branches out of the basin and throws them aside on the trash heap, which will be swept up later. Must one transport plants of some sort along with water? Women carrying large clay pots or buckets bring water only. Why the difference? Nothing simpler, I'm told. The basins are flat and wide—poor for water transport. As a woman walks, the rhythm of her steps sets up a rhythm in the water. In a deep pot, this is unimportant, the water will not spill; but in the wide and shallow basin, it will soon slosh out. The branches are a simple but effective tool. They break the rhythm of the water and it stays in the basin.

Early in field work, I began to learn how and why things were done. After some time, I thought I understood, even felt, as an Abron might. I began to identify with "my people," so much so that during a trip north to "alien" country my attitude toward the non-Abron villagers was colored by the sentiments expressed by my Abron companions. I thought that my feelings of mistrust and hostility must in some way be Abron.

I am white-skinned, but after several weeks in the field, I forgot that I did not look like everyone else. Not shaving, I had little cause to use a mirror. As my identity became Abron, I turned black in my imagination. I tried to convert this into physical change by sunbathing. From the Abron point of view, it was probably one of my most idiotic behaviors. Their country is about six degrees north of the equator, and all normal people seek the shade at midday. My African mother, Afua Morofyé, concerned for my health and sanity, used to ask me why I lay in the sun. If I wanted to get black, she said, I should eat lots of cayenne pepper. This was not her belief but, rather, her metaphor for my stupidity. Of course, I did not really change much. At the end of field work a villager summed it up well when he said to me, "White man, when you came here you were fat and white; now you are thin and red."

How much an anthropologist is really able to integrate himself into a foreign culture, both in his own mind and in the minds of the people he studies, varies from anthropologist to anthropologist and from culture to culture. The task is not self-integration but understanding. This must be translated into scientific discourse, which someday all anthropologists hope will be used to generate a theory of culture and human behavior.

How much of this is self-deluding? What has an anthropologist's description to do with reality? All perceptions are filtered through an established category system. A theoretical structure imposes its own form on data and the analyst may reap what he intended to harvest in the first place. Here anthropologists remain prisoners of their own culture.

Research and analysis are based on assumptions about the scientific method, and current theories determine what data are significant and what are irrelevant. When specific rules of data gathering and reportage are followed, a limited truth emerges based on stated operations. Its validity may be annulled by new theories and new ways of gathering information. New theories may allow old data to reveal hidden things. For example, stone tools collected years ago become new sources of data as archaeological theory and methods of analysis change. Ideas about the significance of social relationships occupy the same place in cultural anthropology as stone tools do in archaeology.

My own orientation is to look at culture as the result of two intertwined processes. The first involves a relationship with nature which, through time, allows a human group to come to terms with its environment. This is the process of ecological adaptation in which information derived from the experience of living within a particular natural setting is employed in the mastery of that setting. This adaptation may occur as the result of conscious thinking and the testing of hypotheses concerning this or that aspect of interaction between human beings and nature, or it may result from an unconscious shaping in which the environment "rewards" particular behaviors and "punishes" others. The speed at which such a process works is affected by the rapidity of feedbacks from the environment and the amount of noise in the system. When the feedbacks are unambiguous, adaptation may be rapid. When the system is noisy, adaptation may be slow. In adaptation to disease, for example, the spontaneous recovery of sick individuals may add noise to the system so that no clear indication of what treatments cure patients will emerge. The pathways involved in disease transmission may also complicate and add noise to a system. When a particular disease is common, severe, has distinctive symptoms, is highly contagious, and is transmitted directly from individual to individual, information about its transmission should accumulate rapidly. The sick may then be quarantined to restrict its further spread. When a disease is rare, when its symptoms are vague or similar to other diseases, and when the mode of transmission involves an agent, such as a mosquito, information may be so clouded as to make the actual source of infection difficult to discover.

The second process that shapes a culture involves the human capacity to think metaphorically—to extend and contract the range of meanings of symbols and to combine symbols into systems of meaning that may be independent of the original inputs. Humans may use environmental information to satisfy behavioral problems that derive from within the behavioral system itself; for example, the objective fact of disease may be translated into a metaphor for social conflict. When this happens, the focus of medical theory and treatment may shift from objective attempts to cure specific pathological conditions, to attempts to cure social pathology such as conflict between social groups. The fact that most illness (at least of a mundane nature) is self-limiting—most patients get well on their own—allows the metaphorical system to work.

Lévi-Strauss and other structural anthropologists have suggested that these metaphorical systems have a logic of their own, that they follow unconscious grammatical rules just as everyday language does. This means that systems of thought are not free to vary in all directions as they change through time and space, but are, rather, constrained by mental processes.

The human adaptation involves accommodation to the external environment and accommodation within an ordered cultural system which follows its own rules of development. The adaptation is therefore both internal (that is, it involves accommodations within the cognitive system, which must obey its own rules) and external (that is, it must prove at least minimally successful as an adaptation to a specific environmental niche).

Our species therefore faces in two directions. The environment does indeed shape behavior (as behavior shapes the environment), but behavior is also shaped from within to meet the requirements of internal consistency.

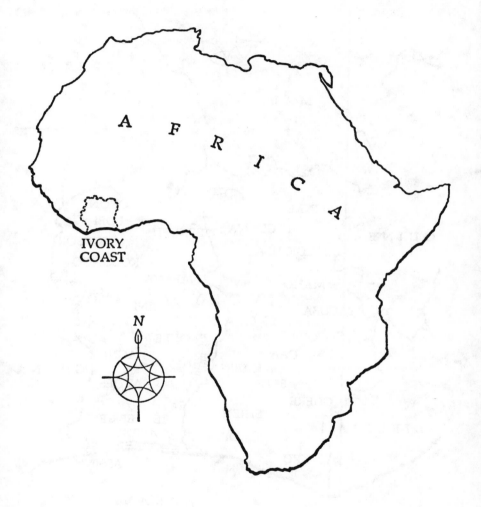

Africa and the Ivory Coast

Ethnic map of the Ivory Coast

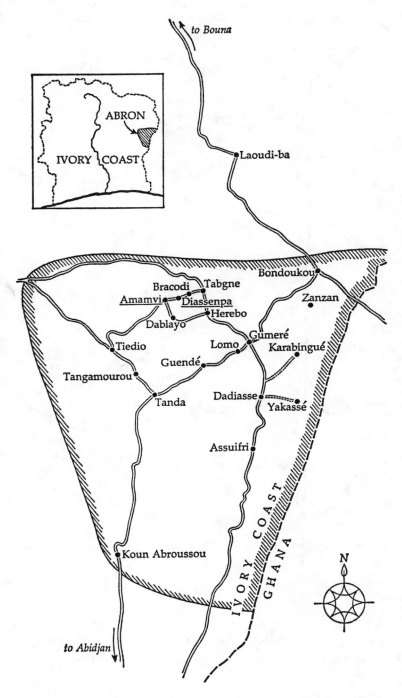

to Bouna

ABRON

IVORY COAST

Laoudi-ba

Bondoukou

Bracodi · Tabgne

Zanzan

Amamvi · Diassenpa

Herebo

Dablayo

Gumeré

Tiedio

Lomo

Karabingué

Guendé

Tangamourou

Dadiasse

Tanda

Yakassé

Assuifri

Koun Abroussou

IVORY COAST

GHANA

N

to Abidjan

Abron area

1
Abidjan

The flight from Paris to the Ivory Coast crosses the Mediterranean by way of Marseilles and Morocco. After the Atlas Mountains, the Sahara spreads southward, an unbroken but changing pattern of sand and rock: reds, ochres, and black. In the rainy season, this view eventually gives way to tiers of gray clouds which are broken only when the plane descends in its final approach to Abidjan. It comes in low over the mat of green that lines the runways, splashes down, and taxies toward the terminal. As soon as the engines die, a line of Africans clad only in shorts and hooded plastic raincoats that stick to their bare, humid backs race toward the plane carrying umbrellas. They look like monks in transparent habits. Each one accompanies a single passenger to the terminal and then disappears into an anonymous crowd of black faces. The passengers themselves begin an ill-tempered push through customs. After the last paper is checked and stamped, new African faces take up the escort again, this time toward the taxi stands. Renaults, Simcas, Peugeots, their drivers competing for space, for fares, and for time, race toward Abidjan. The route is crowded with turbaned herders and their high-humped Zebu cattle from Bamako and beyond; having traveled the trade routes for months, and coming finally to the hungry city, the meat is well seasoned into muscle. Mixed with the animal traffic is the traffic of buses, cars, trucks, motorcycles, bikes, and hundreds of pedestrians. Small houses spotted with fungus and green algae line the road. They smell of decay. This is the unseductive smell of the wet tropics.

The plateau, jutting up above the port, is still the major white neighborhood of Abidjan. It contains the older (and some new) substantial buildings, apartment

houses, government centers, fine shops, and one of two
"European" hotels of the city proper. In 1960, the
richer whites and the new African elite began to move
across one of the lagoons to Cocody, the suburb of the
rich and influential.

Abidjan is engaged in a constant rite of renewal. Like
all cities, Abidjan builds toward urban grandeur impa-
tiently, but solidly, with reinforced concrete. One can
easily date the structures. Before independence, architects concentrated on buildings suited to the tropical
heat. Open hallways running along the outside were
protected from the sun by louvered walls. The apart-
ments, by virtue of this system, were insulated from the
direct rays of the sun. Before the era of air conditioning, there was no such thing as a solid wall in Abidjan.
But with independence, air conditioning became a prestige symbol. In the sixties, government architects spent
a good deal of their time plugging leaks intentionally
designed for ventilation. Sometimes this presented an
almost insurmountable problem of engineering. The
Palace of Justice, for example, an immense structure
almost a block square, had all the solidity of a well-
aged Swiss cheese. It and other buildings like it but on
a less grand scale are obsolescent—antique monuments
of the colonial period. Newer buildings, architected for
climate control, look like some of the familiar offices of
Madison Avenue, although there is perhaps more ex-
perimentation in Abidjan than in New York.

In the daytime, people fill the sidewalks below the
balconies and promenades. Many are engaged in petty
commerce. Street merchants hawk individual cigarettes,
the sale of which yields small profits for the seller and
convenience for those who could never afford the luxury of a whole pack. Everything is sold in small quantities. Other wares include an array of European and African cloth, pens, watches, old magazines (often bought
for their pictures), peanuts, bananas, kola nuts, and
palm wine (which I later discovered is often watered
down in the city).

Vendors trail the pedestrian with loads of badly

carved, mass-produced art ranging from crude copies of museum pieces to the slick items now sold at home in bookshops and drugstores. The name "airport art" has been acquired by these items, since the tourist is deluged with them on arrival and departure at every major air terminal in Africa. Someday an art historian will, no doubt, divide these objects into periods of artistic production—formative airport, Baroque airport, decadent airport, etc. Regional styles will be more difficult to determine, however, since there is almost no variation. I suspect that somewhere, hidden in central Africa, there is a factory that produces these sculptures on an assembly line and ships them out to all parts of the continent. This art style is the combined result of missionary destruction (no idols allowed) and the poor taste of the buying public. The Ivory Coast was formerly one of the major centers of West African art, and even today exciting pieces are produced, their themes a compromise between past tradition and recent history, but much of the country has turned its back on tradition.

This alienation from the past affects the dress of the educated Ivoirian. Middle-class city dwellers prefer drab European clothing. Yet, poor or less acculturated people have not lost their love of color. During their leisure time or in the market, a center of popular culture in the city, they dress, often with great care, in bright robes. The men are draped in chromatic togas, the women in long skirts and blouses of bright cotton. The total impression of flowers, lagoon, trees, and above all, the people, turns the memory of Europe and America into a dull grayness. Even in rain, the color refuses to be muted, as the shiny wet streets reinforce the brilliance denied by cloudy skies.

On Sunday, the shops, businesses, and government offices are closed; the market offers the only morning activity. The only mixed European and African market in the Ivory Coast is on the plateau. It evolved as a convenience for the French inhabitants of the city, for it makes the daily shopping rapid and efficient. The market occupies a large square. The stalls of *petits blancs commerçants* are on three sides, partially enclosing a central plaza. Wine, cheese, meat, canned goods, soaps, and other imported products are sold out of these small shops, which are locked after hours by pulling down the overhead rolling metal doors so common in Paris, where they serve as a protection as much against riots as against thieves. Facing these small stores, and protected from the rain by a roof, is a line of cement tables. These are reserved at a small fee for Africans, generally women, who sell locally grown fruit and vegetables. Piling their produce in enticing patterns, these market women compete for trade vociferously. Few sell more than one variety of vegetable, and there are always several stalls to choose from. Prices are the same from seller to seller. Competition rests upon the size and beauty of the product and the lung power of the women, who shout, *"Bons grands oignons très forts"* (a quality admired locally and so, they suppose, by everyone), *"Poireaux longs et frais, Les jolies oranges douces"* (often bright green but very sweet), and other themes appropriate to their wares.

All sellers offering the same product cluster in a particular section of the market. As one passes down the line of stalls, the colors change from the green of lettuce and peppers to the yellow of bananas, the brown and gold of pineapple, and the brilliant red of cayenne. Young men with boxes follow shoppers, offering them a *caisse* for a few francs. They may also be hired to carry the day's shopping to the buyer's house or car, although most European shoppers come to market accompanied by a servant. The center of the market forms an open plaza. There, women who cannot afford or will not pay the stall tariff, set up trade. They often sell products strange to the European palate: manioc, the long and unsweet yam, millet, short-grain rice, and large green plantains. They cater to the tastes of the other market women, who will exchange part of their small daily profit for an evening's food.

The market opens early, almost with the coming of

daylight, and is closed by noon. The silence of Abidjan during the heat of the day, when all its shops are closed, deepens on Sunday. Africans who during the week remain on the plateau for the afternoon's business, resting and talking in the *jardin public,* go home to their families and friends. The European finishes his Sunday afternoon dinner and sleeps behind closed shutters. The noise and movement flow away from the plateau as the life of the city returns to its crowded quarters.

My first Sunday in Abidjan, I followed the Africans home. The rain had stopped for a time, and although the sky was thatched with heavy clouds, I walked without a raincoat. There is little afternoon sleeping in Adjamé or Tricheville. People visit one another, play, dance, drink, fight, and above all, discuss. Discussion is the end product of every other activity. West Africans value musicality and fluidity of speech above all else. They admire the ability to dance and play the drums and other instruments in youths, but retain their deepest respect for skill in oratory. "He speaks well" is the highest compliment one West African can pay to another.

My curiosity was met by the curiosity of the inhabitants as I walked (white people do not walk in West Africa) from Abidjan past the *château d'eau,* twin water towers that serve the city, and the museum of the Scientific and Cultural Center, toward the army camp that borders Adjamé. The quarter was crowded with the normal traffic of people and cars coming in from the bush, as well as those returning from work.

Adjamé is the terminal for the *rapide,* small Renault trucks that serve as the non-scheduled bus lines for the Ivory Coast. Eight blocks into Adjamé, I heard the sound of drums and began to follow it through side streets lined by windowless houses. Finally, I came to a large open space crowded with people. As I pushed through, I saw a group of drummers and, in the center of the crowd, in a space cleared for them, a man and a woman dancing. Their faces expressed pleasure, ease, and confidence. The woman was purple-black, thin, of medium height, and dressed in a Dutch export print of bright yellow and red. The rims of her ears were pierced from the top down to the lobes and covered with small gold rings set into the skin. Skilled at isolating the movement of her arms and shoulders from the rest of her body, she created her own polyrhythms in dance as she followed the complex drum beat. The male dancer, opposite, imitated her movements, but at the same time translated them into more staccato muscular forms. He was dressed in a toga of green and orange tied at the waist, his arms, back, and chest bare. After several minutes, another man jumped into the circle and challenged the male dancer. Both men danced, sometimes opposite the woman, sometimes opposite each other, until one capitulated and, returning to the sidelines, became a spectator once more. The audience encouraged the best dancer with shouts of praise and approval, but no one criticized any of the participants. The woman remained dancing almost in trance, without tiring for the two hours I stood watching.

Dance is the art form in Africa that persists after all others have given way. African music based on the complex rhythm of a drum chorus provides an emotional background for movement, and the movement in turn inspires the drummers to outdo each other in rhythmic improvisation. Dance and music become merged into a single art as the musicians' syncopation is picked up and elaborated by the dancers, who follow the drum with their bodies. Where Western music has emphasized tonality, African music has stressed rhythm. This is what lies at the divergence of style, and it is the style of each which has in turn affected the evolution of the dance.

Later the same day, on the sidewalk in front of the hotel, a group of Gueré from Man, on the Liberian border, put on a show for the café patrons. These were acrobatic dancers, professionals even in Gueré land, who indulge their audiences with carefully rehearsed tricks. The finale comes when adult male dancers throw young boys into the air over the points of sharp knives and then catch them dangerously close to the long blades. Well calculated to startle, this spectacle has become a secular rite.

The lagoons of Abidjan surround the plateau on two sides. During the dry months, water skiers and dugout canoes compete for space in the bay between the city and Cocody. The French, particular about what kind of water they drink or swim in, ski in an industrial cloaca which is becoming more polluted as the city grows. The canoemen, from coastal ethnic groups, Abidji or Assini, apparently undisturbed by civilization, fish the water with small nets. One can sit poolside at the Piscine Aquarium or at the Relais Arienne (the Air France hotel) and watch the fishermen drop their nets. The difference in the standard of living between these fishermen and the Europeans is astonishing. There were several fine restaurants in Abidjan where one could eat for twenty dollars, and it was difficult to find a European-style meal under three. Even on the Rue de Commerce (the Boulevard Général de Gaulle before independence), which rings the commercial district below the plateau, small cafés charged horrendous prices for simple meals. These prices were striking when compared to the earnings of the average African. Clerks in local businesses earned about forty dollars a month; servants more if they were qualified cooks and less if they were houseboys. Waiters at the big hotels did better, because they got a standard 10 per cent of the inflated prices as tips.

These low wages feed more than just the immediate family of the worker. Jobless relatives come from the bush in search of employment. The major item in their diet is starch: rice, yams, plantains, and manioc covered with a hot sauce of cayenne and okra. Only the coastal fishermen who live in villages close to the city on the shores of the Atlantic manage to eat more than just enough protein.

Meat served in the hotels and restaurants of Abidjan was flown or shipped in frozen, and even Bamako beef was expensive. Eggs ran between $1.50 and $2.00 a dozen. Local fruits and vegetables were cheap in season, but the French inhabitants often bought expensive Moroccan oranges as well as apples and pears from France.

The prices of luxury goods were higher than food. The West African franc (CFA) is worth twice as much as the old French franc (it was 250 to the dollar in 1960–62), but prices in Abidjan shops were marked almost as high as they were in France. For example, books priced at 500 francs in Paris cost 450 francs CFA in Abidjan. Much of this increase was due to the large import duty on manufactured goods, which automatically raised the price on such items as radios, cars, refrigerators, and air conditioners.

The Ivory Coast runs on a dual economy. There is a small middle class and most of the wealth is concentrated in or near Abidjan. It is easy to see the contrast between rich and poor, provided one walks away from the plateau or Cocody. Unfortunately, few Europeans or African visitors do this, partially because of disinterest, partially out of fear. Even on the plateau, however, there are beggars who invade hotel lobbies and local bars, but after a while they fade into the background. Guests are protected by the vigilance of waiters and bellhops, who constantly chase them away.

My first Monday in Abidjan, I set off to meet the American officials stationed in the Ivory Coast. At the time (1960), we had only a small consular office, with a professional staff of three as well as two secretaries and an African librarian, who is still a fixture at the new American Embassy with its staff of over fifty. In addition, since independence, we have added a large mission from AID, a USIA office, and a scattered deployment of Peace Corps teachers. During my first trip, I felt that I had really left American influence behind; today, English with an American accent is common in the shops and recreation facilities of Abidjan, and one is likely to meet an American in almost any large population center in the country.

The best way to travel in Abidjan is either on foot or by taxi. In 1961, a new bus service was introduced by the government, but taxis are cheap and even many working-class Africans use them, a group sharing the common fare. The buses are crowded and restricted in their routing.

I hailed a taxi in front of the hotel, and in my best French requested that the driver take me to the Ambassade Américaine. He nodded and we went off in a direction that seemed a bit strange, away from the plateau and over the bridge to Tricheville. When we had penetrated well into the center of Tricheville, the taxi stopped in front of a bar surrounded by brightly dressed prostitutes, looking rather ghostly with white face powder on their black faces. *"J'ai dit l'Ambassade Américaine,"* I told the driver. He smiled back at me knowingly, obviously sympathizing with my embarrassment, which was real enough but which was caused for reasons other than my supposed sheepish desire to visit a whorehouse. I tried to engage the driver in a meaningful conversation but found his French more limited than my own. When he had heard my request, the word *Américaine* was all the stimulus needed to take me where he had obviously taken others. In my frustration, non-sexual at the moment, I looked out at the bar once again, and this time, over the heads of the ladies, I noticed a sign. The mystery was solved. Painted in red on a white background was BAR AMERICAIN.

Back at the hotel, I asked the desk clerk for new directions and set off again, this time as a pedestrian. It turned out that the American Consulate was only three blocks from the hotel, in an apartment building. There was no sign in red and white, but a flag hanging from a window on the fifth floor announced the location of the American officials I wanted to see.

Americans in distress rarely turn up in Abidjan, and I was welcomed with great courtesy and interest. One of the vice-consuls took me out to meet the government officials necessary for the project I had in mind. This involved both permission to travel in the bush and the

formality of informing the government that I was a visiting scientist. At the time, most of the government
officials were French. During my second trip, in 1961,
most of these had been replaced by Africans, although
Frenchmen still held several major posts as advisers.

The Abron live 250 miles northeast of Abidjan, on
the Ghana border. The one rail line in the Ivory Coast
bisects the country, miles from my destination. I was
therefore forced to find other transportation. In the
rainy season this can be a problem, since most drivers
hesitate to risk the muddy upcountry roads. First I
tried to rent a car. When the rental agency heard that I
wanted to drive in the bush, they offered me a derelict
car for five hundred dollars a month with no guarantees
on maintenance. I then consulted the taxi companies
and was told that no one would take an automobile
north in such weather. Fortunately, a taxi driver who
had taken me to his *patron* to discuss rentals told me
that his brother had a car for hire. I agreed to visit him
that evening in Adjamé.

When I arrived, it was dark and the back streets on
which we drove were unlit. The road was full of
potholes and difficult to maneuver, a preview, I
thought, of conditions in the bush. We finally arrived at
a small house and entered into the gloom cut only by a
small kerosene lamp on a low table. The taxi driver's
brother was asleep and he went to awaken him. I did
not see the driver again until he emerged from somewhere to drive me home. I sat down on a homemade
bamboo chair and peered into the dark. After I got
used to it, I saw several faces looking out at me from
various corners. No one spoke until my host, still partially asleep, emerged from another, darker room and
welcomed me. According to local rules of etiquette, this
was a signal for my official arrival. Suddenly the room
became animated, as each person, perhaps six in all,
greeted me. My hosts spoke a brand of French with
which I was totally unfamiliar and they did not seem to
understand much of what I said. After several minutes
of semi-communication, someone said, "You speak

English?" For an instant, I was relieved. We could communicate through this interpreter who offered himself from the shadows. It turned out, however, that this overture was merely a friendly gesture offered in the only English he knew. Finally, and I am still not sure how it came about, I realized that they would take me as far as the American missionaries in Koun-Fao, forty miles from my final destination. The price for the ride was eighty dollars. Unable to bargain, and considering this too expensive, I refused their offer and the taxi driver took me back to the hotel, where I went to sleep dreaming of my vanishing money, the Africa I thought I would never see, and the angry university that had provided me with a generous grant.

Around midnight, I awoke with a high fever. The thought of being sick in Africa had occurred to me often, but I did not expect to be stricken in Abidjan. My imagination had constructed a more romantic setting somewhere in the forest, to be saved from death by the ministrations of a shaman whose bitter herbal potions worked better than our own medicines. I got up and took some antibiotics bought for such emergencies. Back in bed, I began to enjoy the morbid pleasure that comes with having a fever in the tropics. Even though the surface of my body was hot, I felt cold. I soon discovered that the warmth of my body reflecting off the blankets felt good but the fever amplified my anxiety. Filled with self-doubts, I began to reflect on what had led me to Abidjan. My mind raced back and forth between childhood and my final decision to become an anthropologist. The earliest remembered influence could be pushed back to my fifth year, when I first heard a weekly radio program featuring Joseph Marais. Framed around his travels in South Africa, Marais presented Boer and English folk songs. The initial delight that this ethnic music aroused in me soon expanded to include the more exotic tonal and rhythmic patterns of Indian and black African music. My parents encouraged this interest and in different ways helped to increase my appreciation of the world's artistic tradi-

tions. My mother, a dancer and choreographer, who in
the thirties staged several productions for the Federal
Theatre, drew much of her own inspiration from folk
themes although she was trained in classical ballet and
modern dance. It was her ability to combine the
threads of many techniques that first showed me how
various artistic traditions could contribute to the
enrichment of one's own culture.

My father, a photographer, was fascinated by ethnic
diversity. Between my sixth birthday and the beginning
of adolescence, he worked on two books in which he
expressed the poetry and variety of New York's minority groups. Frequently he took me on his photo explo-
rations, which ranged through all of New York's ethnic
communities, including Gypsies and black Jews. I
learned that the city and its varied neighborhoods contained a fascinating mosaic of human types and cultures. During these years, I was exposed to Korean and
Haitian dancing, Chinese music, and black culture,
which was beginning to enter the consciousness of New
York intellectuals through the writings of Richard
Wright, Roi Ottley, and Langston Hughes. The dancer
Pearl Primus was a family friend.

Parallel to this early ethnic exposure, my interests
turned toward science. My high school was a few
blocks from the American Museum of Natural History,
and I became a frequent visitor to its varied exhibi-
tions. I was particularly interested in microbiology and
remember taking specimens of protozoa cultures
behind the scenes to the fifth floor of the museum.
There I shared taxonomic problems with Libby
Hyman, known to students of comparative vertebrate
anatomy as the author of what was then the most widely
used text in the field. Her book had been written to
subsidize her first love, invertebrates, and she spent patient hours with me peering into the microscope and
consulting Ward and Whipple's masterpiece on fresh-
water biology.

My dual interests made the choice of a profession
difficult. When I went on to college, at the University

of Wisconsin, I "majored" in practically every subject available in the sciences except physics. I was fortunate to have an introductory course in anthropology taught by William Howells, now at Harvard. He was a superb teacher who communicated his subject with ease and brilliance. Anthropology struck me as the only field that could answer my many interests. It combined science with the humanities, and its subject, the human being, could be approached from both biological and cultural aspects.

After graduation, I moved to New York and worked for two years. It was a difficult period. There is no one quite so helpless in the city as a person with an undergraduate degree in anthropology and no further training. Not having enough money for graduate school, I looked for work. I was overeducated for many jobs and undereducated for the rest. Finally I found a position as a group worker in a social agency. Toward the end of this period, I met my wife, Sonia, who had just been awarded a fellowship in French at Yale. Our marriage was followed by a move to New Haven, where I was employed for several months in a mental hospital as a group worker. During Sonia's second semester, we came into some money and I was free to quit my job and return to school. At that time, my interests in science had surfaced again and I was faced with a choice between conservation biology, the humanistic side of a hard science, and a return to anthropology. The latter won out again, but, thinking that it might be useful, I decided to pursue a master's degree in sociology first. I hoped to pick up some of the methodological rigor of that subject, which could be applied later to the more impressionistic but more personally involved kind of work anthropologists do. After a year and a half at the University of Connecticut, where I finished the master's, I was accepted by the Yale Department of Anthropology.

At Yale I was able to follow my interests as they pleased me. Although I took a wide range of subjects, I focused on evolutionary theory as it applied to both bi-

ological and cultural evolution. Because Sonia's field
was French, I thought at first that I would work in a
French village, but was continually drawn to a non-
Western setting. Such an experience would force me to
come to terms with a wider range of unknowns and, I
hoped, produce a deeper appreciation of ethnic variation and its roots in the environment as well as history.
My first trip to the Ivory Coast, in 1960, was made to
search out a field location in which I could study the
relationship between African dance and ritual. By a
series of accidents, I ended up with the Abron. I soon
found out that Abron dancing is not very rich, but a
short stay with them was to reawaken my biological
and ecological interests. In order to integrate myself
into village life and because I felt a strong need to help
my hosts in a way that would have some real value to
them, I was to spend a considerable amount of time
doing simple first aid. This led me to see how the local
hygiene system fit into an adaptive pattern, if only
within the confines of a rather limited theory of disease.
After returning from my first trip, I decided to concen-
trate on health and disease. Thus my field interests
were shaped partially out of design and partially
through a series of accidents.

The choice of Africa was not totally intellectual. As
for so many of my generation, Africa represented ad-
venture. The big game (which I have yet to see) stood
as a symbol of a natural frontier. My familiarity with
African music and dance, including its expression in
American culture, attracted me on the human level.
Dance was still an integral part of daily life among
many West African peoples. When my plane had
touched down in Abidjan, I had felt both the excitement of arrival in a place much fantasized about and
the fear of the unfamiliar. I had the false impression
that I was in some way returning to nature as well as
the real awareness of arrival in a cultural setting full of
unknown challenge. I was about to test myself intellectually and to a lesser extent physically in an alien
world.

My fever was the first sign that it was not going to be an easy experience. Coming field work presented a series of unknowns that were, at least temporarily, overwhelming. I was leaving the rules of my own culture behind to learn a new system. I had to face a void which would, even with the best of luck, fill in only gradually.

As the fever wore off, toward morning, I began to feel warmer and threw off all the blankets; my mind settled down and I was finally able to sleep. When daylight came, I was much better, although quite weak.

Downstairs, the taxi driver was patiently waiting for me in the lobby. Eighty dollars was a lot of money and I was not to be let off so easily. *"Je ne veux pas y aller. Je suis malade,"* I protested. He smiled and suggested that I come out and see the beautiful car his brother had waiting. I was almost dragged out on the street to a Peugeot station wagon. It was brand new and decorated on the inside with plastic birds perched on the dashboard and under the rear window, aesthetically at least a perfect vehicle for visiting the bush. The car was praised to me in the strange semi-French of the night before, and thinking that I feared his driving ability, the driver showed me his license. I began to weaken and tried bargaining over the price, but they held firm. *"Je n'ai pas encore mangé,"* I said in desperation. This struck them as a legitimate protest and I was allowed to go back to the hotel for breakfast under the waiting eye of the driver. I wondered why he was not at work that morning, as I drank my bitter coffee and searched the bar for an escape route back to my room. There was none. My fever began to return. I lingered over breakfast as long as possible, but the time finally came to pay the waiter and decide on my course of action. The taxi driver stood nearby smiling, like a vulture waiting for its prey. *"Je vais monter pour les valises,"* I said, capitulating. He sprang forward to help me, and in five minutes I had checked out of the hotel and was on the road north.

2
The Road North

Ten miles from Abidjan, small settlements begin to line the road. They are inhabited by peasant farmers whose surplus food is sold to the city. Most houses are flimsy, wattle-and-daub structures with thatched roofs. Richer men cover their mud walls with a veneer of cement and their roofs with corrugated iron, but there are few affluent people and few houses of this sort. These villages are ugly. The houses are small, squat, and rectangular. Most of them look as if they are about to crumble. The few streets that wind away from the main road are littered with refuse, which is picked at by freely grazing goats, sheep, and chickens. In each village, the steeple of a jerry-built church rises hopefully skyward, implying somewhat doubtfully that Christianity is the practiced religion.

Adzopé is sixty miles from Abidjan. It is larger than the villages previously described, and, in contrast to them, is built on several low hills, which break the monotony of the countryside. Adzopé is picturesque. As a governmental and missionary center, it has many substantial buildings, several churches, the usual flags and policemen, and, more important to its modest beauty, flowers. These are cultivated with great care and success by missionaries, who, everywhere in the Ivory Coast no matter what their particular faith, are extraordinary horticulturists. The obvious contrast between the floral abundance of mission stations and the bareness of the average village yard may be explained, however, by the African's familiarity with the habits of snakes, spiders, and insects. The missionaries put up with occasional serpents in their gardens for the sake of earthly beauty.

For several miles beyond Adzopé, the forest has been stripped away. Here one finds large banana plantations. Banana trees take several years to mature, so some are planted every year to insure a constant supply of fruit. The life history of the banana tree may be studied as it unfolds along the road. Fields of fledgling plants with small green leaves emerging from fleshy stalks give way to spindly adolescent trees and then to stands of mature specimens ready for harvest. Finally, there are useless lines of bruised stalks waiting to be cut down. The house of the planter stands alone in the middle of one of these fields. It is generally a two-story white cement structure built like a fortress against the heat. The huts or small cement houses of plantation workers line the road away from the planter's own house. On the richer establishments these are painted white.

The road continues to Abengourou, a major way station for the north-south trade. Trucks carrying vegetable produce, the *rapide* overcrowded with passengers, and enormous trailers laden with hardwood logs stop on their way south at the many gas stations in the town. For these, Abengourou signals the beginning of the paved road. Northbound travelers carry cargoes of canned goods, building supplies, medicines, and other manufactured items.

The center of the town opens on a large, square market place. Like the market in Abidjan, it contains European and African establishments, which cater in this case almost exclusively to Africans. European-, Lebanese-, and Syrian-owned trading companies are located in stores that form the lower floor of two-story buildings surrounding the square. They sell rice, oil, salt, sugar, wine, clothing, lanterns, beds, chairs, soft drinks, and other sundry items. The market proper is surrounded by small shacks built of scrap lumber and old tin cans beaten flat. These are stores, usually operated by men who sell tobacco, bread, meat, and an assortment of pins, needles, flashlights, and other small manufactured goods. The open places between the shacks are occupied by women who sell native foods. Business is brisk, but while many work full time at

trade, others come in from the surrounding country
once or twice a week to sell their small surplus for an
equally small profit.

In response to the need of market traders and travelers, there are many eating places in the square. Indis-
tinguishable from the other shacks, these are dark and
windowless with tattered curtains over the doors. They
are furnished with one or two rough tables made of
crates and scrap lumber, a few old chairs, and sometimes a wooden counter that runs along one wall. Food
is served on tin plates and eaten with cheap, aluminum
forks. Frequently a kerosene refrigerator percolates in
one corner of the single room, adding its heat to the accumulated stuffiness. It is likely to contain Coca-Cola,
Fanta, and Yuki soda (produced and bottled in Abidjan). The food, cooked outside over an open fire, is
limited to rice or yam *futu* with a hot sauce of cayenne
and fish or some dried meat. These are penny enter-
prises, but their profit is considerably higher than the
profit of those who sell prepared food in the open
market place. Fried plantains, sweet palmetto soup, a
close approximation to doughnuts, sour corn-meal pan-
cakes, and soft drinks made locally of orange juice,
kola, and cayenne are hawked by women who cry their
trade in the language of the region or Dioula, the lingua
franca of commerce. The market is exceptionally lively.
Information is passed and friendships are occasionally
renewed between local traders and transients en route
from north or south. The chatter is constant, animated
by the frequent clicks of surprise that greet unexpected
news: a flood in the south, a burned village in the
north, tales of witchcraft, or the death of a famous
priest. A new action by the national government that
conflicts with local custom may be debated on the spot,
and those who become embroiled in the discussion may
forget their business for the entire afternoon.

By the time we arrived in Abengourou, I was feeling
better. My temperature was normal and I felt safe
enough to discontinue the display of temperature taking
with which I had indulged myself since leaving Abid-

jan. Not sure just how long we were to stay in Abengourou, I stayed close to my hosts in the market place.
Like any other travelers, they were loath to begin the
real bush driving that was to follow, but finally, after a
couple of hours, we set off again and soon left the city
behind.

Beyond Abengourou, about a hundred miles north of
Abidjan, the paved road gives way to a surface of ferric
clay, a red wound through the otherwise interminable
green of trees, vines, and shrubbery. Left to itself, the
road would heal rapidly, leaving only a scar of secondary scrub, but it is constantly reopened by the clumsy
surgery of road crews and heavy machinery. In the
rains it becomes a slippery, potholed strip of mud. In
the dry season, it is transformed into a line of desert
winding incongruously through the jungle. At such
times, the dust of travel settles slowly. One drives
through a red fog, which, more tangible than water
vapor, sticks persistently to every exposed surface.
When the harmattan, a dry wind off the Sahara, blows,
the dust is carried for miles, giving the horizon a red
cast and, at night, obscuring the stars.

The road between Abengourou and Agniblikourou is
twisty. Since the traffic is light, most drivers stick to the
center of the single lane. This becomes unnerving after
a few close brushes with other cars or trucks, which
emerge at full speed from behind the frequent curves.
My chauffeur was fond of swerving safely away at the
last moment. Clinging to a corner of the back seat, I
was the focus of amused attention for the many passengers we had inexplicably picked up along the way.
They clearly enjoyed the game, which was played out
mile after mile through the otherwise placid jungle. The
roadway itself was littered here and there with wrecks.
Hulks of trucks and cars turned over on their sides or
backs could be seen in all states of decay. The results
of recent accidents, not yet stripped by the combined
hands of man and nature, rested relatively complete in
the weeds. The skeletons of older wrecks lay partially
hidden in the growth that had begun to claim them. We

did not pass a single bridge with its guard rails intact,
and there were many along the way that had none at
all. Taught by Frenchmen, who drive with a malice
nurtured on horsepower, the Ivoirian follows techniques first practiced on the Étoile and the Place de la
Concorde. The anger of the French driver has been
replaced by a love of the unexpected which infuses
West African culture.

I searched the road vainly for wildlife. The animals
of the forest (there are still many monkeys, and a few
leopards, chimpanzees, and elephants) safely avoid
man's path through their forest. An occasional snake
does appear in a hasty attempt to cross the road, but
even they are not common in the daytime. Our car did
hit one, however, a long green mamba, swift and mali-
cious. It was in the middle of the road as we bore down
on it. Unwilling to retreat, it reared up and attacked.
Its head came up over the hood, practically hitting the
windshield before its broken body rebounded off the
car. Such a snake will, I am sure, attack an elephant,
and I was content to have the combat so well in our
favor. This was not an isolated incident with the
mamba. On two other occasions, I killed them in this
way, and each time, they could have avoided the on-
coming automobile. I remembered these encounters
one day as I hitched a ride in a car without a windshield. As we rode through the country, the wind blowing in our faces, I could think of nothing but the huge
green snakes.

We came to Agniblikourou in the late afternoon. It
is the capital of a subdivision of the Agni people,
cousins of the Abron I was to study.

Like all large towns in the Ivory Coast, Agniblikourou is a market center. It is also an important
crossroad and a customs station for trade with Ghana,
to the east. As such, it is a center for smuggling. The
border is closely guarded by the agents of both countries, but it is not difficult for an individual to sneak
through the forest from one nation to the other. There
are no physical barriers between the two countries, and

before European conquest the area around Agniblikourou, including a good deal of Ghana, was merely a part of the Agni kingdom. It is difficult to transport large quantities of contraband any distance on foot, however, so that even if a smuggler crosses an unguarded border he must eventually take to the road. For this reason, both the Ivory Coast and the Ghana governments maintain smuggling checks on major routes. Aside from inspection of the goods people carry, the border between the two nations is relatively open. In principle, Africans need no passport or visa. Travel is officially restricted only for Europeans, but in actuality both countries watch their borders for political agitators.

Aside from its international importance, Agniblikourou is the seat of government for the northern Agni kingdom. Like all native political authorities, the Agni king has lost most of his real power. Nonetheless, his court is interesting for its display of pomp. The Agni, like their cousins the Abron and the better-known Ashanti, of Ghana, are people of the stool and the umbrella. Each chief has a stool carved in a distinctive pattern and a set of umbrellas richly embroidered with the elephant and weapons of war, symbolizing power, and the crocodile, symbolizing fertility. The court, which at present sits mainly to hear minor disputes or to fulfill religious and ceremonial functions, continues with a full retinue. The king has one or more *ochamé* (talking chiefs), who speak for him. In former times these were usually slaves. It is their duty to accept responsibility for royal judgments that go astray: "It is the Ochamé who has spoken, not the King." Other officers include royal drummers, trumpeters, sword and umbrella bearers, court dwarfs, and, until recently, a state executioner, who dispatched those convicted of such crimes as murder, theft, adultery, and gossip. The latter was judged a major crime because it could lead to dissension and eventual war among villages of the kingdom.

Agniblikourou is one of several coffee capitals in the

Ivory Coast. In February and March, the air along the
route is scented with the heavy, sweet odor of the little
white flowers that cover the high, green coffee bushes.
Months later, the mature berries will be gathered by
hand, dried locally, and sold to middlemen who will
truck the harvest into Abidjan, where some will be ex-
ported raw and some will be converted at a new plant
into bitter, French-style instant coffee. There are no
great coffee plantations. Each villager has his own
small plot of trees, which yields a modest yearly profit.
Prices, which would be highly unstable in such a situation, are set by the government so that no grower can
undersell another. This creates tensions between the
local population and the national government. The people, used to an authority to which they can appeal
directly, find themselves unable to cope with the bu-
reaucracy of the modern state.

We reached Koun-Fao at dark. I paid my driver and
set out to find the missionaries. The Freewill Baptists
had just come to the Ivory Coast, and at Koun-Fao
they were in the process of constructing their station.
At the time, the missionaries were living in a small African house. Their situation was cramped and their
time crowded with many duties. In spite of this, they
were extremely hospitable. I was invited to dinner and
was surprised by an American meal of southern fried
chicken and biscuits. I later discovered that this was
unexceptional. Missionaries protect their national identity through cooking.

I was fortunate that other guests included a couple,
Pastor and Mrs. Sparks, who worked farther up the line
in Abron country and were returning home that night.
After dinner, I was loaded up with camping equipment,
graciously lent to me, and we set off in the midst of a
heavy rain. During this last part of my trip, the road
was invisible except for the small strip illuminated by
the headlights. I was unable to perceive the change in
the countryside as we entered the area of open forest
that forms the transition zone between jungle and
savanna.

A few hours later, we arrived at the mission. Pastor and Mrs. Sparks lived just outside Gumeré, in an American-style house. Their guest room, which was open for any visitor passing through the region, was large and comfortable. Its many windows were screened, eliminating the need to put up with mosquito netting and its attendant claustrophobia. As I lay in bed, I could hear the sounds of the forest a few hundred yards from the house. The din is astounding. Nurtured by constant warmth, the lower forms of life in Africa grow to hideous proportions. Earthworms are over a foot long, millipedes over eight inches. There is a scorpion around Gumeré that looks like a lobster. Insects capable of producing noises are equipped with mammoth instruments, which rasp and scrape the air until it fairly bleeds sound. Striking among higher animals is the cry of the bush baby, a small lemur-like primate. It starts off as a low moan and works upward through several octaves to a piercing cry. Monkeys add their voices to the cacophony, but these are mild in comparison to the bush babies' horrendous love call. At dawn these sounds give way to the familiar heraldry of roosters and village dogs, and finally rhythmic clonks as the village women begin to pound their morning futu in large mortars. The replacement of one group of sounds by the other is comforting, as order and familiarity replace chaos.

3
Settling In

I stayed with the missionaries for four days. A young Abron who was their houseboy spoke English, and Pastor Sparks let me begin work on Kolongo, the language of the Abron, with him. During one of our brief lessons, I told him that I was interested in hiring someone who spoke English to work with me in an Abron village. Two days after my arrival, a man who lived in Lomo, a few miles away from Gumeré, appeared at the Sparks' house and offered to work for me. His name was Yao Oppong. In addition to Kolongo, he spoke Ashanti. Educated through two years of high school in Ghana, he spoke no French at all. Later I found out that he was not Abron but, rather, a member of an Ashanti subgroup. Although his English was rudimentary, I hired him immediately. I had only a limited time to spend in the field and was afraid that if I did not soon establish myself in an Abron village I would get no work done that summer. In spite of his linguistic deficiencies, Oppong turned out to be a helpful if difficult assistant, and I employed him again during my second trip.

Oppong performed such daily tasks as marketing, cleaning up, and washing clothes, but his major task was to act as an interpreter. Officially he occupied the position of "boy," which fit the standard definition of an African working for a European, but I let him know that I was more interested in his intellectual skills than his physical labor. He was very intelligent and fascinated by the mathematical nature of kinship data. Once he saw the logic inherent in systems of kin relationships, he worked hard on his own, comparing neighboring systems with that of the Abron. As a Catholic, and non-Abron, his usefulness as an informant was limited to situations in which I wanted to get his point of view concerning certain aspects of Abron culture. Having grown up among Abron, but different from them, he had his own ideas to add to my general impressions. At first I was a bit embarrassed by our relationship, in which he functioned both as servant and as assistant, but I soon discovered that Oppong's talents for organization were applied to recruiting young men of the village to do almost all of the menial work I required. He took on the role of supervisor, to be sure that my dishes would be done correctly and my clothes washed and ironed with care. It was a rare occasion when he himself had to wash a shirt. Apparently because he was my assistant, he acquired a certain amount of prestige, which materialized in a group of young men volunteering to work for us. In Diassenpa, during my second of three trips, two adolescent boys, Kofi and Kwamé, attached themselves permanently to us and turned out to be efficient and useful even as informants. They both spoke good French and were particularly alert and unselfish. Neither of them ever asked for anything from us.

Oppong was about twenty-seven years of age in 1960. His father was a planter who raised coffee and cacao on a small farm near Lomo. Oppong worked for his father, and the wages he received from me during my two trips were in large measure given to the older man. Questions of salary and my offer to give Oppong my refrigerator in lieu of a month's pay at the end of my second trip were discussed with the old man. When I left the field after the first summer, Oppong asked me to bring him a Bible on my return. As far as I know, this is the only thing he kept for himself.

He was very dark, rather short, about five feet six inches, and had a small, barely visible mustache. His complexion was slightly pitted. Physically he was quite undistinguished. What was impressive about Oppong was his firm, rather authoritarian personality, which allowed him, at what was in local society a very young age, to command attention. He was strong-willed to the point where we often came into conflict over details of daily life, and when he thought I was acting unfairly, he did exactly what pleased him. I will have more to say about our conflicts later.

The morning of my fifth day, Pastor Sparks drove me to Amamvi, the Abron capital. The royal village is about twelve miles from Gumeré and the main road north. The King's house, in one of two main streets running parallel through the village, is a fifty-foot-square structure opening on a central courtyard. Three sides of the square contain rooms, the fourth encloses the double-doored entranceway. The King's apartment, consisting of a sitting room and a bedroom, is next to a large, bare room with a raised platform at one end. This and the central courtyard constitute the public areas of the King's house. Another side is divided between storerooms for the various articles of state—the royal drums, stools, and umbrellas—and a lean-to where meat and other products are distributed after a royal sacrifice. The King requires no kitchen or rooms for his several wives and children, since they live and cook in their own houses scattered around the village. Food for the King is prepared by some of his wives and brought to his house, where he generally eats in solitude. Favorite wives sleep in with the King on a rotating schedule. These arrangements, which follow general Abron custom, greatly simplify the housing requirements of the royal family and also reduce tensions among women of the court, who might otherwise quarrel. Members of the King's retinue live in their own houses, and visitors to the court are put up by the richer men of the village.

When we arrived, court was in session. The King, very dark and thin, with his head shaved, was dressed in a yellow felt toga decorated with signs of office. He was talking in a very agitated manner to the assembled elders of the tribe. His ochamé stood helplessly by, unable to keep up with the flow of words. Someone in Amamvi had torn up a national flag, and word of the incident had gotten to the local police. Trivial as such an action might seem, it created a stir in the entire region. The Ivory Coast was about to become independent, and some, it was felt, interpreted this to mean that there would be no more government, no more taxes, and no more chiefs. Furthermore, since the Abron live in both Ghana and the Ivory Coast, there was the suspicion that the action against the flag represented pro-Ghana sentiments. The King was upset not only because the affair looked like a challenge to his authority but because the police had become involved in a case he felt should have been totally within his own rapidly shrinking jurisdiction. The King was haranguing the local police officer. "Who are you in your silly uniform?" he shouted. "Where do you get your authority?" And from a box at his side the King took out a pair of French Navy shoulder boards. Waving them at the crowd, he continued: "Here is my authority." Although uneducated, the King had been an officer in the French Navy during the war. This seemed to be a ludicrous display for a man whose power rested on tradition, but what the King was trying to do was show his own people the influence he had beyond ethnic boundaries. At the same time, he was trying to defeat the police on their own ground. Some of his anger was directed to the crowd at large. "This man must be found, so that we may punish him according to our law," he continued. "Why has he not been brought before me? Cannot one elder among you find out who is responsible?" Later, when the man was caught, the King attempted to hide the fact from the police, and punished him in traditional style by forcing him to sacrifice a cow to the royal stool. This action reaffirmed the power of the King, but the news got out of the village and the culprit was taken off to jail for a few days. Thus the balance of power between the government and the King was restored.

After more than a half hour of this case, the King turned to us and asked why I had come. With Pastor Sparks acting as my interpreter, I explained that I wanted to study Abron history and the Kolongo language. Taking my cue from what I had already seen that morning, I said, "This is a time of great change. It would be a pity if in future days there was no one to remember the old ways." I also pointed out that the Abron's cousins, the Ashanti, had several books written about them and that there was no such work on the Abron. King Adingra was in a mood to listen, and my interest in his people and in the functions of the court seemed to impress him. He called several of the elders forward and conferred with them over a place of residence for me. He said that if I was to study the Abron, I must sit at the King's side, for he had much to tell me. Actually, this was the last place I wished to be. I knew that he would tell me exactly what he wanted me to know and no more. Living in the royal village was another matter, however, since it gave me a chance to observe the workings of the court. The elders conferred for several minutes, and I was then asked to follow them to the dwellings that had room for me. There were two houses, one directly across from the King's, the other on the edge of the village. The former was incomplete and looked very uncomfortable. I chose the more distant house, which gave me a chance to observe life as it took place on the fringes as well as within the village, where I could visit the court when I felt it was important or whenever the King sent for me, as he often did.

Sparks helped me unload my equipment from his truck, and I set up housekeeping in the compound of the ochamé, Pong Kofi, a man of about fifty. Our house was almost as big as the King's. Its mud walls were in the process of being covered with a thin coating of cement. Nine rooms opened on the ubiquitous central courtyard, and two others (unusual for Abron houses) opened directly on the street. I was given two rooms in a corner of the house. These were also atypical, since only one opened on the courtyard; the other, as in a European apartment, could be reached only through the inside. A projecting roof ran all around the courtyard, providing each room with a porch area. This was a convenient place to sit during

the heat of the day or during the rains. I set up my cot
in the inner room and placed what little cooking equipment I had and the stove the missionaries had lent me
in the other. A few moments later, without asking, a
few boys came struggling in with a table made of old
boxes, which, like all wooden objects in the village, was
made of the cheapest and most common hard wood,
mahogany.

As soon as I had settled in, my landlord, who spoke
a little French, introduced me to the other inhabitants
of the house. Directly in line with my rooms lived
Kwasi Yeboah, a son of Pong Kofi. He was tall for an
Abron, five feet nine inches, and very thin. Like most
Abron, he was a farmer. For extra cash, he worked on
the cacao plantations of the King and, whenever he
could, signed on with a trader as a part-time truck
driver. His ambitions, which reflected the attitudes of
his age-mates, were limited to owning a taxi, either in
the bush or in Abidjan. He had one wife, a girl of
about seventeen, and no children. She lived at the other
end of the village with her mother and sisters, but she
was a frequent overnight guest at our house, where
love-making was a frequent and noisy occupation of
the younger men. The most lively in this respect was
Kwasi Appiah, the local playboy, whose reputation
ranged far beyond Amamvi. Attractive to women, he
was constantly getting into trouble with other men's
wives, and there were not many months when he did
not appear in the court of some village chief to answer
charges of adultery. During my stay in Amamvi, he had
a relatively enduring relationship with a girl of about
fifteen, who came to his room almost every night,
where they talked and made love till dawn. Her voice
came at me like a harsh wind over the wall that separated my rooms from Kwasi's.

At the end of the line of rooms opposite me, in one
corner of the house, lived a man who was to become
my good friend. This was Abdoulaye Oatara, a Moslem
who spoke good French, had been sent to school by his
father, and who worked for his great-uncle Pong Kofi.

Abdoulaye was tall, well built, dark, and looked like a black Errol Flynn with a natty mustache. He had two wives. One, about thirty, lived at some distance from our house. She had three children. The other lived half a mile away, in Diassenpa, the village that was to become my home during my second trip. She was a young girl, still in her teens, and had one infant son. Abdoulaye was equally devoted to both, although he seemed to enjoy conversations more with the older woman. Unlike other Abron, perhaps because he was a Moslem, he ate dinner with the wife whose turn it was to bring it. Normally, the women return home after bringing food to their husband's or father's compound. Abdoulaye, although fairly religious, enjoyed a pot of palm wine from time to time and never failed to invite me when there was a good brew available. We became close friends and drinking partners. He volunteered much information on Abron custom and once spent almost a whole night preparing a chart of the royal line for me. This was a painful process requiring a long search of memory, time to question others, and finally, the arduous task of writing everything down in a slow, meticulous hand.

One of the two rooms that faced the outside served mainly as a storeroom, but it was occupied from time to time by traders who had business in Amamvi and needed a place to stay for a few days. All the other rooms around the courtyard were unfinished. Pong Kofi himself lived with his brothers in another part of the village, but pride brought him to his future home often, sometimes as my guest, sometimes to sit in the courtyard, eating, resting, or surveying the work that was in progress.

Anthropologists learn a great deal about the people they study by living according to local custom. Initial weeks in the field are spent testing simple hypotheses about patterns of behavior that appear to be ordered within particular social frameworks. Etiquette associated with the latrine provides an amusing instance of my inability to make a distinction between two types of social situations basic to Abron conduct.

It was not difficult to observe that one of the foremost rules of behavior is the formal greeting pattern. When people meet in any of the innumerable social situations that occur during the day, propriety demands that each greet the other according to the situation, the time of day, and the rank and sex of the two parties. The fact that two people may have greeted each other a few moments previously is no excuse for neglecting this practice. Any new coming together requires a new greeting.

One of my first tasks was to learn the greetings appropriate to the various situations, and I was soon able to practice these in the village with a minimum of mistakes. Quite proud of my linguistic prowess, I went out of my way to greet people and, to show my great familiarity with the language, I always spoke first. There was one situation, however, in which the normal rules gave way to another requirement of correct social behavior. Greetings were not extended to those on their way to the latrine. The silent parade was a twice-daily event. This was marked by the serious expressions of those who marched in determined fashion down the road past my house. For the first few weeks, I managed to greet everyone whose biology was functioning normally. My friends were either too polite or embarrassed to correct me, and it took me a while to realize that my behavior was unusual. Eventually catching on, I asked Oppong if it was impolite to talk to anyone in such a situation. He immediately told me that this was so. One could talk freely only as a member of a group of men going to the latrine together. A few nights later, on the way to the latrine, I had a chance to test my new knowledge. Kwasi Appiah, who was possessed of both a good humor and tremendous curiosity, asked me if I was going to the toilet. I turned to him in mock anger and asked, through Oppong, "What kind of an Abron are you to ask me such a question? Are you not supposed to keep silent at such times?" I capped this off with the usual remonstrance offered by an Abron to any child who violates decorum. "Who brought you up?" Kwasi turned sheepishly away from the gathering of men who were sitting with us outside our house, and the rest exploded into laughter. "He is a better Abron than you," Oppong told Kwasi.

I wish I had been as tolerant of myself as were my hosts. The fact that I had learned the greetings helped me a great deal the first five days in the village, but I made little further progress with the language. Wherever I went, people addressed me in Kolongo. Wishing to be helpful, they pointed things out and made me repeat their names. Differences in tone as well as length of vowel and consonant, unimportant in English, are crucial in Kolongo. I had particular difficulty at first with the words for mother, *nna;* cow, *naa;* four, *na;* and pay attention, *na,* which has a low tone. The unraveling of social customs is also a difficult process. I feared that I was letting my new friends down by learning so slowly. After about a week in Amamvi, I began to avoid people. I spent most of the time in my rooms talking only to Abdoulaye in French and Oppong in English. My major contact with village life was in the morning, when I spent several hours doing first aid. When I did walk through Amamvi, I kept away from the men's gathering areas, where I was sure to get another, now unwanted lesson.

The only time I ventured forth without anxiety was at night in the King's house. Adingra loved music and dance. One of his sons had organized a highlife band (a popular music-and-dance style developed in Ghana) and, every night, people came to the royal house to dance. There I could easily be inconspicuous or, if I wished, noticed on my own terms, since I rapidly learned the local steps. Finally, it was dance that helped restore my confidence and led me back to a normal relationship with the villagers. Abron men compete in good-natured contests of skill on the dance floor. Men and women never dance with each other, and no dancers ever touch. But men attempt to outdo one another with the complexity of their steps. After I had watched a good deal of dancing in the village the first few nights, the King asked me if I would join in. I agreed to try. The King motioned for the drummers to begin. As I started to dance, the other dancers stopped and retreated into the corners of the room to watch. I was not spectacular but I kept to the rhythm well enough. Then the local schoolteacher jumped up to challenge me. He was a man from another region, roundly disliked in the village. He couldn't stand being out of the spotlight and was always intruding himself into the village affairs. I realized that if I could humble him somewhat, I could gain stature. Improvising wildly, I did sailors' bells, jumping and clicking my heels in the air. Then, squatting on the floor, I flicked my legs out like a Cossack, a step I had learned when I used to folk dance as a teen-ager. Somehow I managed to keep time to the music, an absolute imperative, and keep dancing long enough to completely baffle my opponent, who was actually a very fine dancer. As we continued, the King began to smile and nod in approval. Finally, he brushed the other man aside and began to dance opposite me. This was no challenge. It merely signaled approval of my performance, and I let the music take me back to the more conventional steps of the highlife.

My fame as a dancer, if not as a linguist, spread to the villages around Amamvi, and soon people began to come to see me perform. On nights when I was late, the King would send a messenger to fetch me at my house.

Later, when the King and his court set out on an important ceremonial trip, he ordered me to come along with the band. The ceremony was to take place in Sapli, fifty miles north of Amamvi. The chiefs of another ethnic group, the Kolongo, whose language the Abron speak, were to pay their annual respects to the Abron, who have been their titular rulers for several hundred years.

Our trip north was uneventful and the ceremony was performed, without incident, according to custom.

Chiefs from miles around assembled with their stools and umbrellas, each with his ochamé. They spoke long and eloquently of their loyalty to the King and his people. Adingra sat out the occasion on his royal throne, an ornate folding chair covered with brass studding and polished for the occasion to a light gold. He was dressed in his best robes of embroidered felt. The yellow-and-red design contrasted with his black skin.

There were jarring notes in the ceremony, however, anachronisms that were in themselves symbolic of a nation caught between ancient custom and the modern world. When Adingra arrived in Sapli, he was escorted into the village according to custom by his umbrella bearer, who twirled the royal umbrella high over the King. But the King was seated in his automobile, a new Ford. Later, when the King delivered a speech, his voice was amplified by a transistorized public-address system purchased for the occasion. These new items were exploited by the King as part of his dramatic display and fitted in, if a bit strangely, with his image of power. Another feature of the ceremony, which sat less well with the King, was the participation for the first time of the government representative, dressed in a business suit and definitely unimpressed by the entire show. His major function seemed to be the projection of official boredom.

That night, I was put up in the local rest house, a feature of most African villages. Oppong was not with me and I had lost track of my friends in the maze of round houses that made up the village. I wondered whether anyone had remembered to prepare dinner for me. Suddenly, a Kolongo host appeared at the door. He was drunk, dirty, and unpleasantly friendly. He said that he would take me to get some food and led me away through the twisting streets of the village. I tried to get some bearing on the moon so that I could find my way home in case I lost him, an event I both feared and wished. We began to visit his friends around the village. At each house, he would knock on the door, often waking up inhabitants, and introduce me with a low bow. Bleary-eyed, my new host would retreat back into the house for a minute and then emerge with some wine, which we shared in the formal greeting that takes place when any visitor calls. My guide became drunker and drunker, and I, barely managing to remain sober, tried to convince him that I was more hungry than thirsty. He was enjoying all the free drink at my expense and showed no inclination to obtain food or to return me to my house. Suddenly, as we came around the side of a hut, I spied Kwasi Yeboah and his wife walking down the path, she with a pot on her head. They were on their way to my house with food from the King. I thanked my Kolongo host, who could hardly stand up by that time, and Kwasi guided me back to the rest house. My feelings of relief were conveyed, I hope with adequate emotion, to my rescuers, and I suddenly felt that to be an Abron was the best thing in the world. I joked with Kwasi about the behavior of the Kolongo, which he assured me was typical.

The next evening, I piled into the truck with the King's band and we set off for Amamvi. When we were halfway home, a tire went flat. We drove slowly, the tire flapping, into a village about a quarter of a mile down the road, and got out of the truck. Even in the dark, I could see curious faces staring at me. Neither hostile nor friendly, they seemed puzzled by my sudden appearance with a group of Africans traveling together. With nothing to do while the tire was repaired, the band took out its drums and began to play right on the road. I pulled my toga out of my knapsack, put it on, and began to dance. The crowd, which had up to then stood silently, became animated. Arms reached out and I was pulled into the mass of suddenly shouting Abron. I was caught in a flow of people, which moved away from the road toward the center of the village. One group of young men finally managed to separate from the others, and they led a triumphal march into a house where palm wine and African gin were soon produced. As we drank, they explained their excitement. "The French have been here for forty years and they have

never danced with us and never drunk with us. They
have always kept themselves away, except when they
wanted our women. You have shown that you are a
friend." Those few who could speak French asked
question after question about the United States. Their
knowledge of geography was rather vague, and I had to
explain that one could not drive to America. Their favorite question, which was repeated many times, was,
"How many blacks are there in the United States?" I
replied, "Twenty-five million." A ripple of wonder
passed through the room as the figure was translated
into Kolongo. At the time, the Ivory Coast had a population of three and one-half million.

After these experiences, it was easier for me to move
with confidence into the world of Abron. Amamvi was
there for me to explore; its people were willing to share
their experiences with me.

One of the most obvious things about the village was
that there were more than just Abron living there. Segregated from the main stream of Abron life were the
Mossi, laborers whose small village is attached to one
corner of Amamvi. The Mossi, proud subjects of a
northern kingdom, have overpopulated their arid land,
and many have moved south to work in Ghana and the
Ivory Coast. As laborers they work hard, hoping someday to return to their native land. The Mossi are readily identifiable in Amamvi. They scar their faces in a
manner foreign to the Abron, three lines running down
each cheek, with a complicated pattern on the forehead,
and some men file their front teeth. They are also generally taller and huskier than the Abron. As workers
for the richer men of Amamvi, the Mossi occupy a low
status in the village. Not only are their houses segregated, but they use a separate latrine, marry only
within their own group, and associate primarily with
other Mossi. An Abron discussing the Mossi will refer
to them as dirty and say that they love to sing and
dance, feel little pain, and are slow to learn the simple
tasks of civilized life. When calling a Mossi, an Abron
will usually say the equivalent of "Hey, Mossi." Few

Abron bother to learn the names of individual Mossi
with whom they come into daily contact. Since the customs of the two groups differ, the Abron, in their superior position, exaggerate the divergences and thus reinforce their own beliefs.

Wages are low, and few Mossi ever make it back to
their homeland. Children are born at Amamvi—a second generation of strangers. They remain trapped by
the prejudice of most Abron but adhere to their own
proud tradition.

One day, as I was sitting under the big tree, which is
the gathering place for the young men of the village,
the talk turned away from Abron customs to life in
America. Kwasi Ngatia began to ask me some questions about race relations in America. He was a student
at a teachers' college at Grand-Bassam, on the coast,
but spent his summers at home. As a student, his vision
stretched beyond the savanna to world politics. He, like
many of his fellows, was interested in the East-West
struggle and was particularly conscious of the coming
place of Africa and his newly independent nation in the
framework of world politics. "Is it true," he asked,
"that the black man is treated badly in America?"
"Yes." I admitted that discrimination did exist in various forms in the United States. I also explained that the
democratic ideal, opposed to any sort of racial discrimination, was supported by many people in our country.
This did not satisfy Kwasi, nor his friends who sat listening to the conversation. "Why should any American
believe that segregation is just?" "How could state governments condone these practices?" "Why was the
black in particular separated out as inferior?" I had
committed myself to the truth, but I wanted to bring
my friends to some understanding of the problems involved. This was difficult, because there are no good
answers to these questions. If one points out that the
democratic process is slow, one soon finds out that the
African is impatient. In any case where prejudice is
concerned it is difficult, and I believe wrong, to argue
for gradualism. Then I thought of the Mossi. "You

have a similar situation right here in Amamvi," I said.
"What do you mean? We are all black men here. There
can be no discrimination." "You have the Mossi," I replied. "You treat them very much the way black men
are treated in the States." I then compared America
and Amamvi in this respect, emphasizing the stereo-
typic ideas of blacks held by many whites and showing
their similarity to Abron attitudes toward Mossi. Kwasi
was still not satisfied. He looked over at me and finally
said in a hurt tone, "But some of my best friends are
Mossi."

4
First Data

Every morning at first light, I was awakened by the slamming of doors and the swishing of bare feet across the hard-packed clay of the courtyard. The men of the house were going out to urinate. Around the village, roosters called to each other and dogs barked intermittently. People, who according to etiquette could not address one another before their morning bath, added to the mounting noise by much coughing and throat clearing. Now and then a crying baby could be heard. I would get up and follow the men outside to a grassy place just beyond the house. After relieving myself I would check my water supply, brush my teeth, and begin to boil water for coffee on my gas stove. By the time breakfast was prepared, the village chief would be at my door. Bathed and dressed in a fine toga, he would inevitably join me for coffee. We exchanged formal greetings and then, having no common language, would sit silently sipping from our tin cups until, having finished, the chief would get up, say thank you, and slowly walk out.

A bit later, Oppong would show up and ask me what work I required. If I had clothes to wash or needed something from the local store, he would take care of it immediately. Otherwise we would go out together and walk around the village. I would greet everyone, taking note of early-morning activities. It did not take long to build up a general impression of those mundane tasks that make up the daily round for the average Abron.

The Abron are exceptionally clean people. Most Abron women are meticulous housewives. They sweep their houses, courtyards, and the ground between the dwellings several times a day. In addition, they clean public areas around the village once or twice a week, using palm-spine or grass brooms twenty to twenty-five inches long. They bend over their work and inhale a good deal of dust.

Women also take pride in decorating their houses. They spread red, black, and buff clay over the floors and porches of their dwellings. Men care less about decoration, and are content with large, substantial, but plain structures with corrugated-iron roofs and cemented walls and courtyards. They are as exigent as the women about cleanliness, however, and require their wives and daughters to sweep their courtyards out regularly. The men clean their bedrooms themselves, first removing the scant furniture before sweeping out accumulated dust and dirt.

Forest and savanna are not allowed to encroach on the village, and the women are diligent in keeping all weeds away from living areas. While this reduces the insect population, the village becomes a miniature dust bowl whenever even a moderate wind blows.

The garbage that accumulates during the day is gathered up and thrown just outside the village or into pits that have been dug to obtain the claylike soil for house construction. These pits may be close enough to the dwelling area to attract some flies to the village itself.

All Abron villages are equipped with latrines, which are at least one hundred yards from the nearest house. The men's latrines are pits ten to fifteen feet deep, with straight sides fifteen to thirty feet long, about two feet wide. Boards made of split palm trunks are placed at intervals of two feet, and the pits are edged on both sides along the length with palm logs. The paths to the latrines and the area around them are kept free from growth. The latter is important, I was told, because snakes tend to congregate around latrine areas. Although I never saw one there, I never ceased to feel both exposed and defenseless every time I went to relieve myself.

Women's latrines are also outside the village, but they are not dug with the same care as the men's. They are smaller, only a few feet long and four feet deep.

The disparity between men's and women's accommodations is quite general in Abron society, although a man will try to provide his mother and wives with decent housing. In any particular family, improvements to women's houses come only after the men's house has been modified according to rising status and wealth.

The Abron are proud of their hygienic facilities and make fun of other peoples, such as Kolongo and Lobi, who do not have latrines. The latrine has become a symbol of cleanliness that they associate with being Abron, and it no doubt has an effect on the frequency of disease in an area that is known for a wide variety of endemic illness.

The larger market towns, even those which are strictly Abron, contrast with the villages. While standards of personal hygiene remain high and individual houses are kept clean, refuse accumulates in public areas and is rarely removed. Garbage is eaten by vultures, dogs, sheep, and goats; but these animals leave their own waste products scattered in areas frequented by children, who often roll around in the accumulated dirt and feces. In addition, automobile traffic is fairly dense in these centers (at least in comparison with villages), and a plague of red dust is constant in the dry season. When it rains, traffic transforms the roads into a swampy combination of mud and garbage. Again, it is the children who come into most contact with this unhygienic aspect of life, and their infected sores attest to the filth with which they have frequent contact. I found these towns depressing and visited them only when I needed supplies or had patients to take to the dispensary in Tabgne or the hospital in Bondoukou.

There were two customs I found difficult to accommodate to my own sense of proper hygiene. All Abron chew kola nuts. As a consequence, they spit a great deal. There are no social rules about this, except that no one spits directly on anyone else. A person who spits on the floor of a house or in a courtyard is likely to dry the spot with his foot, but this is the only attempt made to clean up saliva. While most Abron realize that certain diseases are contagious, spreading from individual to individual through contact, none were aware that spitting could spread disease. During my stay in Amamvi, the village chief, who visited me every morning, habitually cleared his throat and spat into the corners of my room. Later, when I took up residence in Diassenpa, I discovered that Tchina Kofi, my new houseowner, was a great spitter. Whenever he sat down to talk, he would begin to punctuate his rapid and animated speech with healthy spits which would land close to his chair. He would then remove one sandal and grind the spittle into the floor of the courtyard. For some time, I was put off by this performance and disliked the old man.

More upsetting for a foreigner is the habit the Abron have of blowing their nose onto the ground. They close one nostril with the left hand and clear the other with a heavy snort. Parents wipe their children's noses with their own hands or with the corner of the child's cloth. Like spitting, noses are blown whenever a person feels the need, and no special precautions are taken by sick people who might spread infection to others in the village.

The major compensation for this behavior is the constant isolation of the left and right hands in relation to clean and dirty tasks. The right hand is clean. It is used for greeting and shaking hands and for eating. The left hand is used for personal hygiene. So strong is the separation between right and left, clean and dirty, that the Abron have a proverb that says, "A man who greets another with his left hand is a fool." This isolation is widespread in Africa, the Middle East, and India, where we find a set of associations between left and right, male and female, clean and dirty, and many other dualisms. Among the Yoruba of Nigeria, handshaking with the left hand occurs as part of a ritual in which men, transformed into gods through the medium of trance, greet their audience. This exception to the rule highlights the importance of a taboo that is broken in this instance symbolically, to reinforce the difference between gods and men.

During the rainy season, when water is abundant, it is taken from deep wells, the tops of which are capped with cement and covered with wooden lids. In the dry season, water must be collected elsewhere. In Diassenpa and Amamvi it is taken from holes dug in low-lying areas in the forest. These are three or four feet in diameter and as much as five feet deep. The water from these holes is muddy and often full of algae, which accumulate on the surface of the open pools. The women who fetch water attempt to draw their daily supply without disturbing the sediment, but a good deal of dirt finds its way into it. Still, the relative isolation of water sources acts as a partial barrier to the many parasites common in West Africa.

The digging of these temporary wells is something of a social event. During the dry season in 1961–62 I witnessed the preparation of such a water source. All the young men of the village participated. Some dug in the soft earth with adzes, while others filled buckets with the debris and threw it aside. When the water table was reached, the youths continued to dig into the mud, using pails to scoop it out of the deepening hole. Finally the water was allowed to stand for several hours, and when all the mud had settled, women came from the village to collect it in pots and basins. The digging site was the focus of a large group of village youth, most of whom participated in the work. The participants appeared to enjoy getting wet, and even the mud, which got all over everyone, was taken as part of the fun.

The Abron store water in large clay pots, usually covered, which are kept in the women's kitchens. Rain water collected as the runoff from corrugated-iron roofs is also kept in large catchment barrels.

During the rainy season, they wash clothing in water accumulated in shallow holes dug for that purpose at the edges of the village. Some people carry their clothing to the river, and others, especially in the dry season, do their wash at home in buckets. In Diassenpa, people rarely wash themselves or their clothing directly at the source of drinking water. They take bath water from the same source as drinking water, but prefer to bathe in the privacy of a special bath house or a room set aside for that purpose.

Although, most of the time, both men and women bathe in the privacy of a bath house, a man would sometimes bathe in the corner of a courtyard in full view of residents and guests. He would sit on a stool with a bucket of water in front of him, strip off his clothes discreetly, wet himself, and lather his entire body without getting up. After a thorough soaping, he would rinse from the bucket, splashing the water in handfuls over his body. Finally he would get up, push his penis between his legs to hide it, and dry himself with a towel or bit of cloth set aside for that purpose. Men were amazingly adept at maintaining their modesty in full view of everyone in the courtyard. I was never brave enough to try this method and restricted my own bathing to the more sheltered formal bath house.

Bathing is a major preoccupation of all Abron, but other aspects of personal hygiene also illustrate their approach to cleanliness:

Abron men keep their hair short and many shave their heads. The few razors owned by individuals are widely loaned for that purpose. In the trading towns, hair is cut and heads shaved by professional barbers, who do not clean their tools as well as villagers do.

Women let their hair grow long, but wear it in tight braids coiled close to the head. Members of the same female household usually help each other in the combing, braiding, and tying of hair.

After bathing, most Abron anoint themselves with grease. This may be shea butter prepared in the north of the Ivory Coast and sold by Dioula traders in the local markets, or mentholated vaseline, which is readily available in town. The latter is beginning to replace the native product. The application of either type of grease makes the skin sticky, but until it is dulled by dust, the body shines against the clean, bright togas worn after the daily round is completed and the evening bath finished.

The Abron clean their teeth after the morning and evening meals with a stick of pliable wood which they chew and work around their teeth and gums. While I have no clinical information on Abron dental problems, their teeth and gums appear to be in very good shape and few people ever complained about toothaches of any sort.

The prestige costume of the Abron man is the brightly colored toga, found over many parts of West Africa. Today most of these are of European manufacture, but some native cloths remain. Men wear the toga on rest days, on trips to other villages, on court visits, during ceremonies, and in the evening after work. Adults own at least two, and rich men own several, including specimens of the heavily embroidered kenti made by many Akan peoples and much admired by the Abron. Women give these clothes loving care and wash them often. They also wear this costume, but prefer a long blouse, seen elsewhere in West Africa, which they wear over an ankle-length wraparound skirt.

Work clothes are practical items of everyday wear. Most men own one or two changes of European clothing. The variety of garments amazed me. Women's coats trimmed with fur are a favorite men's item and are worn even in the hottest days over a nondescript collection of shorts, breeches, and shirts of all types, including sweat shirts. The latter often come secondhand from America and are sometimes emblazoned with the insigne of some university or club. These work clothes are kept until they literally fall apart.

The Abron rarely wash this clothing. After work, they hang it on pegs, ready to be worn again when needed. A few men own good European clothing that they wear on special occasions. This type of dress is limited to educated Abron, and in Diassenpa only one man ever wore "correct" European dress.

Women's work attire is plainer than that of the men.
They wear a simple wraparound cloth just over the
breasts, or in some cases, on the waist, which they wash
frequently. Their "underwear" consists of a multi-
rowed string of beads worn over the hips. Little girls
receive a set of these beads at birth and continue
throughout their lives to wear larger and larger versions. After the age of two or three, girls begin to pass
a bit of cloth between their legs, hooking the ends into
their beaded belts. Adult women forgo these cloths except during menstruation. They protect their modesty
by drawing their skirts discreetly between the legs when
they sit down.

Male children run naked most of the time. Some own
bits of togas that have been passed down to them, but
these rarely cover more than their shoulders. Some girls
may also own cloths, but as with the boys, these are
tied so carelessly over the body that they offer no con-
cessions to modesty. School children wear uniforms
standardized by the government. For boys, these are
khaki shorts and shirts; for girls, blue dresses. Both the
boys' uniforms and the girls' dresses are rapidly reduced to rags, but are worn as long as they hold together. Few children wear shoes or sandals.

Adults own at least one pair of sandals, made either
of leather or from used tires. The latter are manufactured in the trading towns by specialists, and leather
sandals are made by skilled workers in either villages or
towns. Both types of footwear are being replaced by
plastic sandals of European manufacture.

Adults often cover their heads when working. Men
wear a variety of hats bought from traders or made locally; women prefer a bandana tied tightly over the
head. Children hardly ever use head coverings. Most
Abron avoid the sun and, except for savanna gardening, are rarely exposed to it for long. My own custom
of taking occasional sun baths was looked upon as a
mild form of insanity and caused not a small amount of
discussion in the villages of Amamvi and Diassenpa.

I was constantly impressed by the fact that the daily

work pattern follows a rhythm in which men never overexert themselves. Even women, although they work hard, follow a pace that includes time for relaxation and conversation, if not rest. Toil is moderate and regular, so fatigue is never pushed beyond the level of honest tiredness. Men often complain about their work load; women, never, except those who have had some schooling and have oriented themselves somewhat away from the core of Abron culture. Children are at constant beck and call of adults, but there is a certain gentleness in the demands older people make upon the young. Abron culture is pervaded with a sense of what an adequate contribution to village life should be. This sense of participation is adjusted to individual ability, the determination of which rests largely on age and experience. No one criticizes an invalid for doing less than a healthy person, and sick individuals are not castigated for their inability to contribute. Truly lazy people are rare, and those few that exist are usually those who have had a great deal of contact with the outside world. Even laziness is tolerated, if not admired, since the Abron believe that a man will gain as much fortune or misfortune and prestige in later life as he deserves. This philosophy is, however, limited by the fact that a lazy husband or wife is very likely to be deserted by an unsatisfied spouse. Marriage requires a considerable amount of economic co-operation, and the slighting of work within the context of marriage will produce deep strains.

The sense of cleanliness and good hygiene that one gets from village life extends to the preparation of food. Few Europeans are fond of West African food, but those who know the Abron can at least be sure that the food is well cooked under hygienic conditions.

After visiting a large number of houses every morning, I would spend the early afternoon in the fields observing farm work or in the village with a group of men who congregated around one of several big shade trees in the center of the village. There they would gossip about village life, discuss local politics, or play *wari,* a

board game. If there was any palm wine available, it
would be shared among the men. With Oppong present
to translate for me, I would pose questions to the men
on these occasions. During my first field work, I restricted myself to questions about farming and other
economic activities, which most people were willing to
talk freely about. Those few times I tried to discuss religion or politics, I was told to ask the King about such
matters.

In the late afternoon, I repeated my rounds of village
houses. This gave me an opportunity to observe the
preparation of food. My presence amused the women
on these occasions, and they went out of their way to
show me what they were doing. Abron women, often
shy in public, are quite relaxed in their own houses,
and I found them both friendly and helpful. My constant prodding about food preparation and my habit of
peeking into pots simmering on the fire were greeted
with great mirth. Frequently I would be offered some
morsel to taste.

Women's fireplaces are on the floor of the kitchen or
on the ground just in front of it. In the dry season, they
cook out of doors, reserving the indoor stove for rainy
days. Women own a variety of pots (of clay and iron,
with an occasional aluminum utensil), enameled pans,
calabash bowls, calabash strainers and spoons, covered
enameled serving dishes, one or two large mortars and
pestles, a screen sifter for manioc flour, a grinding
stone for pepper and salt, and a wooden mixing
stick.

Food is always prepared by the women and younger
children of both sexes who live in the women's house.
The senior female of the household supervises the
cooking. Manioc, rice, and corn are prepared for cooking (dried, and in the case of manioc, pounded and
sifted) and stored in large cylindrical clay bins ranged
along the walls in the kitchen areas. Yams and taro,
which are stored in the fields, are peeled before cooking. Starchy food, which serves as the base of all Abron
recipes, is boiled and then pounded in a large wooden

mortar. The rhythm of this pounding provides a constant background in the early morning and evening of every day in every Abron village. A small quantity of water is added to the pounded starch and it is pressed into a ball called *futu*. A sauce for this futu is made by boiling dried fish or a small quantity of meat with palm oil, okra, tomatoes, salt, onions, and an enormous quantity of cayenne pepper.

The futu ball is placed in a serving dish, and the steaming sauce is poured over it. If it is to be served in a man's house, the dish is immediately covered and one of the women takes it to one of the associated men's houses. People eat futu almost every day, but the Abron also make a stew with rice and chicken and a rather good stew/soup with peanuts and chicken now found in African restaurants in both New York and Paris. This groundnut stew is more common in Ghana than among the Abron, a fact that contributed to my own culinary unhappiness during my stay in Abron country.

The Abron value meat for its taste (*ho dun*—sweet) and would eat it in larger quantities if they could afford it. On the other hand, there is no real shortage of protein, and those families that have little meat make up for this lack with beans and lentils, which are added to the sauce. In addition, they balance their diet with vegetables of various sorts and fruits rich in vitamin C. Palm oil, red with carotene, is loaded with vitamin A, but, unfortunately, one of the signs of acculturation is the abandonment of locally made palm oil for peanut oil, which is bought cheaply in the local market. Otherwise, the only possible vitamin deficiency would lie in the B group. While I found that Abron children were quite susceptible to infection, no other visible symptoms of malnutrition or undernutrition could be found. Never did I see kwashiorkor (protein malnutrition), which is so common in other parts of Africa. The Abron eat a well-balanced diet, and what malnutrition exists may be caused by a heavy burden of intestinal parasites, particularly hookworm, which is caught not from food but from walking barefoot on the contaminated ground.

Pots, pans, mortars, and pestles are washed before and after cooking, but in unboiled water. The evening meal is cooked just about the time the young women of the family are sweeping up the scraps of food and accumulated dirt in the courtyard, so a bit of dust undoubtedly gets cooked into the dinner.

Sick women are not restricted from preparing food. The only taboo on food handling occurs during menstruation, and, in some households, the men prefer menstruating women to keep away from any aspect of food preparation. In such households, menstruating women are also forbidden to enter the men's houses. This taboo is explained in terms of cleanliness: the men say that menstrual blood is dirty.

Although I frequently prepared my own food, I also ate with the men of my courtyard from time to time in order to observe patterns of etiquette, amount of food eaten, and other behaviors associated with the taking of meals. Since it is considered the height of bad manners to observe other people eating, the only way to obtain such information is to participate in a meal. It is not difficult to get invited to dinner. The Abron are generous to strangers and friends, and curious about the eating habits of non-Africans. They were particularly eager to see if I could take the cayenne pepper they love so well.

The Abron do not eat their evening meal until everyone in the household has bathed. Men and women eat separately. Food is taken to the men's houses immediately after it is prepared; then the women gather in their own compounds to eat. Depending on the size of the household and the number of female houses associated with it, the men may be served by a large number of separate kitchens. The two eating units in the men's house are a group of adult men (usually between three and eight) and a group of young boys (usually between three and ten). The men sit around a low table on stools and chairs and wash their hands in a calabash full of water which is passed around the table. They dip the right hand into the water and dry it in the air before dipping it into the pot. The women serve the dishes one by one. The senior man of the house divides the protein part of the meal; then everyone begins to eat the futu ball, taking pieces of it with the first three fingers and the thumb of the right hand. When the men have eaten all they want from a dish, they pass the remainder to the children, who gather in another circle, usually on the ground. If there is any meat or fish left, the eldest boys in this group have first call on it, unless a parent has already given some meat to a favorite child.

The Abron eat rapidly, the length of a meal depending upon the number of dishes and the number of people eating. After everyone has finished, they drink water from a common calabash or an aluminum teakettle. When the meal is over, some of the children wash the table and return the serving dishes to the women, who wash them. Women's meals are much the same as those of the men, except that mature women often eat together with their young daughters or even grandchildren.

Dinner is the only organized meal of the day. Men may gather for breakfast, but this is not a regular routine and men often eat food brought to them by their women when they are out in the gardens. Women and children, at least those children attached to the women's house, eat small snacks throughout the day. Guests eat with their hosts, sharing the common pot with the people of the household. Leftover food is rarely consumed later. Instead, it is either thrown out or given to the animals. There is rarely any leftover food, however, since the Abron are hearty eaters and generally consume large quantities of futu.

I gathered information on pregnancy and the care of newborn children from interviews with the local doctor, as well as from women in Amamvi and Diassenpa. I observed child care during both my trips, but gathered data on pregnancy only during my second visit. For the

sake of clarity, I shall include both kinds of information
here. Men are not allowed to be present at a birth. I
was therefore unable to get any firsthand data on the
process. Although I had to rely on informants for this
information, I was lucky enough to hear the babble of
excitement that the birth of twins engendered in Diassenpa during my second trip to the field. I was
awakened from a sound sleep at about three in the
morning by the voices of a large group of excited
women, who sounded like a flock of clucking chickens.
Judging from the changes in tone that occurred during
the process, the birth itself took about one hour. I
heard no cries of pain from the mother, and in the
morning was invited to come and visit the house of the
new mother and her twin boys.

Birth is an occasion for joy. When a baby is born,
the excitement that begins in the house of the mother
spreads like a wave through the village. People greet a
new baby with skepticism, however. Happiness is tem-
pered by the realization that the first days of a child's
life are the most dangerous. The gods may take the
baby's spirit back to the land of the dead. The formal
acceptance of a newborn into the community does not
come until the end of the first week. At that time, the
parents dress the baby in a fine cloth and take it around
the village "to greet the people." After it is taken
home, the villagers return the visit, bringing small gifts.
Even this ceremony is not convincing proof that the
child is a full member of the group. This recognition
comes only after the child is a year old, when it receives its second name (the first name is automatic and
is merely the name of the day on which it was born).

The Abron place few restrictions on pregnant
women, with the exception of a taboo on the eating of
oranges. Otherwise, a woman's diet remains normal
during her full term. She eats no special foods, but
many women admit to cravings similar to those reported in Western society. Some desire clay, and since
this is a common medication, it is given freely. There
are no restrictions on sexual intercourse during preg-

nancy: a man may sleep with his wife right up to the moment of birth. On the other hand, a long post-partum sex taboo exists: a man may not sleep with his wife, after she has given birth, until the newborn walks. Although no Abron expresses it as such, this is a form of birth control, the woman's fecundity being cut considerably.

Some women prefer to give birth alone in the forest, probably because it is considered dangerous to be heard crying out during labor, for fear that a witch will harm the infant. Normally, however, when a woman begins her labor she is in the company of other women of her household. Older women, experienced in childbirth, willingly assist her.

The mother is not washed or prepared in any special way. She squats over some banana bark softened with lemon juice (if any is available) and crushed. The pregnant woman places her hands on the shoulders of another woman squatting in front of her, who in turn grips the pregnant woman's shoulders. This gives the latter leverage for bearing down. If the contractions are not strong, medication is given that increases their intensity. This drug, which I was not able to identify, is said to be so strong that women with narrow birth canals often rupture the uterus under the violent contractions thus stimulated. If the birth is normal, the baby falls on the banana bark. The cord is not cut until the placenta is expelled, and the woman remains in a squatting posture until all the afterbirth has appeared. The cord is pressed with a stick, cut with a knife or razor blade a few inches from the baby's body, and tied with a bit of thread. The remainder is allowed to fall off by itself.

Some women, especially those living in the trading towns, visit prenatal clinics set up by the government in Bondoukou and by the Catholic missionaries in Tanda. Women in Diassenpa and Amamvi were eager to be taken to the hospital for examination, but would never make the trip on their own. The high incidence of abortions due to venereal disease and other causes, some of them anatomical, has created a great deal of interest in this branch of European medicine. Doctors complain that women who come in for regular examinations rarely come to the hospital to give birth. The women believe that if they have followed the doctor's instructions, they will have a normal birth at home, a situation they prefer. Women who have been delivered by Caesarian section often attempt to have their next child on their own, with predictably tragic results. In an effort to ease this difficulty, the doctors perform low Caesarians whenever possible, as these do not weaken the uterus as much as the more drastic operation. At Berekum, among the Ghana Brong, the Catholic missionaries sometimes perform an operation to widen the pubic symphysis so that a woman with a narrow pelvic structure may have normal births.

As soon as the cord is cut, the child is splashed with cold water to make it cry, and then bathed with warm water and soap. The women in attendance also wash out the infant's mouth with a special medicine to clear the air passages of mucus. After the bath, the newborn is wrapped in a cloth and given a bracelet to protect it from harm. The mother then bathes, and white clay is applied to her body and to that of the child as a further protection. The child's first nourishment is usually taken at the breast of another woman.

Eighty per cent of all Abron women that I questioned believe that colostrum is harmful and therefore do not nurse their infants until the milk comes. The mother takes over the task of feeding as soon as this happens. Sometimes there are difficulties. When the mother does not have any milk, she is given a medicine to stimulate milk production.* If this does not work or

* Information from studies in the United States, particularly by Dana Raphael, suggest that all that is necessary to start milk flow is stimulation of the breast and that such "drugs" may have no more than a psychological effect. Dr. Raphael herself adopted a baby more than sixteen years after her last child was born and was, after a period of stimulation, able to nurse the child for several months.

if for any other reason a mother is unable to nurse her child (the Abron themselves say this is very rare), the baby may be given to a wet nurse or bottle fed from a mixture of canned or powdered milk and water. The water used in this preparation is never sterilized, nor is the bottle, which is bought in one of the trading towns. While I was in Diassenpa, a set of twins were successfully bottle fed in this manner.

Women rest in their houses for one week after giving birth. They may go out only to bathe and use the latrine. Restrictions on farm work last forty days, after which time they may resume normal activity. There are no food taboos placed on either the mother or the father, and no ceremony is associated with birth itself.

Sexual taboos are strictly enforced until the child walks. To hasten this process, the Abron make a walking trainer, a little cart with a handrail. The child is encouraged to walk with the aid of this device as soon as it can stand. Older siblings spend a good deal of time with the babies of their family, helping to speed the first steps.

Contrary to Western medicine, the eyes of newborn infants are not protected unless they are infected with a disease known as *anepaté*. This appears to be a form of mild conjunctivitis and probably clears up in time. Abron treatment consists of painting the eyebrow of the affected infant with clay—white over the left eye and red over the right eye. In spite of a high incidence of gonorrhea in the Abron area, the people do not distinguish gonococcal eye infection from other causes of blindness, and consequently there is no treatment for it. People believe, or at least say, that if a man closes his eyes during copulation, his child will be born blind.

When it is not on a woman's or a girl's back, the infant lies on a pile of cloth which is soft and always clean. A mother will not dry her baby when it urinates, but will wash off feces as soon as she discovers that the child has soiled. When on a woman's back, the infant's genitals are covered with clean rags to catch and absorb waste. These are reused, but are always washed after each soiling. I did not see a single case of anything even resembling diaper rash during my stay. Mothers wash their babies frequently with soap and hot water, usually from the head downward, the reverse of the procedure followed when adults wash themselves. Then they cover the clean baby with a thin dusting of white clay, or, more recently, with talcum powder bought in town.

Young infants are usually cared for by adults, although occasionally they may be watched by responsible children. They are never exposed to the sun, for the adults who look after them and carry them about do their best to avoid direct sunlight, which all Abron dislike. Some attempt is made to keep flies away from the child by covering it with a cloth. This is not sufficient to offer protection against mosquito bites, however, so the child is infected with malaria practically at birth although mosquitoes are common only during the rainy season.

Children are demand-fed and do not eat solid food until they can sit up. After weaning, the only major difference between adults' and children's diets is the relative shortage of meat for the younger members of Abron society. The protein deficiency that could result from such denial is apparently offset by the addition of lentils and beans to the diet during several months of the year.

The infant is always fed by its mother, who tries to see that an adequate amount of food has been consumed. Infants are not burped unless they fuss, and then the process is more or less automatic, as a fussy baby is handled and bounced around until it quiets down.

Infants always sleep with their mothers. Since women are taboo sexually to their husbands until the newborn child walks, the infant has no nighttime contact with the male household. The taboo on sexual intercourse is strengthened by the belief that if one sleeps with a woman too soon after she has given birth, her baby will get a swollen stomach and die.

Infants are the most overtly loved members of the society. They are constantly cared for and played with by their mothers' relatives. Men frequently visit women's compounds, where they play with the babies of the house. Most play involves simple fondling, although the infant may be given some small object to handle. Since children are fed on demand, they seldom put these objects in their mouths or suck their thumbs. Occasionally, one may see a small baby playing with a dangerous object, such as a knife or even a razor. Adults often seem unaware that these objects present possible hazards to children. If an older child deprives a young one of a toy in the presence of an adult, it is usually returned.

Children's dress has been described. Its poorness is a demonstration of the general poverty of children in Abron society. Even though they are loved, they are deprived. This is the result of the heavily age-ranked status system in which people attain certain rights as they mature and come to occupy responsible positions in the social system. Children sit on chairs only when there are enough for all the adults present; they eat food considered inferior for adults; and they are dressed in ragged, insufficient clothing. They sleep several to a room or even on the porches of houses, and must give prized possessions to any older sibling who might demand them.

Beyond necessary tasks, childhood activities are never supervised. Children play as they wish and wander where they will, and it is up to the older children to caution their young playmates about the dangers of wood and savanna. A parent's contact with children lessens markedly after the child begins to walk with ease. Bathing then becomes the responsibility of the child, and most children take care to clean themselves at the proper time lest they be punished or made fun of. Childhood, however, is the time for romping around the village, and most children are covered with a layer of dust mixed with animal feces from shortly after their first bath to the next washing, at the end of the day. As long as they follow the formula and bathe at the proper times, they can be as dirty as they wish, or, at least, as dirty as their activity makes them.

For the Abron, who have no germ theory of disease, something or someone not visibly dirty is clean. Dishes are washed in murky water, as are clothes. Dirty underclothes are the business of the wearer, and work clothes need not be cleaned, as they are not worn after the evening bath.

To get dirty during the course of an honest day's work is a normal state of affairs, but to miss the evening bath is a serious infraction which can actually lead to social ostracism. An Abron does not want to eat with someone who has not bathed. One old man in Diassenpa, a debt slave, rarely washed. His body odor was pronounced and people avoided him. The morning bath is justified on the grounds that sexual intercourse makes one dirty, and although one does not have sexual relations every night, the habit of bathing in the morning is considered a good one. Dirtiness is an emotional subject akin to elimination. People do not like to talk about either, and while sexual joking is open between adults and children of both sexes, bathroom jokes, even those referring to the bathtub, are mildly taboo. One does not talk to people in the morning until after bathing.

Cleanliness appears to be an aesthetic concept. Dirty people and dirty things do not look good. Women and men take pride in their houses, and neatness is as important as decoration. Dirtiness and disorder are roughly equated, as they are in our own society.

The Abron have no formal preventive medicine. Yet, many of their practices include sensible approaches to daily life which reduce the threat of infection. Many of these are related to their concept of order and the aesthetic that is coupled with it. Such concepts furnish them with useful if limited tools that provide considerable barriers to disease. Since the concept of cleanliness touches only surface reality, however, the Abron have no way of judging what goes on in the submicroscopic world of disease organisms. Their hygienic customs work best against diseases that are spread through filth and carelessness. More subtle relations between disease organisms and man are unknown, so diseases such as malaria are impossible to avoid.

5
Emerging Patterns: History, Social Organization, Agriculture

Abdoulaye taught me Abron history. His information is part of oral tradition and as such, no doubt, represents the "official" view of who the Abron are, where they originated, and how they came to rule in Kolongo territory. The story resembles others from many parts of Africa, where the idea of conquest provides the major justification for inequality between ethnic groups. How much of it can be classed as a secular origin myth and how much reflects real history is difficult to say, but a close look at current relationships between Kolongo and Abron sheds some light on the problem.*

According to Abdoulaye, sometime in the sixteenth or seventeenth century (for obvious reasons, he and other Abron are very vague about early dates), the Ashanti empire began to take shape in Ghana. The Ashanti pattern of conquest was to incorporate existing lesser states into a loose confederation of Akan-speaking peoples. The Abron, or Brong as they are known in Ghana, lived in the northwestern part of what was to become Ashanti land. Faced with incorporation, flight, or war, a portion of the group chose to stay in Ghana, where they are now, a subgroup of the Ashanti nation. The rest, under the leadership of a queen, fled to the west into what is now the Ivory Coast and conquered the Kolongo. Abron centralized political authority provided superior military organization to that of the Kolongo, who had no political unit higher than the in-

* A full account of Abron ethnohistory will soon be published by Emanuel Terray in France.

dividual village. The Kolongo could be conquered village by village and incorporated one segment at a time into an expanding Abron state.

I am not convinced that the Abron actually conquered the Kolongo in what we would conceive of as war. I think, instead, that because population density was so low in the area it was not difficult for the Abron to penetrate the territory and take up residence in the empty places. The location of the earliest Abron villages, Zanzan and Yakassé, close to today's Ghana border, suggests that the initial Abron settlement was not far from the limits of Ashanti power. It seems likely that, with their superior form of political organization, Abron power could be slowly imposed on the Kolongo without much actual fighting. In addition, the fact that the Abron took slaves in raids might have convinced nearby Kolongo villages to accept Abron rule and thereby avoid enslavement. Although the Kolongo occupied an inferior position in what came to be the Abron state, they were nonetheless free, and intermarriage between the two groups became quite common. I believe Abron "warfare" was in fact largely limited to slave raiding among the less well organized groups living on the fringes of their territory. Certainly their military strength could never have been impressive. Only a small number of Kolongo villages close to the point of original penetration into the Ivory Coast were incorporated. Today the majority of Kolongo villages lie outside of Abron control or are only loosely touched by Abron sovereignty.

The interpenetration of territory is not a rare occurrence in Africa. The largest town in what is technically Abron country is inhabited by a patrilineal, Islamicized, non-Akan-speaking people originally from the west of the Ivory Coast and Guinea. These people, the Dioula, are traders, and have lived in peace in the area for at least several generations.

Evidence that the Abron moved into Kolongo territory without total war is also provided by the system of land tenure. Villages as units are said to hold land. Thus Abron villages have their land and Kolongo villages theirs. Title may pass to individual kinship groups (lineages in the old days, families today) if they are resident in the village, but such title is based on use: land, to be retained, must be worked. Strangers who move into a village must obtain permission to use free savanna. Permission is usually granted, for there is no shortage of this type of land used for the production of subsistence crops. Forest, however, is relatively scarce and valuable. This has been true at least since the introduction of cash crops. The Abron recognize that forest land belongs to Kolongo groups and, by their own rules, must ask permission of Kolongo chiefs to work it. In addition, mineral rights are, or were, held by Kolongo, and the extraction of gold was undertaken with permission from Kolongo titleholders.

As I have mentioned, the ideology of conquest, widespread in Africa, is found also among the Abron. In the light of what I know about Abron culture, I would be surprised if this ideology is completely true. The Abron do not strike me as a warrior people, capable of mounting concerted offensive action against their neighbors.

Abdoulaye drew a chart for me showing the Abron royal line branching downward through time. He told me about historical divisions that had occurred and placed them spatially on a detailed map of the area which I had bought in Abidjan. His description fit in with what I had learned about African political organization. The Abron represented a single case of a wider pattern which had been described in the anthropological literature.

As in most African states, kinship among the Abron is an overlay on a social organization that depends upon lineage segmentation. Under segmentary systems, groups of kin (lineages) related either through a paternal or a maternal line, constitute the political, social, and economic units. All members of the ethnic group

are related to a founding ancestor, but with each succeeding generation, the number of lines multiplies, each
taking off from one son or, in the case of matrilineal
systems, nephew (eldest sister's eldest son) of the
founder, and in turn the founder's children's children,
and so on. Each member of the ethnic group is a
member of a minimal lineage (the smallest number of
unilineally related kin who form a corporate unit) and
more inclusive lineages up to the largest unit recognized, which is usually the entire group. At each level,
groups are more or less equal in power and wealth.
Relations between lineages are activated on the basis of
social distance between individuals involved in contracts or disputes. For example, two individuals who
are members of different minimal lineages that are both
nested into the group on the next-highest level (a larger
lineage segment) can each mobilize his own minimal
lineage in the commerce between them. If their minimal lineages are in turn members of different larger
groups, a wider group of people (all those who belong
to the two wider units) may become involved.

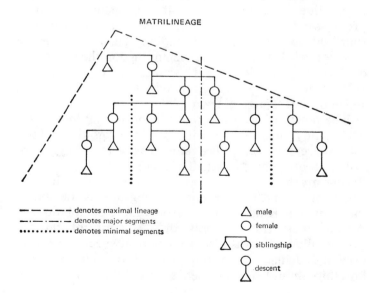

MATRILINEAGE

— — — — — — denotes maximal lineage △ male
—·—·—·— denotes major segments ○ female
•••••••••••••denotes minimal segments △○ siblingship
  ○|△ descent

Through time, the number of segments increases with each new generation. At the same time, some lines are lost and others combined, since the structure is only partially based upon genealogical relationships. In fact, the whole system constitutes an ideology, which in reality responds to political expediency. Lines are folded and genealogies changed in order to smooth out political differences or to give one group an advantage over another.

In African states that are also segmentary in the fashion described, certain lines come to be isolated as royal or noble lineages. They occupy a place in the system against which commoners can be defined. Nonetheless, these royal lines also tend to segment through time. According to tradition, shortly after arrival in the Ivory Coast the Abron elite split into two factions (which either were, or became, royal lineage segments). These factions settled in the villages of Zanzan and Yakassé and are so named. After some dispute as to who was to rule the kingdom, the leaders of Zanzan and Yakassé agreed to circulate royal authority. On the death of a king, the ranking member of the other royal line would take up the kingship. As time progressed, the number of lines increased from two to four and, finally, with the founding of Diassenpa as an offshoot of Tabgne in the beginning of the twentieth century, to five. Today the existing five royal lines reside in the villages of Amamvi, Tabgne, Diassenpa, Herebo, and Tangamourou.

The power of kingship is not incorporated in the person of any ruler. Instead it rests in a "golden" stool, which circulates with accession to power. A king without a stool cannot reign. This was made clear to me during my two trips to Abron territory. The man who was King at that time, Kwamé Adingra, was the son of the previous King. This was a complete violation of Abron rules, for not only did Adingra inhabit the wrong village, he was also a patrilineal successor to the previous King. According to Abron custom, the kingship should have passed to the village of Herebo,

Abron women spinning, 1962

View of Diassenpa, 1962

Tchina Kofi and Oppong prepare snake-bite medicine, 1962

Diassenpa, 1961: woman cleaning her house

Pounding futu, 1962

Young woman preparing yams, 1962

Twins born in Diassenpa, March 1962

Tapping a palm for palm wine, 1962

where the eldest member of the royal lineage was Kofi Yeboa. Adingra was able to seize power with the help of French colonial authorities. He was favored because he and his father had heeded De Gaulle's call to arms against Germany and the Vichy Government in 1940. All through his reign, many Abron expressed dissatisfaction with the situation. This was particularly apparent in Diassenpa and other royal villages, where potential kings looked with disfavor upon the breaking of the normal order of succession. Finally, in the fall of 1961, a group of young men from Tabgne stole the stool from Amamvi, Adingra's village.

At this point the police stepped in. The stool was taken to Bondoukou, the seat of the prefect, and put into a cell in the local jail. Newly independent, the Ivory Coast Government was exerting its authority over the King, and reserved to itself judgment concerning the kingship. As far as most Abron were concerned, he could not fulfill his kingly role because he had lost the stool, which was paramount not as the *sign* of office but as the *office itself*.

This is where the matter rested all during my second stay in Abron land. In January of 1963, Adingra was killed in an automobile accident on the way back from a trip to Bondoukou, and the stool was allowed to pass to Kofi Yeboa, its rightful guardian.

As a resident in Amamvi, I was able to observe the functioning of the King's court. With Oppong as my interpreter, I could follow court cases and watch individual members of the King's retinue in action. In addition, from time to time Adingra himself explained the symbols of kingship from which his power flowed. Other elders, particularly Pong Kofi, provided me with a description of contemporary Abron political subdivisions.

The Abron state is based on the power of the stool, which is shared according to strict rules of succession. The stool is both a political and a religious symbol. As among the Ashanti, whom the Abron resemble in many ways, the stool is said to have descended from heaven to provide the Abron with political unity. The king, acting for the stool, is the religious, judicial, and political head of the Abron polity. He makes decisions about war, adjudicates disputes between parties, and performs those ceremonies, particularly the yam festival, that insure that Abron life will maintain its desired state of equilibrium.

Under the king are the chiefs of five cantons, known as Penongo, Achedom, Anenefy, Fumasa, and Ciagni. These chiefs are charged with the handling of local matters and succeed to office according to patrilineal rules, i.e., the son of a deceased chief takes his father's office. Although this pattern is out of harmony with the general rule of matrilineal inheritance found among the Abron, it appears to be an indigenous pattern.

Below the canton, each village has its own chief, who, following the matrilineal rule, succeeds to office as the eldest son of the eldest sister of the deceased chief. The power of the village chief is limited to local affairs, and his decision-making power is further diluted by the influence of a council of elders made up of old men (formerly lineage heads) and, in some cases, old women of the village. If a chief is rich, wise, and endowed with oratorial skill, his authority is likely to be strong. If he lacks any of these qualities, he may be by-passed or overruled by the elders. In Diassenpa, the village chief was a dull and poor man whose powers of oratory were minimal. Since Diassenpa is also a royal village, the royal lineage chief there assumed the local chief's role in village politics.

In the old days, before the introduction of cash crops, which have eroded the concept of lineage property and lineage organization, the lineage was also a focus of political activity. Each lineage had its chief. Lineage members were responsible to him and to lineage elders in the operation of what was a corporate group, holding common title to land, distributing work and the fruits of work, and providing its young men with the goods to pay the required bride price. The latter function was very important, since no Abron male could marry without a considerable bride payment, nor could he hope to accumulate enough goods on his own to make this payment. The provision of bride price was thus an essential element in the political authority of the lineage. The introduction of private property and cash payments for bride price led to a rapid decline in the power of the lineage. At the present time, kindreds (groups of kin that, unlike lineages, are related through either the father or the mother—the equivalent of a large family in the United States, with a mother and father and their siblings, their children, their siblings' children, along with surviving grandparents on each side) are the effective economic unit, although matrilineal inheritance continues to be practiced.

KINDRED

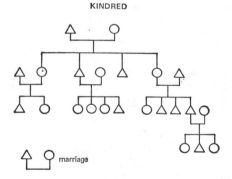

All Abron except the king work as farmers. In addition to subsistence crops—yams, taro, and to a lesser extent maize, dry rice, and millet, as well as a wide assortment of vegetables ranging from tomatoes, cayenne pepper, and eggplants, to onions and lentils—the Abron of today raise three important cash crops and collect a fourth. These are coffee, cacao, oranges, and kola nuts. The latter are collected in the forest. Work depends upon family co-operation and hired hands, usually Mossi. In previous times, slaves (who were captured in war) and debt slaves helped with garden work and the mining of gold, which was an important activity. The riches of the kingdom were also increased through taxes and labor provided by Kolongo who had become vassals of the Abron state.

Social organization is a major interest of anthropologists. This includes regular patterns of interaction among different categories of people, elder with younger, men with women, status group with status group, as well as the system of kinship, by which relatives are distinguished, and the internal political organization of the society. The idea of social organization is built up by the anthropologist from observation of daily patterns of interaction as well as the gathering of rules from informants. Kinship is determined through the gathering of genealogies, in which actual relatives are distinguished and placed in family trees along with the terms appropriate to them. Some of these patterns are easy to determine; others are buried under apparent differences that melt away with careful analysis and reanalysis of gathered material. My initial work in Amamvi was little concerned with these patterns, as I was at first unable to distinguish how individuals fit into regular categories. There were, of course, exceptions. The relationships between men and men, between women and women, and between the sexes, began to emerge early. The court was a place in which I could determine general patterns of behavior among different individuals as they related to the King and to the internal functioning of local politics.

The spatial arrangement of social categories was the most obvious pattern to fall into place. The King's palace, for example, was centrally located in the village of Amamvi. It was a large cement building painted yellow and green with a roof of corrugated iron. Unlike ordinary houses, it contained, in addition to several bedrooms occupied by the King and his sons, a large meeting room. Like the larger houses, it also had a central courtyard. This and the meeting room served as the locus for the court. On most days, these spaces were the gathering place for the older men, some of the older women, and court officers. These included the talking chief (ochamé) and a court dwarf.

While I was in Amamvi, several cases were heard by the King. In addition to the flag incident, these included cases of adultery (in which men had accused their wives of infidelity) and one case of petty thievery. I was not able to follow the outcome of any of these cases in detail, and during my second trip I did not attend court. The general procedures were, however, apparent. In all cases, the King heard the accusation first and then the defense. Witnesses to the alleged crime also were given a chance to speak. Occasionally the King himself would pose a question directly, but usually he would speak to his ochamé, who would then address the witness. After the presentation of evidence, the group of assembled elders would discuss the case with occasional intercessions from the King through his ochamé. In the cases of adultery, the accused were made to stand before the court during the entire procedure. The man accused of thievery was bound hand and foot and sat before the King. Apparently his guilt was assumed by everyone present. Now and then, one of the elders would stride over to him and cuff him on the face and shoulders. This beating was certainly not pleasant, but it was not very severe either. Instead, it looked like a public display of anger and displeasure on the part of one or another elder before the assembly.

Sometimes it was obvious that the King was at odds with the elders over some point in a case. There would be a great deal of argument, often without the intercession of the ochamé. The King would often shout at his adversary, who would bow his head during the tirade. When the court had come to a decision, the King would set the punishment, usually a fine (sometimes in money and sometimes in goods) and, in the case of men, a period of servitude on the King's estates. Later, many Abron complained that Adingra was too free with the latter type of punishment, which, they said, he tended to impose for his own profit.

In addition to previous reading on Africa and preliminary observations in Amamvi, my penetration of Abron social organization was accelerated through conversations with the Sparks, who had a considerable fund of knowledge. They were particularly aware of those patterns that contrasted with their own. Also, the Abron themselves practice a kind of reverse anthropology, in which European patterns serve to highlight the distinctiveness of Abron culture. Abron self-awareness increases as they become familiar with the world beyond their own immediate boundaries. This makes it possible for them to verbalize certain features of Abron culture that might otherwise be submerged in the uneventfulness of daily life.

Certain aspects of social organization were striking. The missionaries were quick to tell me that the Abron were odd in at least two respects: men and women lived apart even after marriage, and they called some cousins on the father's side "brother" and "sister." The missionaries had also noted that, on the mother's side, some cousins were called "son" and "daughter."

The Sparks were correct about both patterns. The Abron are duolocal: men live in men's houses and women in women's houses. Under ideal conditions, this situation continues throughout life and married couples never cohabit. A woman is born into the house of her mother. She grows up in the company of her mother and her aunts (her mother's sisters), her aunts' daughters, her own sisters, and finally her own as well as her sisters' daughters. A man normally lives in his father's house, taking up residence there as soon as he can walk and feed himself. There he finds his father's full brothers, his own brothers, and his father's full brothers' sons. Some men may live with their maternal uncles, but this is not the preferred residence. In any case, a man's adult life is spent in the company of men.

A man may have several wives, but since he cannot marry women who are sisters, all his spouses will come from different women's houses. Each wife prepares food for her husband's table and brings it to his house, where the men eat in common. She then returns to her own house to eat with her female relatives. Because wives come from separate female households, tension between them is partially avoided, although arguments do break out not only between wives, but between whole female households related through a common husband.

When a man wishes to sleep with his wife, he invites her to join him in his room after dark. If she agrees, she will come to his house after the other men have gone to sleep. She will leave before dawn. If a man has more than one wife, and this is true only of the richer, older men, he will sleep with each of them on a rotating basis during the week. If a wife is menstruating or nursing an infant, she is taboo to her husband and will drop out of the cycle.

Both the Sparks and individual villagers were quick to tell me that the Abron are matrilineal. That is to say, title and goods pass down from man to man through a line of females. Instead of inheriting from his father, a man will inherit from his mother's brother and leave his goods to his eldest sister's eldest son. A woman leaves her goods to her eldest daughter. If one compares this rule of inheritance to the rules of residence, we can see that for women the two rules are in harmony, but that for men there is a disjunction between inheritance and residence. Women live only with matrilineal relatives. Men live in a house founded by a group of matrilineally related men (a set of whole brothers, sons of the same mother), but as each brother gets married and has children, the situation changes. The sons of each of these brothers will belong to a different matriline, since membership comes through the mother. In most matrilineal societies, men either live with their maternal uncle from an early age or take up residence at marriage with or near the maternal uncle or the parents of the bride. Among the Abron, a man who inherits from his maternal uncle is, nonetheless, brought up by his own father, and it is between father and son that parental relationships on the male side are most close. As we shall see later, this disjunction between inheritance and residence for men creates tensions in Abron society that have become aggravated since the introduction of private property.

The missionaries' information about kinship was all I needed, to know that the Abron have what anthropologists call a Crow kinship system. Typical of Crow terminology is the merging of generations for certain kin. In one's own generation, the offspring of father's sister (cousin, in our system) are called by the same term that applies to father and mother. On the same side, father's brother's children are called by the same term that one applies to his or her brother and sister. The latter applies also on the mother's side, where mother's sister's children are called brother and sister. Finally, children of one's mother's brother are called by the same terms as are applied to one's own children.

I have been careful to say that a particular kin is called by a term that is also *applied to* another kin (father's sister's daughter, for example, is called by a term that is also applied to one's own mother). I have *not* said that a person *calls* a cousin mother or father, brother or sister, son or daughter. The reason for this distinction is very important. The Abron do not recognize generation as a distinctive feature of kinship as it applies to cousins and the terms for mother and father. They construct their kinship system according to different principles from those we employ in our own system. For someone who has not given much thought to the subject of kinship, it will seem as if the Abron violate some natural rule by which relatives are named. Actually, such terminological systems are rather arbitrary, or, better, are based on sets of rules that become codified by a particular culture. We use generation as a criterion for distinction in all cases in which the distinction exists. Thus, the terms "father" and "mother" are applied only to individuals one generation above ego. "Children" are only found one generation below ego, and "cousins" in ego's own generation. We also separate lineal relatives from all collaterals; that is, we limit our use of the terms "father" and "mother" to a direct line of relatives that includes grandparents, parents,

AMERICAN KINSHIP SYSTEM

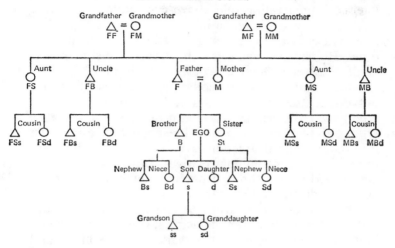

ABRON KINSHIP SYSTEM

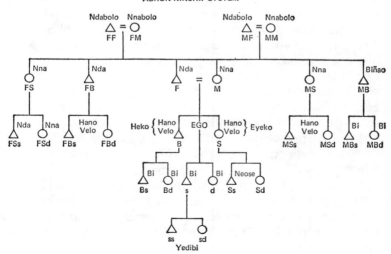

children, grandchildren, and so on. Thus, mother and
father are lineal relatives, while uncle and aunt are collaterals in generation one above ego. Note also that a
distinction by sex is made in our system that applies to
most kin but not to the term "cousin." In French (and
other Romance languages), however, a distinction is
made between female *cousine* and male *cousin*.
Brothers and sisters are collateral relatives (they are
not direct ascendants or descendants of ego) of one
type, and cousins are collateral relatives of another
type, although both types of kin appear in ego's own
generation. The distinction is based on their closeness
to ego in terms of linking relatives. Brothers and sisters
are related to ego through parents, and cousins are related to ego through grandparents.

The Abron system is just as logical as our own, but
it depends upon different principles. Generation may be
blurred and no distinction is made between lineal and
collateral relatives. Thus, the term that is *applied* to father may also be applied to his brother and to father's
sister's son. The Abron also make a distinction that is
not found at all in our own kinship system. They mark
older and younger siblings of both sexes. *Hano* applies
to older siblings and *velo* applies to younger siblings.
The kinship system also contains terms for brother of
any age (*heko*) and sister of any age (*eyeko*). The distinction elder-younger is very important in Abron social life, for the entire society is based on respect for
age, and even slight differences can determine patterns
of respect and responsibility between individuals.

My first few weeks in the field, I was able to check
out the residence patterns without any difficulty.
Kinship would have been much harder to discover if
the Sparks had not provided the important clue. The
Abron system is not unique. I had had it described
many times in classes in social structure and had come
across it in reading. It is almost always found in associ-
ation with matrilineal societies that have a lineage
structure, that is, corporate groups made up of
matrilineally related kin.

My first field trip occurred during the summer rains; the second spanned the long dry season. The two seasons form the basis of very different rhythms of life and present contrasting physical aspects. During the rains, the grass along the roads towers above even the tallest individual. On the paths and smaller trails, one feels as if walking in a tunnel. Everything is green. Except in the village and along straight stretches of the road, there is no horizon. The sky, full of humidity, is lead gray, broken only occasionally in the evening, when the sun drops below the mantel of clouds and provides a rather spectacular sunset. The ground is alive with insects, and one thinks always of rain, even when none falls. Between the constant hum of mosquitoes and the humidity, the night seems long and is partially sleepless.

The rains sustain the growing period. In the dry season, the land looks barren. The grass is reduced to broken yellow stalks. Yet the dry season is a time of plenty, for it is then that the food crops are harvested.

I am fond of neither heat nor humidity, and although I found the dry season uncomfortable, particularly at midday, the rainy season was unbearable. The heat is moderate but I was constantly dripping. My evening bath provided only momentary relief from a constant feeling of stickiness. In the dry season, the heat dissipates after six o'clock, and when the harmattan blows off the Sahara at night the temperature can drop as low as 45 degrees. On such occasions the heat of the day could be washed off. A bath kept me clean-feeling well into the late morning hours.

The Abron, however, prefer the climate during the rains. The houses provide good protection and rain is not so frequent that it becomes depressing. People are much more disturbed by the wide swings of temperature that come in the dry season. Colds, grippe, and even malarial attacks are more frequent when the daily temperature swings in exaggerated loops between 105 and 50 degrees in a twenty-four-hour period.

The rainy season is a time of great activity. Just before the rains, major new fields are burned off. Then, after the first storms, the soil is worked and major crops are planted by the men. When these tasks are completed, Abron men are free to engage in political discussions, to play endless games of wari (the board game common all over West Africa), checkers, and sometimes cards.

From time to time, a man will want to make some *tanga,* or palm wine. This requires a visit to a toddy palm, which is cut at the crown. When the sap is collected, it is placed in clay pots and allowed to ferment. If a man has money, he will prefer to buy tanga rather than make it, and men are always on the lookout for a friend who has a full tanga pot and might be willing to share it. Drinking is never, as far as I could tell, a private affair, and a man with a good pot will readily share it with a group of men. Women are also sometimes invited to drink tanga, but this rarely occurs. Not all tanga turns out well, and the first man to taste it, usually the maker, will comment on its quality, *ho dun* (sweet), or *ha doi* (not sweet). *Ho dun* is the preferred taste, and good tanga is not completely fermented. To me, it tasted a bit like slightly sweetened hard cider. (Sonia found it a bit vinegary, or "spoiled.")

The major burden of daily work falls upon the women during the rainy season. They may be seen leaving for their garden each morning after their bath and after preparing breakfast for themselves, their children, and their men. Gardens are weeded frequently, and each woman will be so occupied until the harvest period.

One rather misty day, Abdoulaye took me to see his yam gardens and coffee trees. We set off on a path that cut across the savanna, dotted with palmettoes. After a walk of five minutes, we came to a cleared area that was marked out by lines of pineapple plants. These were borders between gardens, he told me. We crossed several of these gardens and finally came to one of his own. The yams were planted in neat hills, on one side of which stout poles were stuck in the ground. The young plants, with their bright-green, triangular leaves and tendrils, looked a bit like morning glories. Abdoulaye put down his machete and, working from hill to hill, began to tie the vines to the poles. If this is not done, he told me, the plants will die. Anxious to show me his coffee trees as well, he completed the tying of only a few hills and we set off again, this time into a low-lying area in which the forest had pushed itself up to form an island in the savanna. Adequate runoff from the surrounding high ground provided the water to support a small stand of trees.

The growth was quite thick and, walking along the path, I occasionally had to push a branch aside. After doing this once or twice, I felt a sharp, burning sting on my shoulder, and then another, and still another. I pulled my shirt off and found that I was being bitten repeatedly by a red fire ant, which had dropped off a leaf. Fire ants are capable of multiple stings, which burn almost as badly as a yellow jacket's. They often accumulate on fruit trees, particularly orange trees. Before these fruits are harvested, Abron tie some meat in one of the branches to attract all the ants to one place. Much to my sorrow, I once leaned on an orange tree that, although it had been treated in this way, shook under my weight. Several fire ants dropped into my shirt. On that occasion, I provided my companions with a good week of fun. The pain had been due to my stupidity. Anyone who is silly enough to shake fire ants down on himself deserves to be stung. The story of my misfortune spread through the village so rapidly that it could have given birth to a new proverb reflecting upon fire ants and the stupidity of visiting anthropologists.

Soon the trees thinned out and we came to a part of the forest in which rows of very young coffee saplings grew under the protective canopy of the taller forest layer. Abdoulaye had about thirty young coffee trees planted in this grove, but none of them were yet old enough to bear fruit. He inspected his burgeoning plantation and finally led me to a small lean-to covered with palm leaves, in which he lit a small fire. By this time it was raining and we were both quite cold. We sat down under the shelter and, reaching under the low end, where the leaves touched the ground, Abdoulaye pulled out a pot of palm wine. It was *ho dun,* about two quarts of it, and we sat quietly talking and drinking for some time.

Following people out to their gardens took up most of my time during my stay at Amamvi. Women leave their houses around ten in the morning after finishing their cooking and cleaning. Usually a group of friends and their children set out for the gardens with their tools and some food for a light afternoon meal. One or more of the women carry a charred bit of smoldering wood. This is used to start a small cooking fire in the fields. In addition, most women carry babies on their backs wrapped in the cloth that covers the shoulders and drapes over the long skirt. Babies stay in this position most of the day and sleep as their mothers work. Weeding, which is done with a machete, forces the women to bend partway over at the waist (Abron almost never bend at the knees when they must pick something off the ground or perform such tasks as weeding or sweeping) and swing the machete with a chopping motion inward, toward the body. This is done rhythmically for long periods, and so the baby is rocked, sometimes even jarred, as its mother works. When a child soils itself, the mother swings it off her back, cleans it and herself off, and ties it back into position. Mothers attempt to anticipate when their children are going to defecate. In such cases, the child is taken off the back and held with both hands in front of the mother's body until the child relieves itself. Mothers never get angry when babies soil on their back, but they express displeasure, at least to each other, when this happens. An older child who defecates or urinates in the house is reprimanded, and children who already walk will usually take care of these functions outside of the house. Because the latrines are far away from the dwelling areas and because they are quite deep and therefore dangerous for a young child, real toilet training takes place rather late, about the age of five or six.

Women spend up to about six hours in the fields. After they have finished weeding and/or planting such lesser crops as tomatoes, onions, peppers, beans, or squash, they gather food for the evening meal, place it in a basin which is carried on the head, and begin their walk home. Most gardens are some distance (one to four kilometers) from the village, along paths that run away from the road.

Men do not often go to their gardens during the growing season. Rather, they work when the spirit moves them, although they are aware of their responsibilities and will carry them out as part of the work cycle.

As the yam vines grow long, men tie them to poles stuck in the ground around each yam hill or to young trees frequently left standing in the yam gardens. This is sporadic work and represents only a mild interruption of the leisure enjoyed by men.

The dry season brings about a partial reversal of the work rhythm. In the middle of the winter, men harvest the cash crops. In late December and January, they gather oranges, which grow around the periphery of the village; in January and into February, they gather the coffee beans and cacao (both crops require a good deal of attention, and it is the men who set up drying racks for them). These are loaded with the harvest, which must be turned and spread out every few days so that the beans can dry evenly. In March, the men begin to repair or to make farming tools: axes, hoes, and digging sticks. During this period, women rarely leave the village except to gather firewood or to pick up a load of yams from the farms. Their activity is centered on the hearth, where they may be seen sweeping their houses, cooking, or restoring their fireplaces. In between, they chat among themselves or visit men's houses and join in the general gossip of the village.

Women, and less frequently men, also go to market. Some go once a week on a regular basis to sell a small portion of their harvest and to buy cloth, salt, fuel for lamps, and occasionally a chicken or dried fish. The market provides a pleasant break in the daily round. It is a place to meet friends from other villages and to exchange local news. Commerce is light, and although money is used in all transactions, the amounts bought and sold are very small. Except for the foreign trading companies and Dioula traders, who profit from the market and are tied into the larger, national commerce of buying and selling, most transactions, even though they involve money, represent exchange rather than selling for gain. A few goods are sold for small change, which is soon reconverted into goods to fill simple needs.

The Abron are becoming increasingly aware of economic disparities between themselves and traders, both Dioula and European. They have acquired a range of new needs for commercial goods, and the educated among them are drawn to the city.

Abdoulaye was unhappy. He had two wives, one in Amamvi and the other in Diassenpa, and four children. As one of the few literate older Abron (he was about forty), he felt that he could do better in the city. He was very concerned about providing for his family, particularly his children, whom he wanted to see go to school. He had visions of a large house for himself, and two good houses for his wives as well. He told me that he was going to leave Diassenpa and try his luck in Abidjan. I attempted to discourage him, saying that Abidjan was very expensive and that jobs were hard to find. I compared the life at Amamvi, where no one was hungry, with life in the city slums. He was not convinced. He, like most people from the country, have relatives in the city, and new migrants count on their relatives and other members of their own ethnic group to help them with food and lodging while they look for work. This situation cuts two ways, however. While it is true that a new arrival finds help in the city, the ease with which one can establish oneself tends to attract more people than the labor market can absorb. In addition, as more kin arrive, the burden on those who do work is so increased that the meager pay can provide little more than bare necessities.

After my first return to the States, I received a letter from Abdoulaye, who had indeed gone to Abidjan. He asked me to buy him a wallet from a certain company in the United States. At first I wondered why he had made this strange request, but, when the wallet arrived, it came with a set of magical instructions on how to use it to get rich. These suggested that the wallet be put under one's pillow at night. The user was also told to say a prayer that was included in the package. Of course, the company made no direct claims that the system would work, but the implication was very strong that this was no ordinary wallet. The same company sent me a catalog of other wares, including various kinds of magic rings, which, it was implied, could make the wearer strong, and perfumes that would make the wearer sexually irresistible.

The first thing I did on my arrival back in the Ivory Coast in 1961 was to look up Abdoulaye and give him his wallet. I invited him to dinner at the hotel. He accepted and arrived dressed in his best clothes. I took the menu and told him what was available, because I suddenly realized that I did not want him to see the absurdly high prices. One meal in that modest hotel cost the same as a good week of food for Abdoulaye. I suggested various kinds of meat, which he refused, finally telling me that he was afraid that the animals were killed by machine, therefore violating Islamic law concerning the preparation of meat. Finally he settled for an omelette, and I guiltily ordered a steak. Although very proper and polite and certainly equipped with all the best table manners, Abdoulaye seemed very ill at ease. This was not the place for the two of us to have a conversation. The relative wealth of the hotel, although it was the cheapest in Abidjan that provided air conditioning, and the typical colonial guests really did not sit well with either of us. Besides, it was not a dinner Abdoulaye wanted from me, it was help. He was my friend. He had gone out of his way to guide me through a few difficult weeks in the bush, and he was convinced that I could find him a job with my "friends" at the American Embassy. This was, of course, impossible, but he could not understand how one American could not convince another to do a countryman a favor, particularly in a foreign setting. We parted sadly that night, and I never saw him again. A few months after my final return from the field, he wrote me a melancholy letter asking me once again to find him a job either with the Embassy or some American company. He let me know that he was very disappointed with my efforts on his behalf.*

My six weeks in the field passed rapidly. I had collected data on farming and shot a good deal of 8-mm film. These later served as a partial record of life during the rainy season. Although I did not understand Kolongo, I had some notion of the workings of the king's court, thanks to Oppong. Religion was still a total unknown. The residence pattern and kinship system had fallen into place early. Experience with first aid was already beginning to turn my interests toward Abron medicine and hygiene. Abdoulaye had become my friend, and I was to miss him during my later trips.

I had arranged with the Sparks to pick Oppong and me up on the morning of my last day. After saying good-by to King Adingra at his house, we made a final round of the village and bid farewell to Pong Kofi. At Gumeré, Oppong and I separated. He went to his home at Lomo and I stayed with the Sparks for one night. The next day, I caught a ride with a truck going from Gumeré directly to Abidjan. I arrived in the late afternoon, checked into the same hotel in which my voyage

* Abdoulaye was lucky, however, and he now works for a trading company. His younger wife from Diassenpa, has joined him in the city, and they are raising a large family.

in the Ivory Coast had started, and made straight for the shower. The water flowing over my body was a real luxury, the thing I had most missed in the field. The dust that had covered me during the ride south left a stain around the bottom of the shower stall. It had turned into sticky red clay.

In the early evening, I went down to the café to observe city life again. The only impression I remember well is that white people looked exceptionally pasty, even sickly. The next day, I left Africa for Paris, and a week later was back in the United States.

The following months were spent in New Haven. I completed a final year of course work and began to prepare for the study of Abron medicine and hygiene. I had little time to analyze the data already collected and did not feel confident enough about Abron culture to do much with it anyway. Too many spaces had to be filled in during the next trip. Much later, I was to find that my notions about the Abron were to change with the flow of my thinking about anthropology in general. As the school year passed, I became more and more anxious to return to the Abron. Amamvi had left a deep impression and I was eager to become entangled in the life of Diassenpa.

6
Diassenpa

My first stay in Abron country was very brief. I left
with only the barest understanding of how the culture
worked. But I had made several good contacts and left
many friends behind. Amamvi was a bit large for my
research needs, so I determined to work in Diassenpa,
a smaller village about a half mile away. This would
give me the advantage of knowing everyone in a single
village and, because of the nearness to Amamvi, the
opportunity to continue observations there. Smallness
meant that I could collect medical data on every
member of the community and follow disease patterns
as they emerged in the village. In addition, because I
had only a limited time in which to do field work, I felt
that the restricted setting would allow me to collect
more material in depth on the social behavior of a limited range of individuals.

A little more than a year passed between my first
and second trips. When I arrived in Gumeré, I stayed
for a few days with Dupont, a French trader, revisited
the missionaries, and made contact with Oppong, who
appeared, as he did before, out of nowhere, the day
after my arrival. After buying some supplies, we set out
for Amamvi.

We were greeted with an eerie silence. No men sat
under the big tree; even the courtyards of the women
were deserted. Not even a single curious child came to
the car. We drove to the King's house and went in, but
it was also empty. Then we heard the sound of drums
coming from one end of the village. "It's a funeral,"
Oppong told me as we approached the sound on foot.
Everyone was gathered in and around a large men's
house on the outskirts of the village. In the courtyard,
people were dancing in honor of the dead in front of a
row of mourners sitting near the drummers. As we en-

tered the open place through the compound door, the men gave out a yell, the drummers dropped their sticks, and everyone rushed toward us shouting, "Alex." We were engulfed by the crowd, everyone trying to embrace us. The children jumped up and down in delight. I had kept my word and returned. Those who were not directly involved broke away from the funeral and took us to the house of my former landlord, Pong Kofi. The funeral itself was not a very serious affair, since the man being honored had died twenty days before. Funeral ceremonies take place for three days and nights at death, for one day twenty days after death, and again for a single day forty-three days after the first funeral.

We sat in the middle of Pong Kofi's courtyard and, for the first time in my experience, the greeting pattern was ignored by the crowd. Literally half the village came up to shake hands, asking if I could identify them. A child whose finger had been badly infected and whom I had treated every day up to my departure, came to show me that he was completely healed. Pong Kofi himself took me to my old rooms to reminisce about my former stay and to show me the improvements that had been made in the house since I had occupied it. A goat and several yams were brought as gifts of greeting.

The warmth of welcome made it difficult to mention my decision to stay in another village. I began slowly. "I am happy to be back with you, and I thank you for this greeting." "How long will you stay this time?" I was asked. "I shall remain with the Abron for several months." "Will you live in my house?" asked Pong Kofi. There was no other way out to tell them of my decision. "No, I have decided to stay in Diassenpa, because it is smaller and I will be able to know the people better. But I shall visit Amamvi often." Kofi looked hurt, but said diplomatically, "Amamvi and Diassenpa are one. If you stay there, you are still in our village, but you must visit this house often." My embarrassment was solved through a typically Abron diplomatic maneuver, but, for months afterward, people from Amamvi would ask why I had chosen to live in another village. I repeated my explanation again and again until the question was no longer asked, and I also made it a point of visiting Amamvi often. If I had hurt peoples' feelings, it was never mentioned directly. One of the reasons beyond friendship that people had wanted me to live in their village was my large supply of first-aid equipment. During my first stay in Amamvi, I had managed to cure many minor ills, particularly hundreds of tropical sores, which plague the children. I told the people of Amamvi that they should come to Diassenpa for treatment.

Pong Kofi himself took me to Diassenpa, where he helped to set me up in the house of a relative. The centrally located compound was one of the more substantial Abron dwellings, cemented and roofed in corrugated galvanized iron. Even the courtyard had a cement floor, an accommodation that served well in the rainy season. We arrived in the early evening, just before mealtime. The young men of the house had just bathed. They were joking with a woman who had brought a pot of food from her compound. The men greeted us as we entered, and then, apparently without paying much attention to me, went back to their joking. But this time, I soon discovered, I was the butt of the humor. Sexual joking is allowed between brothers and sisters, providing a non-relative is the object of the joke, and I served as a perfect foil for the young men.

The gist of the fun was the suggestion that the young girl, Ajoa Badu, and I have sexual relations. When she protested, her brothers said that she was afraid of my penis. This sexual joking continued for two or three days, until I began to call the girl "sister." This was a reasonable kinship designation, because she was a sister to my age-mates in the house. Once our kinship was accepted, any suggestion of mutual sexual relations became a matter of poor taste, and the joking stopped. My solution to this problem eventually led the members of my household to accept me as a son or brother to the men of the compound. Ajoa Badu's mother also began to call me *mi bi* (my son), so I became an accepted kinsman in her compound. Usually, the anthropologist waits to be adopted into a family. I had forced the issue to avoid embarrassment.

My house was owned by an old man, Tchina Kofi, who had inherited it from his elder brother a few months before. He shared it with two younger brothers and the sons of the original houseowner. The older men became my fathers, the sons of the original houseowner my brothers. These relations tied me to several female houses as well. The first houseowner had had three wives, my mothers. Each of these women had their own houses, inhabited by their sisters (also my mothers) and daughters, who became my sisters. In addition, Tchina Kofi had two wives, again my mothers.

Tchina Kofi was tiny, but muscular. His face was gray-brown, like old leather, usually covered with a short growth of white bristles. During the working day, he dressed in a pair of shapeless old shorts and a brown double-breasted jacket, undoubtedly bought years before, secondhand. After his bath, he would emerge from his room with a brown-and-red toga draped over his skinny body. He loved to chew kola and consequently spat frequently. Whenever he spat, he would rub the glob of saliva into the ground with his bare foot. My first impression of him was negative. He looked like a cranky and dirty old man, but he became one of my favorite people. He was kind to his family and to me and had a marvelous sense of humor, which bubbled over at the slightest provocation. He was also a master of mime, and although at first we could not communicate through language, he could always act out what was on his mind. Our relationship was such that, after a time, I thought of him as a real father and a close friend as well.

His slightly younger brother, Azumana, was one of three Moslems in the village. Like Tchina Kofi, his outward appearance was at first somewhat unappetizing, but also like his brother, he was a man of good disposition. Azumana was under five feet two inches tall and as thin as a stick. His head, always shaved to the skin, was a brown, shiny dome. He moved in rapid, mincing steps, like a rodent, and was always talking to himself. I never saw him wearing anything but a single dirty blue "Arab" robe. He washed as often as the other men of the village, but, unlike them, he never seemed to change his clothing. Azumana and Tchina Kofi were the best storytellers in the village, and there were many nights when they would gather the children around them for a long session of Abron folk tales. These brothers were also hard workers, each spending long hours in the yam fields or cacao plantations. When they returned home in the evening, they both wore the tired expression of men who had used their bodies in hard physical labor. Tchina Kofi would settle down under a tree and nap before his bath, but Azumana, bowed and weary, would continue to scurry around, mumbling to himself until prayer time. He would then bathe, spread his mat on the ground, and offer his respects to Allah.

Tchina Kofi was a traditionalist. His gods were the old deities of the Abron. These were not often worshiped, unless there was some need: a request, a wish to know the future, or a payment for some past service rendered. On one occasion, Tchina Kofi left Diassenpa for a few days, and when he came back he sacrificed to Tano, the river god the Abron share with their Ashanti neighbors across the border. His wife brought a chicken, a bowl, and a plate to his door. He cut the chicken's throat and let the blood run down the wall outside his room. The chicken was then given back to his wife to cook, since only blood was necessary for the sacrifice. He then placed something I could not see under the dish and left it outside his room for a few days. My curiosity soon got the better of me. The Abron are quite casual about their sacrifices. I had eaten many eggs that had first been given to the gods, and so I asked Tchina Kofi if I could see what was under the dish. He willingly let me look. I found two

Ghana pennies. "Why did you sacrifice Ghana money?" I asked. "Because Tano lives in Ghana," he replied, puzzled by my inability to think logically.

One day, Tchina Kofi was squatting in front of his door cutting up a length of palmetto spine into sections. The end product was a cylindrical piece of pulpwood six inches long and two inches in diameter, with the consistency of balsa wood. I asked him what he was making, but he refused to answer. When I pressed him, he began to laugh. This was a clue that what he was making had something to do with the latrine. The Abron joke freely about sex, but elimination is a strictly taboo subject even among close friends of the same sex. Because he was amused and because he understood that I had come to learn everything I could about Abron custom, he finally broke down and explained rather clearly through mime that he was preparing Abron toilet paper. As he went through the motions, he could not control his mirth and finally gave way completely to his laughter. Tears came to his eyes as he fairly rolled on the ground.

Kwasi (Tan) Daté, the first son of the original houseowner, was the hardest worker in the village. He was up before dawn and gone from the village until the evening bath time. He took care not only of his own fields but those of his recently dead father. Kwasi was a black Apollo, muscular and handsome with a broad smile. Although only in his thirties, he had been married five years and supported two wives. He was always on the lookout for another wife, but he approached matrimony with responsibility, making sure that he could provide for his scattered families. One of his wives was a priest, a woman of considerable power. She was opposed to any new spouses for him, but he seemed determined to marry again anyway. Unfortunately, I left Diassenpa before the situation resolved itself, and I have no idea if she was able to influence her husband.

Although Tchina Kofi was the legal head of our household, Kwasi was the real leader. As the eldest

youth and son of the founder of the household, he com-
manded respect from the other junior members of the
house. Tchina Kofi generally followed his decisions, because he was a man of serious purpose. He was also
outgoing, wise, thoughtful, and a good talker. Kwasi's
personal characteristics helped him maintain prestige
within the village even though he was only a junior in
comparison with most village elders. Kwasi loved to
buy presents for his wives and children. His major
weakness was clothing. He kept a good supply of bright
togas, the most expensive of which were made in
Ghana by Ashanti weavers. Even his work clothes were
extraordinary, in both size and choice of secondhand
wardrobe. One of his favorite items was a pair of heavy
woolen breeches in a red lumberjack plaid. They were
held up by a pair of thick red suspenders and worn
even in the hottest weather. Kwasi had learned how to
run a sewing machine, and he often made his own
shirts from cloth bought in the market. Weaving is a
traditional men's occupation, and when sewing ma-
chines were introduced it was only logical that men
continue their monopoly.

Kwasi loved palm wine as much as any other man in
the village. When there was a good supply of well-fer-
mented, cool brew, he could be found among the
drinkers. It takes a lot of tanga to intoxicate an experienced drinker, but, on some days, there is enough
available from the tapster to affect most of the adult
men of the village.

The Abron have adopted a special drinking day
(*Sopeh*), which comes once in the Kolongo, six-day
week. Every Sopeh, Kwasi Daté was the center of the
largest drinking group. Some Abron get abusive when
drunk, but Kwasi mellowed into a state of exaggerated
good nature in which he loved the entire world. Drunk-
enness also made him generous, and I was often invited
to share his pot of wine. The first time he offered me
tanga, I was unfamiliar with its alcohol level and drank
too much. I could hardly walk by the time the pot of
wine was down to the dregs. The mild misfortunes of

others are the gist of Abron humor, and while the people are not overtly cruel, except occasionally toward small animals, they do enjoy real-life slapstick. A wavering drunk is considered a capital situation for humor. It was many weeks before Kwasi let me forget that first drinking bout and its effects upon my equilibrium.

Another aspect of Abron humor involves a game of strategy. Strangers are asked for impossible favors. If they grant them, so much the better not only for the recipient but for all witnesses, since the gullible victim becomes the butt of jokes. Anthropologists have a tendency to be gift givers, hoping in this way to gain entry into society and friendship. Among the Abron, this is not always wise, since the more one gives the more one is asked for. Nor is the giver respected, for it is against the rules of Abron culture to get something for nothing. When I finally learned to refuse all but reasonable requests, my prestige in the village improved. It is a silly man who throws away his wealth; presents are donated for services or to gain prestige and power.

Sometimes the game of strategy can be quite complicated and pragmatic as players attempt to gain some advantage. Kwasi Daté and Tchina Kofi involved me in one of these games quite early in my stay in Diassenpa.

The cacao crop had been poor that year due to a lack of rain. In an attempt to earn some extra cash, Kwasi and Kofi decided to buy a cow, slaughter it, and sell the meat in the village. A group of Fulani herders passed through the village with a few thin animals for sale, and Tchina Kofi began to negotiate for one of them. The Fulani wanted sixteen thousand francs for his cow. At first, Kofi offered him twelve thousand. The Fulani refused. Tchina Kofi squatted on the ground and said nothing. Kwasi offered thirteen thousand francs, but the herder remained adamant. Kwasi then also squatted down without another word. The herder then joined them on the ground, each staring at the animal, each waiting for the other to make another offer. The

silence lasted for several minutes, and all the while a
crowd began to gather to watch. Finally, the Fulani
said that he would take fifteen thousand but not a franc
less. Kofi offered him fourteen thousand and the owner
refused again. Other men in the crowd began to discuss
the value of the animal and the amount it might fetch
in the village as meat. Kofi's friends made fun of the
animal, saying that it was nothing but skin and bones
and not worth the price. The herdsman countered that
it was a fine cow and that it could be used for breeding
if it was not bought. Fairly sure that the Fulani would
accept his last offer, Tchina Kofi ployed by getting up
and slowly walking away from the group. The herder,
knowing that he would do no better, stopped him and
agreed on the price. The deal seemed to have been con-
summated, but it turned out that Tchina Kofi had no
money to pay for the animal. He turned to me and in
an assured tone demanded that I lend him the money.
He said that he would repay it the next day with interest. I had already decided that I was not going to turn
into the local bank, and refused. Kofi then suggested
that the owner sell him the animal but not take payment until the meat was sold. The herder, knowing it
was a risky venture, refused to part with his cow until it
was paid for. He was anxious to sell, however, and he
agreed to wait until Kofi could raise the money. Although Kofi had told me that he had no money, he
managed to produce six thousand francs between himself and Kwasi. He had finally decided that the cow was
worth risking his own capital. He and Kwasi then spent
the rest of the afternoon borrowing money from other
villagers. By evening, they were still two thousand
francs short. They appealed once more to the herder,
asking him to wait for the rest of the money. He again
refused, wanting to leave the village that day. It began
to look as if the entire deal would fall through. Wishing
to see what would follow, I gave two thousand francs
to Oppong and told him to lend the money in his name
so that I would not be involved. The cow was finally
purchased. The Fulani left with their other animals and

the money, and the two men proceeded to kill the cow. The carcass was cut in a haphazard fashion and divided into approximately half-kilo portions, each with a share of bone, fat, and meat, and laid out in the center of the village. Buyers came forth to purchase these portions at a price slightly under that of the local market. By the end of the day, the meat was beginning to smell and had attracted swarms of flies. Still it was not all sold. That evening, Kofi came to me with a present of the kidneys, a choice, tender part. He had respected my decision not to invest in the purchase. The remaining meat was hung in the storeroom of our house, where, by morning, the smell was overpowering. That day, Kofi and Kwasi continued to sell what was left of the animal, this time at a slightly lower price. Thankfully, by the second evening all the meat was sold. The total profit was under one thousand francs, but it was not bad for two days' work. Kofi and Kwasi had accurately judged the value of the animal.

Some of the men who had lent money to pay for the animal had bought meat. In effect, they were paying for their own meat, but evidently none of them saw it that way, and they were repaid only after the entire animal was sold off.

An episode of strategy that did not come out well for me concerned a goat that Pong Kofi had given me on my arrival in Amamvi. Wishing to give a gift to my new family, I donated the animal to the common table, and asked to share in the meal. Everyone agreed, but after the animal was slaughtered, they decided not to cook the meat until the next day. I am not sure, but I think they knew that I would not eat day-old meat. In any event, I was out a goat. The affair did not end there, however. After accepting the animal with much thanks, most of the men informed me that the goat was a taboo animal for them. They pointed out that if I was to give a gift to the house, it would be unfair of me to leave them out. They demanded two chickens in lieu of the goat. Not exactly by coincidence, the chief of Diassenpa had given me two large cocks as an arrival gift in the village. These were turned over to my house-mates, who had a feast while I dined on canned goods. None of this means that the Abron are ungenerous. On other occasions, I was given gifts of food not only by Tchina Kofi but by other men of the village. One man went out of his way to hunt guinea fowl for me. But none of this generosity was shown until I had proved my own worth through first aid and other services.

Abron names lead to a good deal of confusion among visitors. There are only seven first names for males and seven for women—one for each day of the Abron week. Kofi was a Friday, and Kwasi, a Sunday. There were two Kwamés (Saturday) in my house and Oppong was a Thursday (Yao). The remaining day names for men are Kwajo (Monday), Kwabena (Tuesday) and Kwaku (Wednesday). Girls' names from Monday to Sunday are Ajoa, Abena, Akua, Yawa, Afua, Ama, Kousia. The days of the week are Joda, Benada, Ukwoda, Yaoda, Fieda, Memeneda, Kwaseda.

Living in my house were two half brothers by the same father, Kofi and Kwasi, with the same last name, Apo. (Last names, however, do not follow family lines.) The elder, Kofi, was one of the few plump Abron men. He was of average height, five feet six, and in spite of his paunch, quite muscular. He had an extraordinary disposition, one side of which was reflected in his constant broad smile. The other side emerged when he was drunk. At such times, and they were frequent, he became surly, particularly with those against whom he held a grudge. His family was involved in a feud with another family of the village, and Kofi was almost singlehandedly responsible for keeping it alive. Whenever he got drunk, he would go out of his way to insult members of the other family. Such insults do not go unnoticed, and he was often brought before the village chief and fined. As an unmarried youth, he was allowed some leeway in his behavior. His ill humor was better tolerated than it would have been in a married man of full adult status.

Kofi Apo liked to hunt. Whenever he could get away

from the village for a night of hunting, he would. All
the capital he could accumulate went into ammunition
for the antique shotgun he treasured above all his other
possessions. Night hunting involves the use of a jack
light, worn on the head like a miner's lamp. Kofi owned
one of the few such lights in the village.

Kwasi Apo was a sad-faced boy of fifteen. Thin and
weak, he brooded around the house and did little farm
work with his family. In the middle of my stay, he
came down with a respiratory infection, which was
cured after a short stay at the hospital, but if anyone in
the village was likely to get tuberculosis it was he.
Kwasi looked like a lonely philosopher. When something amused him, on some rare occasion, he would
break into a weak smile that made him look like a
kindly old man. Most Abron, even children, enjoy a
good argument, and when age-mates are together there
is a constant stream of conversation. Kwasi sat in the
background most of the time and listened silently to
what was said. He was a late child of his mother, who
had been unable to conceive for several years after giving birth to his elder brother. In desperation, because
his father and mother wanted more children, they appealed to a powerful Kolongo god, Eboah, to grant
them a child. Shortly after this, Kwasi was born. He is
considered the son of Eboah, and on that god's day he
wears a red toga to honor his paternity.

Kwamé Kosinu and his half sister Ajoa Badu were
the most deviant young people in the village. Ajoa had
attended school through the sixth grade and left only
when she had become pregnant after a liaison with one
of her teachers. She had a daughter and returned to the
village, where she kept house with her mother. She was
about seventeen, her body already spent from child-
bearing. Ajoa had a lovely face, her beauty spoiled only
by her smile, which revealed a large gap between the
two upper incisors. She had a good sense of humor and
could not be angered, although she was often the victim
of sexual joking, more because of her own forward behavior than the fact that she had an illegitimate child.

Ajoa had a selfish streak; although she loved her
daughter she would often steal meat from her. She was
the sloppiest housekeeper in the village, and when her
mother was not home, household order degenerated
shamefully. She loved to dress up and had dreams of
marrying a rich man from the city. Ajoa was a useful
informant for me, because she enjoyed speaking French
and had a loose tongue, which could always be stimulated to reveal some village secret. She was vain, always
admiring herself, and was very pleased when I
presented her with jewelry. She was also the only
Abron who ever expressed to me the desire to be white.
Ajoa's charm came from her easygoing, relaxed nature
and an innocence that, to a great extent, made up for
her bad traits.

   Ajoa's half brother Kwamé was a handsome youth,
also about seventeen. He was enrolled in the Cours
Complimentaire, a high school for those considered unable to go on to the *"Bac,"* the French academic di-
ploma awarded at the end of secondary school. He had
been studying to become a teacher but had come home
because of his father's death. He was the village, perhaps even the district, Don Juan, and had affairs with
women much older than himself. Kwamé often got into
trouble with other men's wives and had a reputation for
stealing. In one instance, he not only slept with a man's
wife but, to add insult to injury, stole the man's pants
and money. During my stay in the village, he spent a
few weeks in the district jail.

   Few Abron steal, and Kwamé's behavior was looked
down upon by his entire family. At one time or another, his relatives, even Ajoa, warned me about him.
But his dishonesty was not total. When I first came to
Diassenpa, my light meter disappeared. A few weeks
later, when, as a gift for interpreting for me, I gave
Kwamé a pair of shoes he admired, he emerged from
his room with my meter, which he claimed one of the
children had found that day. His family was particularly annoyed by his laziness. Most of the time, Kwamé
sat around doing nothing or chased after the girls of

other villages. He ate from the common table, but except to go on occasional group hunts, which were considered more of a sport than work anyway, he never contributed labor to food production. Kwamé and Badu were caught between worlds. Having had considerably more schooling than any of the other members of the village, they were typical products of such circumstances. Kwamé acted out the role of playboy; Badu dreamed away much of her time.

Badu's mother, Afua Morofyé, a woman of about fifty, was an extremely competent woman. She had lived to see all nine of her children grow to adulthood, an amazing record in an area where infant mortality is 30 per cent. She was familiar with the vast pharmacopoeia known to West Africans. While many of these drugs are of little value, others work well for simple complaints. Among these, the Abron have several effective fever depressants, an abortant, and many vermifuges. They also know various formulas for laxatives and analgesics. Afua Morofyé was a repository of such information. She was also a patient woman, who taught all her children, including myself, with a gentle calm. I spent many days in the courtyard of my Abron mother learning about food preparation, cleanliness, medicines, and religion. She was proud of her children, all except Badu, whom she loved nonetheless. Badu was her great failure, and yet they got along well, because they were mother and daughter and because this mother could only love her offspring.

When I was finally installed in Diassenpa, I decided to invite the Sparks to dinner in order to repay the kindness they had shown me during my first trip. Since I had limited stores, I offered them a choice between beef burgundy, which I could prepare with local meat and cheap table wine available in the local market, or sweet-and-sour chicken, the ingredients for which could be easily put together from my collection of staples. When I told them that the beef would contain wine, they settled on the chicken although I assured them that the alcohol would evaporate during cooking. On

the day before their arrival, I set about making chopsticks from lengths of dried elephant grass, which could
be found around the village. The next day, I precooked
a tough village chicken, and by evening was ready for
my guests. When they arrived, I set up a table in my
corner of the courtyard and the four of us sat down to
eat. The adult members of my household kept themselves discreetly busy, for, as noted earlier, to watch
others eat is one of the worst breaches of Abron etiquette. The children, however, could not contain themselves, and soon the area was teeming with a large assortment of village youngsters. I picked up my
chopsticks and began to eat the food. Many New
Yorkers are fully adept with these tools and I am no
exception. The Sparks, however, who had never tried
them before, soon gave up and asked me if I would not
mind if they used forks. Their chopsticks were put
aside and they ate the rest of their meal apparently
satisfied with my cooking.

The next evening, I noticed that about half the village children were carrying lengths of elephant grass.
By mealtime many of them had successfully cut the
grass into chopstick-size lengths. They were soon amusing themselves at dinner trying to eat the slippery futu.
A few of them managed to manipulate the sticks quite
well, and although I usually averted my eyes when people ate, I must confess that the children's efforts in-
trigued me enough to violate my new code of manners.
The novelty apparently wore off after one meal: I
never saw any Abron eating with chopsticks again.

7
Beginning Again

The first few weeks in Diassenpa, most of my time was spent doing first aid and taking the more seriously ill to the hospital. Village children were covered with sores, and many were also suffering from other sicknesses, particularly malaria. Afternoons were reserved for anthropological work, which began with a village map and a census. At the same time, the village chief, Kwaku Adjé, offered his services to me as an informant. He would tell me about Abron history and customs, and answer any questions I might have, for a small fee. He spoke a peculiar French picked up during the First World War, but it was good enough so that I could work with him without an interpreter. I prefer to get data from groups in informal situations rather than from single persons. In fact, I often obtained useful information during drinking sessions, when I could get several men to discuss their culture together. I used single informants to check data obtained from other single informants. In the beginning, however, when I knew few individuals, I used Adjé. We spent several hours together for two or three days, but it soon became obvious that I would need Oppong's help. Adjé's information confused me. Even though there are vast differences among cultures, all good data display an internal logic that in turn reflects a general structure. Adjé's material just did not fit together. I continued to work with him for a while because he did give me leads that could be checked with others and because I felt trapped by the relationship. At the same time, I began to make inquiries about Adjé. He was far from popular in the village. His authority as chief was bypassed by the council, and most cases were taken directly to the head of the royal line or the Queen Mother (the sister of the maternal uncle of the royal lineage chief and a

powerful political figure). Most people considered him
a silly and selfish old man who had degraded himself on
several occasions by arguing with younger men. Adjé
was also criticized because he lacked eloquence. While
the position of an Abron chief is hereditary, the power
that goes with the office is not. A good leader, one
whose authority will be respected, must prove he has
chiefly qualities. He must be wise, rendering fair and, if
possible, eloquent decisions, and he must be a good
talker, able to convince the audience as well as the
plaintiffs in a case. A few years before my arrival, Adjé
had lowered himself before the entire village: A
younger man had insulted him publicly. Adjé took him
to court before the King, in Amamvi, where he was
fined a considerable sum. Adjé's honor would have
been restored if he had accepted the decision. Instead,
he set fire to the man's orange groves. If he had not
been chief and the original plaintiff, Adjé would have
been liable to a court summons. His action put life
back into a dispute that had been settled by the courts.
While there are vindictive men among the Abron, only
the King can reign and show such a disregard for law
and custom.(And even kings can be overthrown. Adjé's
behavior suggested abnormality. Eventually I found out
that he had been gassed during the First World War,
when he had served in the French Army.)

In the beginning, there was general resistance to
questions about religion and kinship. After a few
weeks, Oppong found out that no one would tell me
anything essential until the Queen Mother had given
her permission. She was away on a visit to another village and would not be back for two weeks. When she
finally returned to Diassenpa, the elders were called together to decide my case. The Queen Mother was old
by any standards. For the Abron, she was ancient.
When she gathered her family together, great-
grandchildren sat at her feet. She was a large woman,
heavy-framed, and bent like a thorn tree. Her brown
skin was tinged with gray, and her large breasts hung

flat against her chest like empty leather bags. She wore a man's cloth draped either over one shoulder or around her waist. As a woman of great age and status, she could wear the cloth like a man. Her brown eyes were lost deep in the loose wrinkles of her face, but when she looked directly at someone, or was making a point to the court, they glowed like two distant lights. Her head was covered with gray moss, cut very short; her hands were gnarled with arthritis. She had a very large head and prominent chin, which made her look like the Red Queen in *Alice in Wonderland*. Her bearing was as regal as that of any queen. She spoke slowly, in a cracked voice, which, like her eyes, was buried deep in her head. Oppong acted as my interpreter and ochamé. This was a role he liked, and he was magnificent. I had come, he told the court, to rescue Abron customs from oblivion. My books would preserve the dignity of the royal lineage and of her people and make the Abron equal to the Ashanti. But I was to do more than this. Was she not told that on my first day in the village I had saved the life of Atta Kwasi, who had lain ill for days? (I had taken him to the hospital for treatment.) I was not like other white men, who come to change the Abron. I was neither missionary nor merchant, but a friend. I had come once before and had returned to my friends. I was accepted by the King. After Oppong had finished, other elders rose to speak. I sat tensely, understanding little. What kind of information did I want, demanded the Queen Mother's ochamé. Through Oppong, I explained that I wanted to find out how the Abron lived and believed. I emphasized medicine, telling the court that there was much Europeans could learn from African medicine and that they could help by sharing their secrets with me. After the cross-examination was finished, the elders conferred with the Queen Mother, and then she spoke directly to me. "You have proved your friendship to this village," she said, "and we shall share what we can with you." And then to the assembled villagers,

"Tell this man everything he asks you. Do not be afraid; you have the permission of the Queen Mother." I had passed the test, and real work could begin.

From then on, people were willing to talk to me and it was no longer necessary to pay for information. But there were areas that many Abron did not feel comfortable talking about. Religion was still a vague domain. Kwamé Kosinu, who was Catholic, told me that there were three other Catholics in the village and that the other villagers no longer worshiped the old gods. This was untrue, but I could not get any useful information on beliefs. My breakthrough came with the aid of the missionaries, who gave me the words for "witch," "priest," and "devil." My knowledge of these words unlocked many tongues. I used the first in conversation with Badu and her mother. When they realized that I knew something about witchcraft, at least that it existed, they opened up. It was then that I began to get a feeling for what went on beneath the composed exteriors of these people.

 The Abron are pragmatic. Religious observances do not occupy much time in an individual's daily life. There are few ceremonies, and the gods do not bother those who do not have a specific obligation to them. But Abron culture is witch-ridden. Most villagers actively fear the attacks of witches (*deresé;* plural, *deresogo*). The strangest thing about this fear is that it is focused on members of one's own family: witches can harm only their own kin.

Deresogo are supernatural beings. Unlike gods, they live with people but are unknown to them. Deresogo fly in the night and eat the souls of their victims. Like the witches of medieval Europe, they gather to celebrate their own sabbath. They kill at night through magic and are able to change into animals at will. No ordinary Abron can do anything against them. They strike swiftly, bringing disease and death down upon their victims. They kill out of personal envy. Their motive is to destroy any individual who makes them jealous. Ordinary villagers live in constant fear of attack. Attitudes are colored by the realization that some close kinsmen may be witches.

Ranged against deresogo are *kparesogo,* or priests. Only kparesogo know which individuals are deresogo and they only can combat witches. Kparesogo never reveal which villagers are deresogo. This would bring them into general combat with the entire community of witches—a great risk.

The Abron pantheon is divided into good and evil gods. The high god, *Nyamé,* stands alone as the Creator and Prime Mover. Although he is responsible for epidemics and some other manifestations of disease, he has little to do with the affairs of men. Below Nyamé is *Tano,* the river god. He is often appealed to in time of need. After Tano there is a wide range of gods, or *gbawkaw,* who inhabit various natural areas such as mountains, rivers, or even trees and objects such as specially prepared gin bottles and crudely carved statues. Every kparesé and deresé have their own gbawkaw, through whom their power is derived.

When a man dies, the Abron tie a bit of hair from his head and nail parings from the fingers and toes in a small bundle which they place on five bamboo poles. Two men carry these on their heads as they walk around the center of a circle bounded by a group of villagers. A man chosen for his age and wisdom directs a series of yes-or-no questions at the bundle. If the answer is no, the men continue to walk without difficulty, but if the answer is yes, their heads dip from side to side under the influence of the bundle, which becomes agitated. It is thus that the Abron are able to determine the cause of death and also whether or not the individual was a witch in his lifetime. The first question generally put is, "Were you a witch?" If the answer is yes, the rite is over and the corpse is disposed of without ceremony.

Deresogo do not always bring serious illness upon their victims. A Kwamé Apo, who was the uncle on the mother's side of the young men of my house, was one of the richest men in Diassenpa. He had a large cacao plantation and owned several orange trees. In a good year he could make over one thousand dollars, a considerable sum in a country where the average income was fifty-two dollars a year and in a village where he had few necessary expenses. Kwamé's main desire in life, the desire of most adult men, was to build himself a fine cement house with an iron roof and then to provide his wife with a similar house. When I lived in Diassenpa, Kwamé lived in a rented room in the house of the Queen Mother. His room looked out on a large shell of a house that was eventually to become his. The mud walls stood ready for their veneer of cement, and the roof had been finished. Every time Kwamé saved enough money to complete his dwelling, he would inexplicably and compulsively squander his funds and find himself penniless until the next harvest. He and his wife became so disturbed by this behavior that they consulted a kparesé. After divination, the priest told them that a jealous deresé did not want Kwamé to complete the house. Every time he accumulated the necessary capital, the deresé would bewitch him and he would lose all his money. The priest promised to help him against his adversary, but the deresé was evidently quite powerful. Nothing the priest did could stop Kwamé from wasting his money.

Although the sexual joking about Badu and me stopped when I was adopted into her family, my kinship relationships were incomplete because my wealth (the Abron assumed that I was very rich indeed) suggested that I should have many wives. Since my wife, Sonia, did not join me in the field until very late, I was wifeless, as far as my friends were concerned. This abnormal state of affairs must have caused some conversation, since even during my first trip, my lack of female companionship became a matter of public interest. Abdoulaye, who had taken it upon himself to be my friend and confidant, came to me one evening and asked me very frankly if I wanted *"une jeune fille pour la nuit."* I replied that this would not be neces-

Attawa, 1973

Two Abron between yam storage racks; Afua, daughter
of Kofi Apo, at left (photo by Marilyn Paul)

Etienne, 1973 (photo by Marilyn Paul)

Cousins teasing, 1973 (photo by Marilyn Paul)

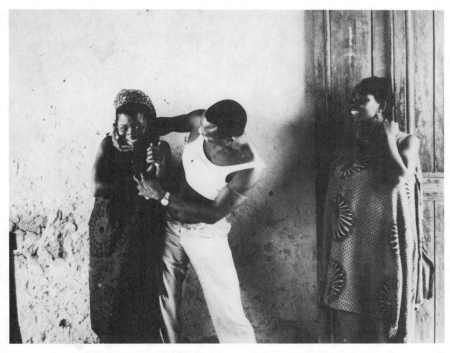

My mother, Afua Morofyé, 1973 (photo by Marilyn Paul)

Fofyé, a religious ceremony in Assuifri, 1962

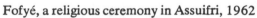

sary, and he apologized, sensing the delicacy of the situation. Feeling that I had embarrassed Abdoulaye, I said in response to his apology, *"Ah, ça va,"* meaning only "It's not important." This was not his interpretation, however, and several minutes later he returned to my room with a young girl and an older woman. They were mother and daughter. Neither spoke any French, but Abdoulaye told them to shake hands with me, and the girl, after some prompting, managed to say, *"Bon soir, monsieur."* The girl looked very embarrassed; the mother, very determined. For a long time, she and Abdoulaye kept up an animated conversation, the subject of which was obviously myself and the woman's daughter. Finally, Abdoulaye said to me, "This woman will give her daughter to you if you will take her picture with your Polaroid camera." For a moment, I did not know what to say. Then I realized that I could get out of the sticky situation easily. "I'm very sorry," I replied, "but I have no more film." Abdoulaye relayed this response to the woman, who, with a frown, quickly pushed her daughter out of the room and disappeared.

On the surface, this anecdote undoubtedly begs several questions. Was, for example, Abdoulaye soliciting for the girl's mother; did he lack respect for Abron womanhood? Was the mother loose with the sexual favors of her daughter? Was I unnecessarily prudish in this situation? These questions put one ethic against another and beg still another set of questions. Abdoulaye was my friend and was concerned with my comfort. As a man, he had a man's view of sexual needs and an Abron's view of white behavior. Except for missionaries, I met few unattached white men in the Ivory Coast who did not have either African mistresses or casual sexual liaisons with local women. Dupont (the French trader in Gumeré), who himself had an African mistress of whom he was quite fond, once pointed out a small, wizened Frenchman who worked for the Ivory Coast Government as a supervisor in the building and repairing of roads. "You see that man," he said with

wonder and humility, "he sleeps with a different woman
every night."

In addition, it is abnormal for an adult man who can
afford to get married to remain single. For those who
cannot afford wives, there are potential liaisons with
married and unmarried women of the village. Abdoulaye quite correctly judged that I did not know how
to go about getting a woman, and so put himself in the
position of arranging things for me. What he did not
count on was the fact that I did not want to sleep with
an Abron girl. This is not because I am a prude, but I
am prudent, and several factors weighed against my
giving into what were real sexual desires and frustrations during field work. First of all, I did not want in
any way to be associated with the white colonial world,
which comes and takes what it wishes without regard
for local feelings and customs. My reasons for this were
both practical and moral. It can lead to strained relations and make field work more difficult, and it is immoral in the ethical and political sense, given the colonial context. It was not sex that was immoral in this
situation, but the situation itself. Doubly so since the
girl herself was given no choice.

What of the woman and her daughter? Frankly, I am
still puzzled by the event from their point of view.
Abron do *not* casually offer their children to strangers
or other Abron. Affairs are carried out *sub rosa,* without the approval of relatives on either side. Adultery,
although it occurs, is considered disruptive at the very
least. The only thing I can think of is that this woman
had some debt to Abdoulaye, which induced her to
make me an offer. Perhaps for the sake of her own
honor, she felt that she should gain at least a token reward in return for her daughter. The girl had nothing
to say in the matter; when she shook hands with me, it
was with her eyes averted. I'm sure that she was scared
to death by the entire encounter.

Early in my second trip, Atta, an Éwe mason from
Togo who had become my friend, came rushing into

my house. "Alex, come quick, Abdoulaye's daughter is very ill." I picked up my first-aid supplies, and the two of us rushed down the road to Amamvi. When we arrived, he led me through a maze of women's compounds to a small, round house at the edge of the village. We entered a dark room lit only by light filtering in from the doorway covered by a tattered cloth. The room was full of women talking in low, excited voices. Against the rounded wall opposite the door, a small child lay on a mat. She was covered with a wool blanket, but was shivering. I took her temperature; she was running a fever of 104. The most likely diagnosis was malaria, and so I gave her mother enough anti-malaria pills for a full treatment and asked Atta to translate the directions for dosage and time of day the pills were to be taken. She agreed to follow my directions and the girl took her first medication in my presence. Nonetheless, the women of the house seemed unsatisfied with the treatment I had given the child. I told Atta that I would come back the next day to look in on the girl.

The next morning, I returned to the house to find that the child had not taken her pills. The women had expected me to give the child a shot and, when I did not, refused to continue the therapy. The child was still quite feverish, and this time I asked Atta to take care of her. He promised me that he would make sure the child took her medication, which he did assiduously, and in a few days the girl was playing with her friends in front of the house. When I returned to find the child well, I also found a grateful mother and a houseful of thankful women. I told them that not all diseases needed a *"picure,"* and that next time they should follow my directions. My attention then turned toward the girl. She was smiling happily and played with an energy which I could scarcely have thought possible a few days before. Since she was my friend's daughter and because I had successfully cured her, I decided to call her "little wife." When I first used this appellation, the women looked up in surprise, and then chuckled together.

Thus, Abdoulaye's daughter, Yawa, became my first "wife."

But Yawa lived in Amamvi. In order to complete my family, I began to call another girl wife. This was Attawa (female twin), a girl of about ten who was adopted by the Queen Mother and worked for her. I chose her primarily because if I had been free to take a wife and if she had been older and willing, Attawa would have been my real choice. She was an emotionally mature young lady with tremendous poise, who worked very hard and well for the Queen Mother. She was also very beautiful. In my eyes, she looked like a black Leslie Caron. When she was doing service for her stepmother she was very serious, but in her free moments she smiled easily. She was amused when I first called her wife. Since she was under age and knew it was a kind of game, she accepted the relationship readily without making any effort to act out the role I had assigned to her. The idea of Attawa as my wife was a gentle village joke which was accepted in a half-serious way but never considered a social fact.

Attawa had a sister, Tewia, also pretty, but only about five years old. She lived in the household of her mother. Several weeks into my stay, Tewia got sick and I treated her successfully. After her cure, I began to call her wife also. This was accepted on the same level as my "marriage" to her sister Attawa, but since the Abron do not allow a man to marry sisters, this marriage served to underline the symbolic nature of all my marriages.

Thus I completed my family. I had a full set of blood relatives and a full set of in-laws, although I never did interact much with the latter. The marriages established my status as adult but did not involve me with a whole new family. This situation worked well for the short time I lived in Diassenpa. If I had stayed much longer and if Sonia had not finally materialized for the villagers, I'm sure my status would have once more come into question.

I was sure that everyone took my marriages as a

good-natured joke and as a symbolic affirmation of my position among the villagers. I was wrong in one instance. When Sonia came to Diassenpa, Attawa began to act like a jealous wife. For two days before my wife's arrival, Attawa sulked around the village shooting poisonous glances at me whenever I passed. On the same day, she got into a fight with a village boy about her age and almost pulled his penis off. This kind of aggressive sexual play is common among preadolescents and adolescents, but is never so violent. When he pulled himself free, the boy set off for his house holding his groin and wailing as if he had been castrated.

The day I left for Abidjan to pick Sonia up, I did not see Attawa, and since we returned to the village late at night she did not see us until the next day. Early in the morning, however, as Sonia and I were having coffee on the terrace in front of our room, Attawa walked quickly into the courtyard. At first glance I thought that she had suddenly matured, for she had stuffed some cloth into her tunic to give the appearance of breasts. She walked over to the far side of the courtyard, away from our house, and for the rest of the morning, as I performed the daily medical tasks, she shot angry looks at Sonia and me.

Sonia was able to spend only three weeks in the field. At the time, we had two small children and agreed that their health should not be endangered by a trip to Africa. By the spring, Sonia felt comfortable enough to leave them for a short time with a good friend.

Our first night together, as we set off for bed in the Volkswagen camper, the Queen Mother came toward us, gesturing that we should wait. She took Sonia by the hand and pulled her quite forcibly away from me. "She can't sleep with you; she's your wife," she said with a broad grin. Her remark, made in jest, had the desired effect on the bystanders, who burst into gales of laughter. The Abron had become adept at playing their culture off against our own.

The first week of her stay, Sonia was subjected, as I had been, to a hazing, particularly as concerned the greeting patterns. No matter what forms she used, the replies consisted of variations she had not heard before. Although I had coached her on the formalities of greetings on our trip from Abidjan, I had not had time to cover all the possible forms. Still, everyone was happy to finally meet my wife and to see that she really existed. Her physical presence dispelled the nagging doubts that were held by some. Ajoa Badu and her mother, Afua Morofyé, were particularly kind to her. She and Badu soon struck up a friendship, which led to some good data on women's customs. The loquacious Badu seemed pleased to have a woman with whom she could speak French.

8
Religion and Ceremonies

One day, after visiting another village, Oppong and I returned to Diassenpa quite late. The streets were deserted and it seemed that everyone was asleep. As soon as the motor quit, however, we heard the sounds of drums coming from Amamvi. I turned to Oppong. "Someone has died," he said, and without another word we set off for Amamvi. I parked the car near the King's house and we followed the drums in the dark. A man had died that evening and this was the beginning of his three-day funeral. The mourners, who had come several hours before, were in a state of high excitation stimulated by the constant drumming and the liberal flow of gin and palm wine provided by the hosts. With the exception of the immediate family, no one seemed particularly distressed. The atmosphere was similar to an Irish wake, except the music, dancing, and drinking would continue after the interment. To dance at a funeral is to honor the dead, and so while all Abron enjoy dancing it is also a serious display of respect.

The dead man was laid out on a bed placed under a projecting portion of the roof. Dressed in a fine cloth, he appeared to be sleeping. Close relatives sat in the center of the courtyard with their cloths pulled up over their heads, crying copiously. Their keening could at times be heard over the boom of the drums, which beat out distinctive funeral rhythms.

The man had been preceded in death by three of his siblings. Their funerals had been simple affairs, with little ceremony and no dancing. His death marked the beginning of the funeral cycle for his remaining siblings. From then on, all his brothers and sisters would be honored with the full ceremony, which continues for two days after the burial, which takes place within twenty-four hours after death.

The funeral of an infant is a strangely silent affair. One occurred during my first trip. The entire village came to pay its respects to the bereaved parents. The dead baby was not laid in state, because it had died so soon after birth. It was not yet counted as a member of society. Women gathered in the courtyard with the mother, while men lined up outside, where they waited calmly for the signal that the mother was ready to receive them. The men then entered the courtyard in single file, and addressed the gathered women with the evening greeting, *"Nna men, nna men."* Then they turned and filed out. A silence hung over the village that evening, replacing the usual sounds of the women pounding.

The funeral of the dead man, like the funerals of all adults, centered on the deceased rather than the family. The mourners were largely ignored. As the corpse lay in state, people presented it with gifts of food and cloth. Money was also donated by more distant relatives, to help pay for the cost of the funeral. When gifts of cloth were presented, they were torn in half. One piece was buried with the body, and the other was returned to the donor to wear from time to time as a reminder of the dead person. The continuity between the living and the dead, an important aspect of Abron belief, is made real by these gifts. Such customs remind the living that they have obligations to their ancestors which must be fulfilled.

After a night of dancing, the body was placed in a wooden coffin. Before the coffin was lowered into the grave, the pallbearers turned it rapidly around several times. This is supposed to confuse the spirit, so that it will be unable to find its way back to the village.

The dancing continued all night, and it was not until dawn began to break over the roof that people began drifting away one by one to their own houses. When it was light enough to see clearly, the drummers ceased their beating and placed their instruments in one corner of the yard. Children who had been sleeping during the revel (Abron children have an amazing ability to sleep in the midst of noise) were awakened by their now impatient parents and pushed homeward, where they would sleep for a few hours. Their parents, in spite of the night's activity, would be off in their garden early. Without much sleep, they would return the next evening and again the next, to dance in honor of the dead man.

Mourning relatives cover their heads for six days and wear old, dark-colored cloths. The wife of the deceased stays in her husband's house and eats only once a day. After the funeral is over, she is taken out by an old woman and bathed with special water.

When a priest or a member of the royal family dies, the funeral is more elaborate. The ceremony lasts for seven days and nights, and several villages participate. When the king dies, the entire nation mourns and everyone tries to get to the funeral.

Once, during my stay, an important priest died. News of the impending funeral spread rapidly around Abron country and I was implored to take as many villagers as I could to Assuifri, twenty miles away, where the ceremony was to be held. Filled to overflowing, my car bounced heavily out of the village and onto the dirt road, where traffic was unusually heavy. Those who could not find or afford motor transportation were going on foot from miles around. About one hour from Diassenpa, we entered the dead priest's village. It was crowded with an assortment of Abron ranging from local people and commoners to chiefs and other priests. Groups of men were huddled around the village trees discussing the cures the dead man effected and his general power over witches. The reputation of any priest comes from his works. The dead man had been one of the wisest and best known of a group of particularly powerful kparesogo.

After my introduction to the local village elders, I was taken into the house of the dead man. He lay in state on a brass bed, with his symbols of office around him; these included a pair of gilded swords and several gilded fly switches. The man's brother danced in the

center of the courtyard. The drums used in the ceremony were elaborately carved with sacred Abron symbols, contrasting with the plain drum I had seen before,
in Amamvi. The most popular design was the alligator,
which appeared in the carvings to straddle the drum
vertically. Snakes added a spiral design to some of the
instruments, which appeared to be held together by the
twisting bodies.

At first, the funeral proceeded like any other I had
seen. Then, suddenly, a group of priests rushed through
the crowd up to the corpse. They stood swaying before
the body until one of them became possessed and fell
to the ground. The other priests lifted him up, and as
he revived, he began to writhe violently. They attempted to restrain him but he worked himself loose
and rushed out of the courtyard. The other priests followed him, sweeping the area before them with the
leaves of a tall plant that grows near the water. The
possessed priest was taking the dead man's spirit back
to the river, from which it had come. The other priests
were sweeping away any loose remnants of the spirit
which, freed of the body, might become dangerous.
Then a man rushed into the courtyard with a young
chicken dangling from his mouth. His eyes bulging, he
ran wildly around the edge of the crowd as some of the
spectators tried to restrain him. Others attempted to
force his mouth open and to extract the dead bird. This
apparently contributed to his agitation, but after some
minutes he, too, left. The bird held in his mouth
represented the truth, which had been guarded by the
priest in his lifetime. The man with the bird was followed by the priest's wife. She entered as the others
had, dancing wildly toward the body. She was held by
two women, members of her family. She had a small
piece of braided grass in her mouth, which she would
keep there except during meals for the forty-three days
of mourning, to insure her silence and testify to her
grief. The wife was led from the courtyard just as the
priests who had swept the area returned, this time with
a sheep. The animal was placed before the corpse and

slaughtered. Its blood was allowed to spurt over the floor in front of the funeral bed. The sheep was then removed and butchered; its meat was later distributed to some of the more important guests. After the sacrifice, music began and the funeral settled down to the usual dancing and drinking. Just outside of the village a grave was dug, and after sunset the body, in its coffin, was placed in the open pit. The grave was not filled in for seven days, and during this period the dancing continued. I was later told that if the people did not dance for seven days, the soul of the priest would return to haunt the entire village and kill everyone there.

Funerals are the major events in Abron society. They constitute the single most important social activity in the entire culture. I think this is so because death creates a social rupture which, unlike divorce for example, has supernatural overtones. The break is not only between a married couple or social groups, but between an individual and an entire village. Funerals reaffirm social ties in the face of separation. Abron dead continue to occupy their established place in the social order. They continue as lineage members and may influence the course of events, particularly the fortunes of society in economic and social life. The ancestors insure rain and good weather and can also intercede with the gods in personal matters. In addition, for the Abron, death brings only a temporary separation, even in the physical sense. The dead are reincarnated—born again into their own families.

It was difficult to get people to talk about Abron cosmology. The concepts involved are quite complex, and only the older men and some of the women priests grasped all the subtleties. In addition, many Abron, even those who had not converted to Islam or Christianity, displayed some embarrassment when talking to me about their religious system. My marginal linguistic skills inhibited conversation on these topics, and even Oppong had difficulty finding translations for some of the ideas. What follows is a synthesis drawn from many conversations with a wide range of individuals.

An individual is made up of *bodgya* (blood) and *kra* (spirit). Blood comes from the female line and spirit from the male. This concept represents the combination of male and female elements: of sperm and blood, of the spirit and the body. When someone dies, the body deteriorates, but the spirit continues to exist. The spirit may become a ghost (*puni*)—literally, corpse. The puni continues to inhabit the earth and appear in physical form. They are seen, it is said, by travelers outside of Abron land. They appear and disappear in crowds, always vanishing before they can be addressed. These ghosts can also take animal forms and haunt a village for a limited time, but there seems to be a short temporal limitation on the period during which puni are active.

According to those informants who practice Abron religion, when a person dies the soul (*ngose*), as distinct from spirit,* breaks into two parts. One of these, the *punungo,* goes to heaven, and the other, the *punungo bo bokogo* (stool spirit), goes into a stool that was carved for the person during his or her lifetime. Other informants said that there was only one soul, which lived in heaven but visited the soul stool on sacrificial occasions. The latter information is, I think, an attempt by Christian Abron to reconcile their new religion with the old system of beliefs. In any case, the soul stools are cared for by members of the defunct's family and receive sacrifices on ancestors' days, the *Adae,* and once a year at the great yam festival.

Punungo can behave like ghosts. They are "like the wind" and cannot be seen. Punungo may visit their relatives in the night to demand service, and may kill them if they are lonely in *punu* (heaven).

People are given good funerals to please their punungo, and one of the ways to punish a witch is to deny it the last rites. This can be done without fear, be-

* The translations of such terms as *kra* as spirit and *ngose* as soul are only approximations. They are meant to confer the sense in which I understand the complex set of beliefs surrounding the Abron conception of life and afterlife.

cause the spirits of dead witches are unable to revenge themselves on the living. Some informants told me that the souls of witches eventually become *bonzam,* or bush devils. Bonzam menace everyone but do not seek revenge against specific individuals.

The punungo of priests, on the other hand, are very dangerous. Special care is taken to put them to rest with dignity and honor. A less than perfect funeral for a priest can lead to death and havoc for an entire village.

I did not find out until my last trip, and then by accident, that the Abron have, or at least had, puberty ceremonies for both males and females. I was never able to uncover any details of these ceremonies. Willing to talk about birth, weddings, and even funerals, the subject of puberty was blocked by a wall of silence. It is, I think, worth speculating about the reasons for this.

First, on the purely pragmatic side, it is easier to hide scheduled puberty ceremonies from general view than such public events as births and funerals, which may occur at any time of the year. Second, when a system is threatened by change brought about by pressures from the outside, people may become uncomfortable about revealing more than they have to about their lives, particularly those aspects which might seem strange or even absurd to strangers. Third, secrecy itself reinforces a custom. By hiding it from outsiders, an aura of mystery is created around it and its sacredness is strengthened. Also, puberty is a time of biological change which is potentially disruptive on the social level. It is in the context of these ceremonies that children become adults, often full members of the society. Among the Abron, full adulthood does not come until marriage, but puberty ceremonies must at least recognize coming adulthood and prepare the young for major responsibilities to their kinship groups and society at large. In most African cultures, puberty ceremonies mark a time of concentrated instruction in which children are initiated into sacred rites and knowledge. In many cases, this knowledge is essential not only on the religious level but on the secular as well, for it provides a core around which social life articulates.

Another reason why initiation rites might fall into a particularly sensitive area of custom is that the transition from childhood to adulthood is often seen as a dangerous period for the individuals concerned. Victor Turner, who has written much of great interest on ritual, calls these periods liminal, for the initiates exist, at least on the symbolic level, outside of their society. Caught between statuses, they have no place in the normal social order. The purpose of these rites is to move the individual from one level to another and to protect him or her during the period of change. To share them easily with an outsider would immediately secularize them and threaten their effectiveness. Puberty rites are probably more sensitive in this respect than funerals. The Abron, at least, are very open about the latter, because death marks a transition in which an individual's position is concretely altered by the physical reality of death. Although the spirit of a newly deceased individual may be dangerous for a period that can also be considered liminal (as the soul seeks its final resting place, for example), death itself as an immediate change is not something people normally have to "lead into" on a metaphorical plane. Generally, there is no instruction associated with dying, as there is with puberty.

My sister, Ajoa Badu, loved to talk French with me. Besides her brother Kwamé, I was the only adult in Diassenpa who spoke that language, before Sonia came. So eager was she to have conversations with me that I could exploit the situation by asking her questions that would have embarrassed other women. When I brought up the subject of female puberty, she answered freely, at least about current practices.

At the present time, she told me, the period of adolescence for girls is marked by instructions in feminine hygiene, which they receive from their mothers on the occasion of first menses. No further notice is taken of the event except that menstruating girls and women are not permitted to cook or carry food to some of the men's houses. This, however, is a matter of some choice, and many men do not restrict the women of their family in this way. Puberty ceremonies, or even instruction for men, no longer occurred, I was told, but I have no way of evaluating the truth or falsehood of this information.

There were no marriages while I was in Diassenpa, and I therefore had no opportunity to observe a marriage ceremony. The following description is second-hand, but comes from several informants. These ranged in age from old people to younger adult residents of the village, and included both converted and pagan Abron. Although marriages follow a regular series of stereo-typic symbolic behaviors, and therefore may be classed along with other life-crisis rites as ceremonies, inform-ants were generally willing to talk about them. It was my impression from these conversations that this rather relaxed attitude reflected the secular nature of marriage as compared to other rituals.

When a marriage has been decided upon between two families, the groom's parents and other relatives provide the bride price, which is paid to the bride's kinship group. In general, a woman's father chooses a husband and her mother is not consulted. In the case of a man, it is preferred that his mother's brother "give" him his wife. In some cases, this means that men marry their mother's brother's daughter (a type of cross-cousin), and some Abron actually express this as a pre-ferred marriage. Cross-cousin marriage of any type is rare, however, and generally the rule merely means that the mother's brother has approved the marriage, per-haps even playing a role in finding a girl for his nephew to marry. In the past, when a man actually married his mother's brother's daughter, he was allowed to pawn her for debt payment. The latter pattern is, however, no longer practiced. The Abron follow a strict rule that a man may not marry sisters. The one exception to this applies to the King and to cantonal chiefs; these may

marry twin sisters. Twins are considered lucky among
the Abron. Marrying twins is one symbolic way of reinforcing the difference between royalty and commoners.
In a cultural sense, twins represent a rare commodity
and are valued as lucky. They are *naturally* exceptional
and provide for an instance of exceptional marriage in
the *cultural* system.

The day of the marriage, the groom receives gifts
from his brothers and friends. Toward evening, he gives
his sister a white cloth. She hides the cloth behind her
back and goes to the house of the bride's mother. When
she gets a chance, she throws the cloth over the girl's
head, saying, "It is your husband who gives you this."
The bride then falls to the ground and begins to cry
out. Her friends try to calm her, and after they succeed,
wash her and comb her hair. She then eats dinner alone
and is afterward summoned by her friends. When it
gets dark, she is put on the back of a female friend and,
accompanied by two old women, is carried to the
groom's house. The groom stations himself in front of
his house, where he may be found talking to his
friends.

A few steps from the groom's house, the woman carrying the bride on her back stops and says, "The horse
has a broken leg." At this point, the husband must give
her a small gift of money, about one hundred francs
(CFA). The woman then enters the groom's house,
puts the bride down on the bed, and leaves. The two
old women who have entered with the bride encourage
her to go to sleep. They put out the light and make believe that they are leaving the house. Actually, they
take up positions in two corners of the house. After the
light has been put out, the groom enters and has sexual
intercourse with the bride. Afterward, he is supposed to
verify her virginity to the two old women. If the woman
is a virgin, the husband is ordered to circulate around
the village with the blood stained sheet proclaiming the
purity of his bride. The villagers gather at the groom's
house and everyone sings and dances until dawn. Before going to sleep again, in the early hours of the

morning, the husband gives gifts of palm wine and tobacco to the assembled guests. During the dancing, the
relatives of the groom put money in a calabash which is
later distributed to the old women of the village. The
fete continues for two more nights and all costs fall on
the husband.

According to some informants, on the fourth day the
husband presents the bride's family with a series of presents that represent an additional payment of bride
price. These are usually small quantities of yams, one
or two sheep, possibly some gin, and some cloth. This
gift is followed by more dancing. Finally, on the fifth
day, the young girls of the village go to the river with
the new bride, where she washes her husband's clothes.
Each morning, the bride goes back to the house of her
mother, where she spends the day. Each night, she returns to her husband. Finally, after ten days, the husband's sister goes to the bride's house and brings both
the bride and her mother back to the groom's house,
where he sacrifices a goat or a chicken to his personal
god. This sacrifice brings good luck to the marriage.

If the woman appears not to be a virgin at marriage,
she is given a chance to prove her innocence. If she
fails, an attempt is made by the groom to discover the
identity of the man who slept with his bride. When a
culprit is discovered, he is forced to pay a fine. A man
may refuse marriage with a non-virgin, but it is easy to
fake the evidence by staining the sheet with a bit of
chicken blood.

Marriage involves the participation of two individuals, two social groups, and the entire village. For the
individuals, it marks the beginning of a new social relationship. For the social groups, it may strengthen old
bonds created at former marriages or set up a new relationship between lineages. For the village at large, it
provides an occasion to reaffirm its social cohesion.

In contrast to marriage, divorce, which marks a
break in the social fabric, has no ceremonial aspect. If
a man finds that his wife does not suit him, he may end
the marriage. Women have equal rights of divorce, but

if a woman initiates this action, her husband's family may demand repayment of bride price. On the other hand, a divorced man has no rights over the children who have issued from the marriage.

The usual reasons for divorce include adultery and lack of attention to marital duties, particularly with regard to adequate provisioning of the family. Since this is a dual responsibility, a harmonious union involves the economic participation of both spouses. A woman may threaten divorce if her husband decides, against her wishes, to take another wife. Since wives live in separate households and since the husband's responsibilities to all his wives are equal, many polygynous unions are harmonious.

In addition to life-crises ceremonies, the Abron celebrate three major fixed religious events. These are the great yam festival (Odiwera), in October, the Adae, or tribute to the ancestors, and the Fofyé, or tribute to local gods and the punungo of dead priests. The yam festival combines a first-fruit ritual, during which the taboo on eating yams is lifted, with ancestor worship, and is by far the most elaborate ceremony. It unfolds in various villages by turn, according to a fixed chronology. The festival begins where an ancient chief is said to have first tasted the yam, proving it was edible. According to legend, long ago a hunter walking through the bush found a yam. When he saw it, he took it home. After some days, he noticed an animal eating it. He went to the chief of Guendé and told him what he had seen. The chief of Guendé then took the yam and cooked it. The people waited forty days and nights, and when they saw that their chief did not die they knew that the yam was good to eat. And so the yam festival is held every year at Guendé, and it is the chief of Guendé who eats the yam before the King.

Another story says that after the chief ate the yam it was then given to the children of the village as a further test. After another week with no bad results, the yam was accepted as fit to eat by all. Today a children's yam festival may follow the one at Guendé, but it does not occur every year and is not an obligatory part of the festival.

Forty days after the Guendé fete, the new yams are taken to the temple of Tano, where they are offered, along with sheep and goats, to that deity. A week later, yams are offered to the punungo bo bokogo of each household. These offerings take place in the context of local yam festivals, one of which is usually held in the village of the King. After the final yam festival, the tuber is declared ready for eating.

The Adae takes place every forty-three days to the nearest Wednesday. According to Abron custom in Ghana, sacrifice is made on the Adae to the lineage ancestor stools, thus honoring past lineage chiefs. In Diassenpa and Amamvi, the Adae is more a family affair, in which people honor their close relatives on both the male and the female side.

The Fofyé takes place every forty-three days on the Friday following the Adae. Sacrifice is made directly to local gbawkaw and may vary from a goat or chicken to small amounts of kola nuts. Priests consider the Fofyé to be their day, as it unites them not only to their gods but to their priestly forerunners. The Fofyé is particularly important at the temple of Tano, where many visitors gather to witness the dancing of the priests.

Friday is a day of rest for the Abron. No one is supposed to work in his or her gardens, and if the rule is violated the offender may be punished. This punishment is accomplished by the earth, which has its own supernatural powers, or by bonzam, who roam the bush looking for unsuspecting victims.

Besides these calendrical ceremonies and rites associated with periods of life crisis, the Abron may convoke their priests to public action if they feel threatened by potential natural catastrophe. When a collective need develops, the village chief may ask a priest to dance. Dancing is the sacrament that provides communion with a god through the mechanism of possession. During possessive states, the body of the priest is inhabited by the spirit of the god. As the priest dances, the gbawkaw may speak through him or her, warning the village of impending trouble or offer advice to counter evil forces.

One such dance took place in Diassenpa during my stay. The Queen Mother asked the priest Ama Pirao, Kwasi (Tan) Daté's senior wife, who had recently arrived in the village, to dance. The ceremony took place on a night chosen by Ama Pirao and was attended by the entire village.

The village drums were taken out of their storage place and, as soon as it became dark, the music began. At first this consisted of a steady rhythm calling everyone to attend the ceremony, much like church bells calling the faithful to services. Then, with the arrival on the scene of the priest, the rhythms changed, becoming more complex and varied. The priest, dressed in white, her face and arms covered with white clay, began to dance on the margin of the light provided by my lantern. She circled around the inside of the group of spectators with small, mincing steps, her head bobbing up and down as she moved. She then retreated to one side of the circle and began to move forward and backward, always facing the same way, always performing the same steps. After several minutes of dancing, she began to chant and, according to my informants, speak in tongues; she had achieved trance and was now possessed by her god. During possession, her dancing continued but the movements were interrupted every few seconds, as she would dance forward into the group, break her dance, and walk back to a set place and begin again. At one point, she shouted over at Sonia and me, saying that we were dangerous to her and that we should move farther back. We moved away, out of the light, and she continued singing and dancing. Her gbawkaw warned the village that a severe epidemic was coming to Diassenpa and that if action was not taken to prevent it, many people would die. The gbawkaw then told the crowd what steps would be necessary to ward off the evil. After about two hours of dancing and speaking in tongues, the priest came out of trance and the ceremony ended.

The next day, acting on the advice of Ama Pirao, the women of the village performed a "cleaning ceremony." They marched around Diassenpa seven times, singing a sacred song and dragging medicine plants behind them. In addition, sacred plants were placed across the road at both entrances to the village as a barrier to the disease.

On another occasion, a man from Bracodi, a neighboring village, whose son had fallen and seriously hurt himself, called a dance to find the guilty party. In this case, a male priest from another village was asked to perform the ceremony, since at that time there was no priest resident in either Bracodi or Diassenpa.

During those times when witches are particularly active, a village may call in dancers for a special ceremony. Called the *Gban,* this is usually performed by Kolongos, although its origin appears to lie with the Senoufu people, who live in the north-central Ivory Coast. The dance, which I was not allowed to see, evidently differed strikingly from Abron custom. First of all, unlike all other Abron ritual except puberty rites, it is held in secret. Women, children, and non-African males are excluded. Secondly, according to informants, it involves the use of masks. The mask worn by the chief priest is itself a powerful gbawkaw. Other participants wear black anthropomorphic masks with antelope horns carved at their tops. Although these masks are an integral part of the ceremony, they have no individual power and may be seen in public or even sold. I have seen children playing with these masks, while not even an adult would dare to mishandle the main Gban mask, which is hidden except during the ceremony itself.

The Gban is not only a ceremony originating outside of Abron territory, but it is run by foreigners, for Abron do not like to catch their witches. They say that this is because they are too afraid of them.

The activity of the Gban is usually highest in the dry season, when many people die. During the winter of

1961–62, the Gban dancers were an almost constant feature of the secret night life of Gumeré. Before the ceremony begins, heralds run through the village ringing bells to warn non-initiates that the Gban will soon be performed.

In general, the Abron are quite secular in their daily approach to life and the world. It is only at times of crisis that they apply to their gods; most ceremonial life is associated either with placation of the ancestors or protection from witches. Ancestors occupy the position of the once living who still play a major role in regulating the lives of every Abron. Their power comes to them only in afterlife, when they continue to exert an influence on the living through supernatural acts. In contrast to ancestors, witches are evil forces, emanating from the living, who lose their power when they die and pass from the world of men. Ancestors and witches are the axis around which the Abron universe revolves. They provide the philosophy that accounts for good and evil and for the responsibilities of living Abron toward their fellow creatures. Both witches and ancestors are more important, in this respect, than the high god who acts in Abron cosmology only as the Prime Mover now remote from man. God can be reached only through the intercession of less powerful deities or ancestors. The gbawkaw are also important in daily life, but relations with them generally take the form of a specific contract in which an individual agrees to serve a god in return for some specific service done in his or her favor. One does not enter into such contracts with witches, but the contract with ancestors is obligatory and part of an ongoing social system.

The fact that funerals and marriages (I do not know the place of puberty rites) are among the major life-crisis rituals in Abron society fits in well with this structure, since the funeral, which is loaded with religious overtones, makes real a specific supernatural transition that in terms of social structure is no transition at all. The dead continue as part of the system they were born into; marriages, on the other hand, are secular ceremonies that involve only minor sacrifice without the intercession of priests. They mark a real change in status for two individuals and the linking of two social groups. They are therefore a powerful mechanism of changing status within the social system, but, at the same time, they reinforce social cohesion and mark the recognition of oneness shared by all Abron.

9
My Car

Early one morning, I received notice that some money had arrived for me in Abidjan. I told Oppong that I would make the trip that day and he asked if he and his wife could come along. Oppong was fond of fish and, whenever he could, would buy a load of them, sun-dried and smelly. He saw a trip to Abidjan as an opportunity to buy enough fresh fish to satisfy himself and make a profit in the village as well. The thought of two hundred and fifty miles in the heat with a carload of fish did not appeal to me, especially since the car was also my home and I could imagine the smell pervading it for days and days. For that reason, I agreed to take Oppong only if he would promise not to buy any fish for the return trip. I told him that if he had as much as a single fish with him I would either leave him in Abidjan or make him throw it away. He swore solemnly that none would be bought and we piled into the car, along with some passengers who wanted to be left at a nearby market, and set off.

The trip was the usual misery of dry-season traveling. My Volkswagen camper was quite slow, and every time someone passed us we were obliged to shut the windows for several minutes until the dust kicked up by the passing car settled. It was a poor choice between suffocation by heat or by dust, but after one experience with the latter, I learned that the heat was slightly less noxious. There were always official cars along the road. These were preceded by police in Land-Rovers who would make everyone else pull over so that their charges could ride in comfort. These conditions and the expectation that we would rarely meet anyone going in the opposite direction turned me gradually into a reckless driver and road hog. I pushed the car to the limit of its meager power. Often, I would manage to do sixty. Occasionally, all four wheels would leave the ground as we sailed over a bump on the deeply rutted dirt road. Encounters with cars coming the other way were always moments of suspense, as we would swerve off center and begin to skid on the sand that covered the apron of the road. It was almost as bad as driving on snow. Arrival at Abengourou, where the paving began, was always greeted with relief and I would settle back into the routine of relatively safe driving. Whenever I could, I passed. Success was limited to heavily laden trucks forced by their burden to travel slowly. Many of these were lumber carriers, which transported one or two enormous hardwood logs as big as adolescent redwoods. These were chained on top of telescoping trailers, whose length could be extended to accommodate the length of the particular trees they carried. It was always difficult to judge how long it would take to pass them. Once, as I was at about mid length of one of these giants, I saw a car coming in the opposite direction. I immediately slowed down, and fortunately the truck driver kept his speed up. I managed to get back in line just as the car came past. If the truck driver had panicked, my camper would have been crushed.

The trip to Abidjan took about eight hours. As soon as we arrived at the outskirts of the city, Oppong asked me to let him off. We agreed to meet two days later at the bus depot in Adjamé, one of the African suburbs that flank the plateau. I continued on to the hotel to see if there was a room available, dreaming of a hot shower and air-conditioned sleep. Abidjan is, however, particularly crowded with businessmen and some tourists in the dry season, and I was unable to get a room. I went to the bank to get my money and then to the swimming pool, where I got rid of my usual covering of red dust and spent the afternoon happily swimming and resting in the sun. That evening, I drove the car to a deserted part of the bay, pulled over, and went to sleep. The following day was a holiday in Abidjan. A well-known French football team had come to play in the Houphouët-Boigny stadium, and everyone who could

afford the price of entry was there. Those who could
not, ranged themselves along a sloping hill just over the
stadium, where, although the distance was great, one
could see the game. France won with the aid of their
many African stars. The crowd broke up rapidly, making off for the various neighborhoods—defined by
affluence, by ethnic identity, and by color. I drove back
to my bay and slept. The next day, the debris of celebration or remorse was scattered over the roadway. I
have never seen so many wrecked cars in my life. All
that mayhem had occurred while I slept.

Oppong was waiting for me as I pulled up at the
edge of the depot. His wife had a suspicious-looking
basin in front of her, covered with a large piece of
blue cloth. "No fish, Oppong?" "No, sir," he said as he
and his wife climbed into the back of the bus and settled on what served at night for my bed. We set off in
the heat. About two hours later, a heavy oily odor
began to waft up front. I said nothing for a while, but it
was not difficult to identify the smell. Oppong was just
too good a businessman to let my foolish inhibitions
stop him. Fish were cheap in Abidjan and dear upcountry. Commerce is founded upon transportation,
and Oppong had decided that my stupidity could not
stand in his way. For my part, I did not have the heart
to make him get out and take the bus or to throw away
the fish, and although my anger grew in proportion to
the rising stench, I said little. On returning to Diassenpa, Oppong, contrite, silently set about cleaning my
car and was especially polite and attentive for about
three days after the incident. The odor of fish lingered
about the same length of time and, as it disappeared,
our testy relationship returned to normal.

During my first visit, I had no car and was therefore
dependent upon the capricious schedules of the local
buses. My American sense of time was constantly upset
when I was forced to wait two hours for a bus to start
off somewhere. The car, then, in spite of all the dangers
inherent in driving on narrow dirt roads, contributed to
my relaxation. Without it, I probably would never have

been able to accustom myself to the other hardships of living in the bush.

Being a social chameleon is not one of my favorite pastimes, and I was frequently unnerved by the constant need to present a friendly face to everyone. Anthropologists working in the field have no right to choose friends, but although I had warm attachments to many Abron, there were some individuals I did not like. There were even a few whom I came to detest during my stay. Abron culture forces one to live a fishbowl existence. Solitude is considered undesirable, so people are rarely alone. Abron eat, sleep, and defecate together. One is constantly surrounded by family, friends, and children. Add to this the natural curiosity generated by the presence of a stranger, and you find yourself in a situation in which privacy is impossible. One day, I experimented with my power as a social magnet by moving from one seating area in the village to another. One by one, without saying a word to the others who had been sitting around me, even those who were engaged in activities totally unrelated to the conversation in which I had been engaged—activities I had not initiated—got up and slowly walked over to my new spot. This type of surrounding behavior is common in West Africa, and, my colleagues tell me, many other parts of the world. No doubt it is we who are unsociable.

Every once in a while I had to escape. The car enabled me to leave alone—providing I was quick enough. Now and then I would jump up, make a quick run for the car, get in, and roar off. I'm sure this convinced everyone that I was a madman.

On one of these small trips, I drove to Soko, a border town between Bondoukou and Ghana. Soko is noteworthy for one reason: Its small population is augmented by a troop of vervet monkeys, which are sacred in the district. All the villagers, even the customs men who come from other regions of the Ivory Coast, say that anyone who harms one of these animals will go insane the same day, "before the sun sets." As a consequence, they are very bold. Running in a group of about seventy-five, these animals often cross the main street, stopping traffic, and then line up more or less regularly to watch the movement of humans across the frontier, which they themselves never breach. When hungry, they sometimes forage in the tall grass around the village, but are more likely to beg food from the village stores, or steal. Watching them, it is hard to decide whether they are to be counted, with the human population, as regular inhabitants of the village or as a group apart, invaders who, having conquered, now tolerate the men who live among them.

Monkeys make Europeans self-conscious. They are our captives, but they act their parts ambiguously. We class them lower than ourselves and watch them for amusement or despise them for their dirty habits. When they notice us at all, they mock our actions, sometimes grimace or spit, even urinate on us. Thus they maintain their dignity. In Soko, men define them as representatives of the gods. Their mocking and thieving underline man's humble status vis-à-vis the gods. The people of Soko live a perpetual charade which, to our eyes at least, might parallel the story of Job.

My room, roofed with corrugated iron, became too hot to sleep in in the dry season. The metal would soak up heat all day and then reflect it down on me at night. For the Abron, who are more accustomed than I to heat, it was a perfect solution to the cool nights, which came with clear skies and low humidity, but for me it was torture. I discovered that the car cooled off much faster than the room. With its skylight open, covered with a screen I had borrowed from the American missionaries, it turned out to be a much better place to sleep. There was still one problem, however. A flock of goats had the habit of milling around my parking area at night, and they would frequently bump against the bus and wake me. Finally I made my escape total by leaving the village every night—driving down the road and sleeping next to the schoolhouse, which was between Amamvi and Diassenpa. For a long time, nobody knew where I slept and I was able to stay in bed much longer than was possible in the village, where the noise of daily activities began with the faint glimmer of dawn. In order to function, I had to have an unbroken period of sleep. No arrangements other than the car seemed to work out.

For the Abron, the Volkswagen bus was a tremendous status symbol. The fact that it was equipped with living accommodations was absorbed slowly and with fascination. When I returned to Amamvi, the King asked to take a ride, and made me set the bed up for him so that he could try it out.

However, I did not always ride. Every afternoon, when everyone was sleeping and before beginning the daily process of note typing, I would go for a walk. Every once in a while, I would meet someone on the road, usually a person returning late from the market or the fields. Each time, I had to go through the same routine. First the usual greetings: *"Beri kouri, nda,"* "Good afternoon, father," *"Nda, beri kouri,"* "And a good afternoon to you." *"Ow ya, bruni?"* "Where are you going, white man?" "I'm taking a walk—" "Why, is your car broken?" "No, but how can I take a walk in the car?"

The car also functioned as a roving ambulance. Medical cases too complicated for first aid were taken on a regular basis to the hospital at Bondoukou. Several emergency trips were also forced by circumstances, including a miscarriage and a few bad accidents in which individuals out working on their farms had cut themselves with machetes. Going to Bondoukou allowed me to perform an important service for the villagers, in whose debt I constantly remained, and also gave me an opportunity to keep a check on the prevailing diseases in the village. The Bondoukou doctor was kind enough to allow my presence during diagnosis and treatment. Since I was engaged in a study of medicine, hygiene, and disease, these trips were of tremendous benefit to my own study.

During the first months of my stay, I noticed a dis-

tinct coldness on the part of the Catholic missionaries
in Tanda, a trading village about forty miles from Diassenpa. There they operated a maternity hospital, and,
when I could, I would take pregnant women in for examinations. Once, I rushed a woman in early labor to
them, and although she was received, the sister in
charge treated me with open hostility. My few attempts
to talk with the local priest, who was fluent in Kolongo
and who had lived in the region for forty years, were
fruitless. At first, I thought that their hostility was an expression of anti-American feeling, but after much questioning of local people, including a few French traders
who were quite friendly, I discovered that the problem
stemmed from my VW Micro-Bus. The Catholics have
been established in Abron territory for many years and
have had no competition from other Christians. In
1959, a group of Freewill Baptists from the United
States began to move into the eastern Ivory Coast from
Agni territory in the south all the way up to northern
Kolongo and Lobi country on the Upper Volta border.
I don't know how the Catholics felt originally about
others coming into an already functioning mission area,
but much of their present ill feelings come from the active anti-Catholic activity of the Baptists, who, in addition to converting "pagans," actively pursue the "idol-
worshiping Papists." In addition, they poach on local
Catholic converts and distribute such tracts as *Le
Prêtre Qui a Choisi Jésus Christ,* i.e., converted to
Protestantism. Such behavior does not endear them to
the Catholic community, but they are convinced by
their sense of Christianity that Catholics are, if anything, worse than pagans. They are also convinced that
Jesus lived according to standards of mid-twentieth-
century rural Oklahoma. The fact that the local priest
liked his Gauloises and an occasional glass of wine convinced them he was an agent of the devil.

I finally discovered that the Catholics, and a good
number of the local African population as well, took
me for an American missionary. This confusion
stemmed not from my nationality, nor from the confu-

sion over what an ethnologist was, but from my bus. All the Freewill Baptists in the eastern Ivory Coast are equipped with Volkswagen Micro-Buses.

In order to disabuse everyone of my supposed identity, I made a point of drinking palm wine and smoking in public. This behavior proved better than words that, automobile notwithstanding, I did not share the missionary zeal of the other Americans in the territory.

In addition to hospital trips, escapes to Abidjan, and short journeys for necessary provisions, I used the car for two excursions: one to Ghana, and one to upper Kolongo-Lobi country to check on kinship data as well as to survey the northern tribal area for possible future field work. Not only Oppong, but a whole group of people from my family, including Tchina Kofi, accompanied me on that trip. They wanted to visit friends in some villages not too far from Diassenpa and were curious about the north, where no Abron lived. At first, they were quite happy to be on the road, and Tchina Kofi was pleased to point out certain sites that he knew but had not seen for a long time. He also got a great deal of enjoyment out of meeting old friends whom he saw only rarely, when their visits to the market in Bondoukou coincided with his. But the farther we got away from Diassenpa, the more miserable he became.

Wherever we went, we were greeted with courtesy and given shelter as well as food, but Tchina Kofi, as we drove north, began a kind of auto-ethnography in which he compared the Abron way of doing things with local customs elsewhere. The more the local culture deviated from his own, the more critical he became. In one town, just over the border from Abron territory, when I asked where the latrine was, Tchina Kofi, who had already visited that facility, looked at me with a deprecatory grin and said, "Wait till you see it." As it turned out, the latrines were located at a respectable distance outside the village, just as they were at Diassenpa, but they were very shallow and fly-ridden. I had to agree that toilet facilities were indeed better "at home," but I had seen far more primitive conditions around Abidjan, where people on their way to work in the morning stop alongside the roads to relieve themselves. Tchina Kofi was scandalized, however, and talked about these dirty people for days afterward.

We did make it all the way up to the Upper Volta border, and for the sake of crossing a frontier without a customs control for once in my life, I drove into Upper Volta a short distance before returning to Doropo, near the border.

The farther one gets from Abidjan the worse the roads get, but, except in the far north, I never had any difficulty passing over rough spots or finding gas stations. Doropo, however, has no garage facilities, and it was lucky that on my visit I had filled the tank at Buna. I have no idea where the first place is that one can buy gas in Upper Volta, except that it must be far from the desolate scrub land that I saw stretching out before me for miles in all directions.

Doropo is an interesting area because of the variety of ethnic groups that have interpenetrated each other's territory. The town itself is populated mostly by Dioula, a trading people whose origin is in the western Ivory Coast and Guinea. Scattered irregularly around Doropo are small villages of Kolongo, Birifor, and Mossi, the latter migrants from farther north. The Kolongo and Birifor are both matrilineal peoples and have, for the most part, been converted to Islam in this region. Their staple crop is the yam, which grows poorly in the district, and famines occur from time to time. These have been aggravated lately by the selling of yams at harvest time to commercial buyers who transport them farther south to be resold in the markets. What appears to be an abundance of food at harvest turns out to be barely enough to meet local needs until the next growing season.

Low, flat-roofed mud houses are scattered across the arid plain. These are inhabited by single large families of Lobi, a cattle-raising people who, to the European eye, are the most exotic and therefore the most "African" of the local populations. Lobi houses are interesting structures. They are made of dried clay. Entering, one descends partway below ground level into a series of dark, cool rooms. One of these communicates by way of a ladder with the roof, which is flat and divided into separate spaces by low walls about eight inches high. In hot weather, people sleep on the roof in their appropriate places. Outside the house, smaller clay structures are used for storing grain. A family god, rather crudely sculptured out of a log, is planted in the ground in front of the entranceway. The Lobi, unlike other groups in the eastern Ivory Coast, are patrilineal. They live in what anthropologists call scattered family homesteads, much like the ranchers in the western United States. Each house is surrounded by pasture land and millet fields. Cows are milked, and no meat is eaten except on special occasions or when an ill cow dies. Lobi women wear small lip plugs (or labrets) in both the upper and lower lips, and the men often file their teeth. The Lobi are resistant to outside influence and have refused both Western medicine and Islam up to the present. Their appearance, particularly that of the men, gives one a mixed impression of cultural tenacity and change. Driving along the road, one frequently comes across a Lobi man on a bike or even a small motorcycle. His usual dress consists of ragged shorts and a long, very used overcoat frequently of French Army issue. Slung over one shoulder, he will carry a bow and quiver of arrows, the symbol of manhood. In 1960, a group of Lobi men killed a game warden in the Parc National de Bouna. He had been interfering with puberty ceremonies, which involve the killing of an elephant. These ceremonies, which occur at intervals of several years, are very important to the Lobi, for one cannot assume the responsibilities of manhood until they have been completed. In order that no one man be judged guilty of murder, a group of adult men agreed to the killing, which was done with these same arrows. Those involved were arrested, tried for murder, found guilty, and sentenced to death under French administration. But, in 1960, the Ivory Coast became an independent nation and the men were quietly let go.

I was warned that, if I happened to hit a Lobi cow along the road, I should keep on driving. These animals are both status symbols and valuable possessions. To kill or injure one is a serious wrong, and the Lobi will shoot anyone who harms them, even by accident.

I arrived in Lobi country in the midst of a virulent meningitis epidemic. The local missionary doctor was loaded down with cases, as the rate of infection was around 30 per cent. I saw frightened parents carrying empty-eyed infants on their backs, sick children lying listless or rocking in pain on their beds. In one village, a male nurse lay trembling in his hut afraid that if he treated anyone he would get sick himself. His training had prepared him to use methods appropriate only for sleeping-sickness control and was therefore quite useless. His fear was completely comprehensible. The doctor gave me a large supply of sulfa pills, a standard prophylactic, which I administered to my company until we left the area. Although fairly sure that no one would contract the disease, I was hesitant about staying in an epidemic area with my Abron charges. This worry, plus the growing discomfort displayed by Tchina Kofi, led me to cut the trip short and return south. I later found out that such epidemics generally occur every few years in the dry season and die out with the first rains.

Lobi rain makers begin their activity in late March or early April, by starting brush fires. Ivory Coast authorities told me that their general success in bringing rain can be attributed to the natural end of the dry season, but there is some evidence that heavy burning, which produces smoke over a wide area, may in fact stimulate rain. Such a practice may be another good example of the pragmatic knowledge that comes with long-term experience within an environment.

One afternoon during my exploration of Lobi country, I came upon a bridge over a dried-up river bed. About halfway across, I saw that the center section had rotted away. I was forced to back up, which was particularly difficult because the bridge consisted solely of parallel planks of wood spaced just far enough apart for the wheels and only about two tires wide. Moving forward was hazardous but not difficult, but the negotiation of these boards in reverse was a nerve-wracking affair. When I had finally succeeded in backing off, I tried to cross the dried river bed. The car immediately sank into the sand up to the tops of the wheels. Tchina Kofi, Oppong, and the two boys we had with us descended and tried to push the car out of the sand. The task was beyond all of us. I began to have images of my vehicle sitting there all through the dry season, finally to be swept away with the coming of the rains in the spring. Suddenly, a large group of Lobi men and women appeared. As the women chattered, the men lifted the car out of the sand and pushed it back on the road. I have no idea where they were going or where they came from, but the experience constituted the one exciting rescue of my voyage in Africa. I am still grateful to those anonymous Lobi, whose kindness belied their ferocious reputation.

10
Folklore

One day, after the first rains had wet the savanna enough to protect the village from fire, the men organized a group hunt. Ten men and most of the village boys set out for an area a mile from the village. The men separated downwind from the children, who, on a prearranged signal, lit the savanna grass in a line three hundred yards long. The flames grew rapidly, leaping almost as high as the tops of the palmetto trees that grow scattered in the grass. These are rarely damaged by fire. Palmetto trunks are insulated with thick fibers, and their foliage grows only at the top of the long trunk, where a fire cannot reach. After a burn, the trees are left scarred below but green above, scattered in the midst of black, parched earth. Once the fire begins to move forward with the wind, the usual hawks appear and circle overhead, hunting for small rodents, which flee the fire with the other game.

The men at the other end of the fire waited for the larger game to emerge. Those armed with clubs raced about after large bush rats, which taste like pork. Occasionally a man jumped back in surprise and fear as a snake disturbed by the fire slithered by. Mambas, cobras, and vipers all inhabit the dense undergrowth. Those few older men who had guns waited patiently for the various species of antelope, which, although thinned out by overhunting, still make their home in the savanna. Occasionally a shot rang out, but hunting was bad that day and only one bush rat and a small pigmy antelope were bagged. After the fire, a group of laughing, shouting boys ran over the still-hot cinders in their bare feet to see what game if any had been killed. The old men were disappointed by the small take, but the boys were content to have been on a hunt, to have seen the great fire, and to have played with the dead bush rat, which one of them was allowed to carry home.

When the hunt is good (a rare event), much meat is brought back to the village. The kill belongs to the hunter and his family. He also gives some to the children who set the fire. Surplus meat is sold to other villagers. There is no wide distribution of game to villagers at large, as there is among those peoples who rely on hunting for their major source of protein.

On an average day, by about five o'clock everyone is back in the village. The women, hot and tired, return from the fields and their last trip of the day to the water hole. The men come back from their plantations or the hunt. Everyone feels dirty: perspiration and dust have mingled to cover the body with an uncomfortable red coating. Relief comes with the evening bath. The village is outfitted with various types of bathrooms. The richer men's houses have rooms provided with a drain and a cement seat and foot rest. Pails of water are taken into these private areas, where bathing is a moderate luxury. The less rich and the women retire to wickerwork enclosures located near their houses. These have earth floors, and it is quite a trick to bathe without getting the feet and a good part of the body muddy. Those used to it, however, are quite adept. By six o'clock, everyone in the village has emerged from the bath. The men put on their best clothes, for their work is finished for the day. The women must prepare supper, and soon the sound of the mortar and pestle vibrates through the village again. As the women cook, the men groom themselves further. Some shave their faces, others their heads, and most coat their skin with shea butter or vaseline. When they have finished, their bodies glow brown under the waning light. Children, who, by the end of the afternoon look particularly dirty, are also preened. At such times, they are most appealing. Adults remain clean for the rest of the evening, but the children begin violent play as darkness comes, bringing cool air, and their shiny skins are soon dulled again by dust.

On moonlit nights, the village is animated by the talk of the adults, the games of the young children, the mock fighting of the adolescents, or if there is some occasion for it, the dancing of the entire village. The energy of the children, which has built up during the day and begins to find its expression in the late evening, explodes with the coming of the moon. The boys run races or fight with each other, while the young girls, led by an elder sister, gather to dance and sing. These songs and dances usually mime some daily task. Sexual teasing becomes a major sport for the adolescents. The boys assemble, and attack one or more of the girls in an attempt to undress them in front of their friends. The girls fight back, kicking and biting, and occasionally one of them succeeds in disrobing a boy. When they can, however, the girls run away from the boys, yelling insults. This is only a part of the game, and in a few minutes they are back again. When not engaged in this sport, boys wrestle among themselves. A group of youths attack one of their number and attempt to pick him up over their heads. During such mock battles, the village resounds with the hollow thud of punches. The favorite site is the lower back, primarily because of the sound a punch there produces. Married men and women watch the adolescents, ready to stop serious fights.

Sometimes the pattern is broken. One rather cold night, well after most of the village had gone to sleep, a group of girls organized by the granddaughter of the Queen Mother, an exceptionally poised girl of about thirteen, invited some of the young men to share an impromptu yam feast with them. I contributed some onions for the sauce and was allowed to join the party. My status in the village was helpfully ambiguous. As a married man, I could interact as an equal with the village elders, but since my wife was not present, I could sometimes slip into the role of the younger men and join in their activities. We sat quietly around the low fire as the yams were peeled and placed in an iron pot to boil. The talk was low and unexcited, as the girls prepared the sauce by grinding the onions, pepper, and salt with a stone mortar and pestle. When the meal was ready, the yams were distributed around the group and a pot of sauce was placed in the center of the circle, where everyone could dip his or her slice of hot yam. The food and the fire felt good, as they warmed us against the harmattan, which was blowing fiercely around the courtyard walls. There was an aura of camaraderie and friendship in the group that is rarely expressed openly between males and females. There appeared not to be any sexual overtones in the activity, since most of the young people present were closely related.

While most Abron have small kerosene lamps with simple wicks, these shed little light and are suitable only as bedside lamps. Just before the village settles into sleep, the soft glow of these lanterns is seen in the doors of most village houses. My Petromax lantern was of a different order. Operating under pressure, the mantle was at least as bright as a one-hundred-watt bulb. If I wanted to gather an evening crowd, all I needed to do was light my lantern and set it out in the courtyard of my house. Adult men and children of both sexes would soon come drifting into the light. Adult men sat close to the lantern, while the children ran around the courtyard. Sometimes, however, one or another of the old men would recite traditional Abron tales. On these occasions, the children settled down in a circle on the periphery of the light to listen.

Some of these tales explain the origin of various creatures, including human beings, while others explain or justify Abron customs. Still other stories end with riddles for the children to discuss and solve. These riddles are often complicated and can generate long, animated discussions.

Azumana was one of the best storytellers in the village. Dressed in his tattered robe, he would perch himself on a stool, his feet drawn up against the base, project his knees outward, and bend his body forward. This posture accentuated his thinness and angularity. His shadow against the far wall was a maze of angles broken only by the curve of his back. He spoke rapidly, but in an animated tone, changing his voice to imitate each character in the story.

There was once a woman who had no children. For ten years she had none. And then, one after another, she had three sons. She loved her sons very much, but after several years they died. After this, the woman could do nothing but cry.

One night a dog came to her and said, "God calls you; follow me." She followed the dog, and when she came before God, he said to her, "Woman, why do you cry so much?" "It is because I lost my three sons," she replied. God then asked her if she would recognize her three sons if she saw them again. She answered that she would of course know her sons. Then God said, "Go with the dog and find them in my village." The woman was led by the dog to God's village. Soon they came before a leper who had no hands and feet. "Is this one of your sons?" asked the dog. "No," replied the woman. They went farther. The dog took her before another man, who was destitute, a man who was despised because he did not pay his debts. "Is this one of your sons?" asked the dog. "No," replied the woman. They went farther into the village. The dog took her before a third man, who was mad. "Is this one of your sons?" he asked. "Surely not," replied the woman. The dog then took her back to God, who said to her, "You have seen your three sons and you may take them home with you if you wish." "No," replied the woman, "I prefer to have no sons." She returned home to her village and recounted all that had passed to the villagers. After this, she had many daughters, all of whom were beautiful.

This is not only a moral tale. It also reflects the Abron fear of leprosy and madness, and their normal attitude toward people thus afflicted. A man who does not pay his debts is placed in a category equally negative. He is as unworthy of his mother's love as the other two sons. The mother receives nothing from her trip to

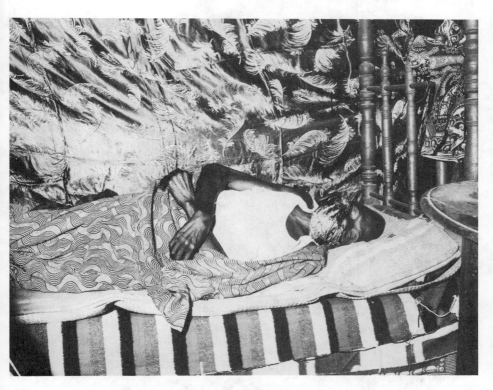

A dead man in Amamvi, 1961

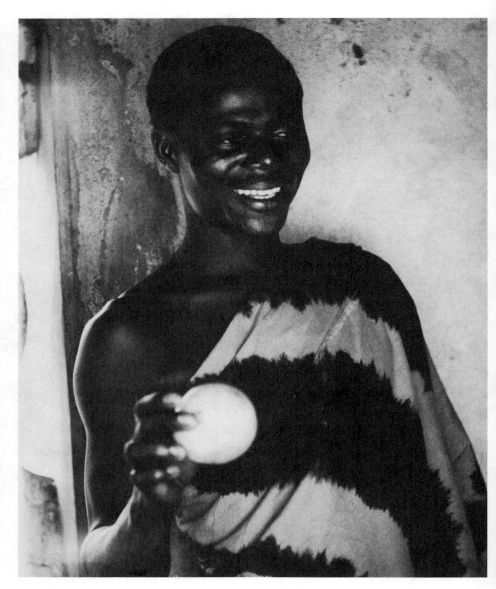

Célestin, 1973 (photo by **Marilyn Paul**)

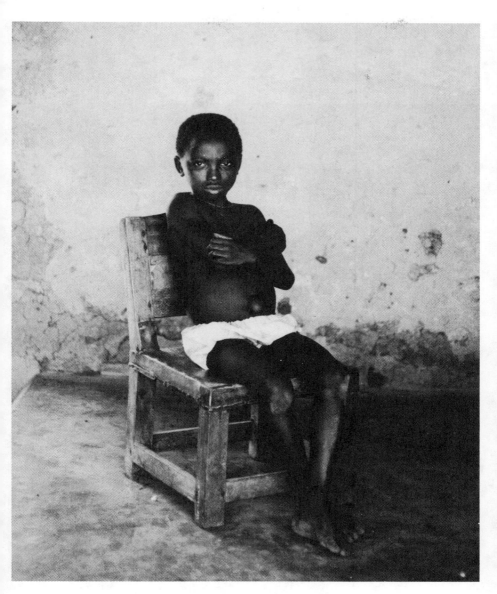

Afua, 1973 (photo by Marilyn Paul)

Kofi Apo, 1973 (photo by Marilyn Paul)

God except wisdom: there is no point in grieving for the dead; they are better left where they are. Once she accepts this, she is blessed with many beautiful daughters. Beautiful daughters attract good husbands, who become allies of a woman's house and because of the residence pattern, husbands do not separate women from each other. A woman who has many daughters has a full and prosperous house.

Azumana asked the children, "Do you know how man got sores on his body?" "No," they replied, and he told this story.

One day a spider heard a woman crying in the bush. Her manner of crying pleased the spider very much. The spider tried to imitate it. When the woman heard the sound of the spider, she began to search for it. The spider began to move toward the woman. Finally, their paths crossed. The woman asked, "Why, when I cry so, do you repeat my sounds?" "It is because the way you cry pleases me." The woman said, "I cry because I have a sore. Would you like to have a sore like me?" "Yes," said the spider. "Then you must sing and dance with me," said the woman. They sang and danced together, and as they did so, the woman's sore healed. At the same time, a large sore began to form on one of the spider's legs. The sore hurt the spider very much and it began to cry. After this, the spider wandered through the bush for many days, crying as it went. Finally, it came to a village of men. The spider gathered the villagers together and said, "I shall teach you a beautiful song." It sang, and as the villagers sang with it, the spider's sore healed and the men in turn became sore, and this is how the misery of sores came to men.

The French anthropologist Claude Lévi-Strauss has suggested that myths fall into structural patterns in which sets of oppositions play a major role. The basic dichotomy is that between nature and culture. He has also noted that the contrast between nature and culture is often mediated by an ambiguous creature. In this simple story, these patterns are particularly obvious. In the beginning, a spider representing the natural world meets a woman in the forest. Although she is human, she appears in the domain of the spider. The spider itself is an interesting animal. Although it is not human, it lives in two worlds: in the wild, and among humans. In addition, it weaves—a behavior otherwise exclusive to humans and thus a part or sign of the cultural world.

When the first encounter occurs, the spider is well and the woman is sick. The woman "dances" in pain. The spider mistakes her pain for a dance (which is itself an aspect of cultural behavior) and, as a result, her sores are transferred to its body.

In the next scene, the spider leaves its realm and enters the world of humans. Now humans mistake the spider's cry of pain for singing, and in their efforts to learn the "song" they, in their turn, become covered with sores.

Illness and its cure are bound to an interaction between the domains of culture and nature. Trickery and misunderstanding lead in each case to the transfer of disease across the boundaries of the human and animal worlds. Finally, the interaction takes place between a spider, an ambiguous creature because it can live with or away from humans and because it spins, and, in the first case at least, with an ambiguous human, a woman who appears in the forest, the animal world. The last encounter is between the spider and humans within their own context, a village. In each case, misunderstanding takes place during communication between two separate domains.

Spider stories are common all over West Africa. In most cases, the spider character is a trickster who, frequently with the aid of magical power, manages to win out over both human and animal adversaries. Most of these stories also reflect a whole series of ambiguous relationships between humans and animals in which the separation of nature and culture is breached.

The ambiguity that exists in contacts between the human world and the world of animals is apparent also in the next tale, in which domestic species, those which have been made part of human society, refuse to act according to the rules of culture. The story reinforces the worth humans have for each other.

There were once three young men in a village. The first one felt that his fields were too far from the village. He went to God and asked for a horse. The second man said that, whenever he went to hunt, he caught nothing and therefore had no meat. He went before God and asked him for a dog. The third man said that he had no woman and asked God for one. God granted each man his request.

The first man, proud of his fine horse, set out for his fields. The horse began to run through the bush and would not stop. It carried the man for many miles beyond his fields, through trees and thorn bushes which tore his flesh.

The second man, proud of his fine dog, set out to hunt. The dog was very large and beautiful, but it would not chase animals. That day, the man saw many fine animals but caught none, because the dog would not help him.

The third man, who had been given the daughter of God, took her home and was happy with her. After three weeks, she became pregnant, and after three months she brought forth three fine daughters. The man was very happy. The other men, seeing his happiness and reflecting on their own misery, went before God once again, this time to return their own gifts and to ask for wives for themselves. God told them to go to the third man, who was happy with his wife, and ask for his daughters in marriage. This they did and were happy. This is why Abron parents give their children in marriage.

Social ties are derived from God, but operate in the world of men. Not all God's gifts are beneficial. Man must choose well. The giving of children in marriage is a social tie that provides harmony within the community. Little violence occurs in Abron tales. In this case, men who are unhappy with their gifts are not jealous of the man who is happy with his. They do not aggress against him, but, rather, by marrying his daughters, find their own happiness. Remember also that sores came via the animal world and not (at least not directly) from the action of other humans.

Other Abron tales reinforce social rules and explain social tensions. The following two stories involve the betrayal of humans by humans. Actions that go against human law and therefore against culture are contrasted in the first tale to the admirable behavior of animals that are usually dangerous (here they act according to cultural rules). In the second tale, an unusual event (the laying of an egg by a goat, an unnatural act of a natural creature) leads to the discovery of wrongdoing and the punishment of the wrongdoer.

There was once a poor hunter. He did not have enough to eat, and he had not even one good cloth. And so he left his village. One day, in the midst of a hunt, he found a large hole in which had fallen another hunter, a cobra, a lion, and a rat. The hunter asked that his life be saved and the first man helped him out of the hole. The rat then asked to be saved and the hunter helped him out of the hole. Then the cobra asked to be saved and he was helped out of the hole. Finally, the lion, in his turn, asked to be saved and the man helped him out of the hole. One day, several days later, the man met the lion carrying an antelope in its mouth. "This antelope is for you," said the lion, "because you have saved my life." One week later, the man met the lion, and again the lion gave him some game. A bit later, the hunter met the man he had helped out of the hole. The man was carrying a large pot of palm wine on his head. "This is for you because you have saved my life," said the man to the hunter.

One night, the first man heard a noise under his bed. It was the rat he had rescued. "Look under your bed; I have brought you something," said the rat. When the hunter looked under the bed, he saw that the floor was covered with gold. He was now rich, and he bought many slaves and founded a village. One day, a messenger came to him with a summons from the King. On the way to the court, the messenger told the hunter that someone had stolen the King's gold and that the King had been told that the hunter was the thief. He was taking the hunter to the King's court for execution.

The hunter asked the King's messenger if he could go into the bush to urinate. He was granted permission, and as soon as he stepped off the road he found the cobra he had rescued from the hole. He explained his plight and asked the serpent to help him. "This is a simple matter," replied the serpent. "The moment you arrive at the King's court, I shall bite the daughter of the King and she will become very sick. You must ask the King's permission to treat her wound. You must then treat her with this antidote, which I give to you. When you have cured the King's daughter, demand of the King that he kill the man who reported you to him, for he has lied about you." The hunter then left the cobra and made his way to the King's court. Just as he arrived in the royal village, a great cry of grief was heard. The people cried out that the daughter of the King had been bitten by a cobra and was sure to die. The hunter rushed before the King and asked that he might be allowed to treat the wound. The King, who loved his daughter very much, was desperate, and, willing to try anything to save his daughter, granted the hunter permission to try. The hunter then gave the girl the antidote provided by the cobra, and she was soon well. "Now," said the hunter to the King, "you must do something for me." "I shall indeed," said the King. "What is your request?" "You must put to death the man who has falsely accused me of stealing your gold." "It shall be done," said the King. And the man who had spread the false story was brought before the hunter and the King. It was the man whom the hunter had rescued from the hole along with the lion, the rat, and the cobra. In no time at all, he was put to death by the King's executioner. And this is why the Abron always punish those who spread false witness.

There were once two friends. They had an agreement between them never to tell anyone their private secrets. One of them took the wife of the King as his mistress. Now, in Abron land, this is indeed dangerous, because if the King hears of it, the man will be put to death. One night when the King's wife went to her lover, she died in his bed. The man was very upset. He was afraid that the King would find him out. He went to the house of his friend and told him what had happened. His friend told him he had nothing to fear, and together they went back to the house where the dead woman lay. Working hard all night, they buried the woman right under the floor of the man's house. The next day, the King could not find his wife. He sent people to search throughout the village, and still no one could find her. Finally, he called all the men of the village together and asked each one if they knew the whereabouts of his wife. The two friends were called before the King and each said that he had seen no one the night before as they had spent the time drinking palm wine together. And so the King did not find his wife.

Sometime later, the friend of the man who had had the King's wife as his mistress died. The man mourned him long and hard, because he had indeed been a good friend. When the family of the dead man saw how much he grieved, they came to him and said, "Here, take your friend's younger brother as a new friend." The man asked the boy if he could keep a secret. The boy said that he could and so he was accepted by the first man, who longed for a new comrade. One day the two men went to sacrifice a goat to the god Tano. Along the way, they stopped to drink. The goat was a troublesome animal, so they tied it to a tree. All of a sudden, the goat sent up a terrible cry. The younger of the two men went to see what had happened. He found that the goat had laid an egg. He picked up the egg and ran back to his friend. "Look," he said, "the goat has laid an egg." The first man took the egg and said, "Let this be a secret between us. No one will believe that this could have happened and we shall be mocked." The youth agreed to tell no one, but when he returned to the village, he went directly to the King and said, "The goat of my friend has laid an egg." Now this news greatly excited the King, because, when his wife had disappeared, he had gone to a Marabout [a Moslem scholar and magician] to ask how he could find his wife. The Marabout had told him that he must look for a goat that had laid an egg. The King therefore called the owner of the goat before him. "Is it true," he asked the owner, "that your goat has laid an egg?" "No," said the man, "how could this be true, the egg which I have, I bought from an old egg seller." The egg seller was then brought before the King, who asked her if she had indeed sold the egg to the man. Now this egg seller was also a friend of the man, and so she replied that she had sold him the egg. But one of the old men sitting in the King's council, listening to what transpired, remembered that he had seen the wife of the King enter into the man's house on the night she had disappeared. He told the King of this, and the King ordered that the man's house be searched. It was not difficult for them to find the grave of the King's wife, and so the man's secret was found out and, as a result, he was executed. This is why one must never take the younger brother of a friend as a friend.

Tales that involve trials for their heroes are frequent in Abron folklore. In the one to follow, the moral is a simple one, explaining the strong bond between husband and wife in Abron society. Since Abron married couples live apart, and family bonds compete with stronger kinship ties within the lineage, it is not surprising that such stories form a part of the Abron repertoire.

Once there was a couple who had no children. They went to a Marabout and asked that he make it possible

for them to have a child. He said, "I can do this for
you, but the child will die before he is fifteen unless you
are able to keep him hidden in the house away from the
sight of women." The Marabout told them that the son
would be liked by women, but that if he should have
intercourse before the age of fifteen he would die. He
said that it was for this reason that they would be unable to protect their son. They said that they could manage, and again demanded of the Marabout that he give
them a son. The Marabout agreed.

The couple were very happy. In order to protect the
child, the man built a house with two stories, and kept
the son hidden upstairs. One day, however, when his
parents were not home, the son discovered that he had
no kola. Now he liked kola very much and so was very
unhappy. He went to his window and saw a young girl
selling kola nuts in the street below. He asked her to
pass him some nuts through the window. She refused
him, saying, "I will only give you the kola if you let me
in the house." The young man went downstairs and let
her in. She gave him the kola, which he immediately
chewed. After he had chewed the kola, the girl refused
to leave, but made love to him instead.

When the young man's parents returned home, they
found him lying dead on the bed. The unhappy couple
returned to the Marabout and told him that they had
found their son dead. The Marabout told them that if
they wanted their son to live again, they must build a
big fire and then enter into it. The parents prepared the
fire but were afraid to enter. The girl who had sold the
kola to the son stepped forward and said, "I shall enter
in your place." And so she did. As she entered the fire,
it went out and she emerged with the son alive and
unharmed. Ever since, man has loved woman.

This story reflects the passing of responsibility from
one generation to the next, as well as the strength of
the marriage link. The man in the tale plays a passive
role in both instances. He wants kola, so lets the
woman in the house, but it is she who seduces him. She

causes his death, but it is she who brings him back to life. The parents are given a gift by a Marabout, but, as in many magic tales, the magical gift comes with a special difficulty that must be overcome if the outcome is to be fully successful. As is frequently the case, a setback occurs before a final, positive outcome.

Not all Abron folk stories are cautionary tales. They are also fond of riddles, some of which are quite complex. The story that follows is about riddles and is itself a riddle.

There was once a King who had only one child, a daughter. When she was still a little girl, she told her father that she wanted to marry a man who was wise in the knowledge of riddles. When she became old enough to marry, her father called the chiefs of all the Abron cantons before him to see which one knew the most riddles. Before they arrived at court, each chief called the men of their villages together and asked them to teach all the riddles they knew. When the chiefs arrived at the house of the King, each in turn recited all the riddles he had collected. None of them was accepted as a husband by the girl.

Some months later, two young men of a distant village decided to go to the court and try their luck with the King's daughter. The journey was long, so they took a youth with them to carry their belongings. When they arrived at court, the daughter of the King said that they must wait three days, and then, on the fourth day, she would accept one of them in marriage. The first day, she made futu for them and in the center of the ball of dough she put a red kola nut. When the two men found the kola, they threw it away, but the youth saved it. On the second day, she again put a red kola nut in the center of the dough ball, and then again on the third day. Each time, the two men threw the kola away and the youth recovered it. On the fourth day, the King's daughter once more prepared futu for the men, but this time she put a small cotton ball in the center of the dough. When the two men found it, they threw it away just as they had thrown away the kola on the three previous days. The young man saved the cotton ball as he had saved the kola. The men then came before the girl. The first man recounted all the riddles he knew, but when he finished, the King's daughter said, "I cannot marry you." Then the second man recounted all the riddles he knew, but when he had finished, the girl said, "I cannot marry you." The youth, who had stood silent all this time, then asked to speak. The two men refused to give him permission, but the King's daughter said, "You must give him a chance also." The youth stepped forward and said, "I have very little to say and so I will not take much of your time. The first day of our arrival, the King's daughter put a red kola nut in the middle of the futu. On the second and third days, she did the same thing, but on the fourth day, she put in a cotton ball. Now I say that on the first three days she was menstruating, but that on the fourth day she had finished." The King's daughter responded by saying that the youth was indeed wise and that she would marry him. The other men were jealous and they said, "We are going to leave you, but the youth must come with us, for he must carry our things." The King's daughter replied that they must stay one more day, so that she and the youth could get married. They agreed, but after the marriage they set out with the youth for their own village. Along the way, the first man said, "We must kill the youth." The second said, "No, we cannot, but let us take him back to the village and give him to his parents." The first man disagreed and suggested that they tie the youth to a tree and abandon him. After some argument, they finally agreed to do this, and so they tied the youth to a tree and left him. Although the youth was tied to a tree, he did not cry, but waited. After some time, a vendor of kola came by. The youth said to him, "Go to the daughter of the King, my wife, and say to her, untie this kola and guard it or it will surely rot." On hearing this, the girl, without saying a word, ran to her father and asked him to give her two horses. "My husband is tied to a tree, and if I do not go and free him, he will surely die."

And so she rode off and freed her husband. From then, they lived happily. Now, my children, which of the two, the youth or the King's daughter, was wiser in the knowledge of riddles?

This tale is perhaps distantly related to the Cinderella story, which does occur in African versions. The poor youth wins the daughter of the King, although he is considered unworthy by the two men for whom he works. Of course, there is a sex reversal here, but remember that the Abron are matrilineal. It is the offspring of the King's daughter who will be in the royal lineage, and so, as in Cinderella, future issue of an ideal marriage will be royal. Kola, which is revered by the Abron as a luxury and often sacrificed to the gods, figures in this story, as it does in many others. Red kola appears to have a sexual symbolism for the Abron.

11
Christmas Eve and Christmas Day

I had two invitations for Christmas Eve 1961: one
from the Protestant missionaries to see their play in the
early evening, and the other from the few Catholic
Abron in Diassenpa to Midnight Mass in the new
church at Lomo, Oppong's home town.

The Sparks had borrowed the use of a small building
on the main street of Gumeré and had spread a few
sheets on a wire running around the small, mud-walled
porch. Costumes were fashioned from other scrap material and scenery from assorted tables and chairs. The
scene was appropriately tropical and there was no
difficulty collecting palm fronds and banana leaves to
finish the décor. The play was lit by flashlights held by
a few members of the audience. Actors were recruited
from among converts' children, and although it was
their debut, they had memorized their lines well and
performed eagerly. The curtain parted to reveal the
biblical characters, all black and half adult size or less.
Mary and Joseph, dressed in white (the Abron color
for priests), came before the door of the inn and were
refused shelter by the owner. They were soon led to the
stable by a "kindly servant," obviously aware of his
coming place in history. The Holy Child was born between the acts and when the curtains opened again, the
Three Kings, their heads turbaned in missionary family
towels, presented their gifts to the Child. The play,
translated into Kolongo by the pastor, came off without
a hitch and was enjoyed by the rather large crowd of
curious spectators. Although unfamiliar with the Bible,
most of the audience were regular patrons of the local
movie theater set up in the back yard of Alhaje Baba,

the rich Moslem chief of Gumeré. The gentle story of Christ's birth was an undoubted change from the blood-and-thunder Indian potboilers. The sincere acting of the children was better than the pompous mannerisms of the professionals, to which they were accustomed. After the brief play, Pastor Sparks delivered a brief Christmas sermon stressing that Christ was neither black nor white, but, like "Syrian traders, a man of mixed parentage." By the time the service had ended, it was dark. I groped around the village looking for my friends and finally found them in the house of the local carpenter, a Ghana Brong with whom I had drunk palm wine and who had made shelves for me. This man had the habit of calling me "master," a term the British in West Africa had taught Africans to use in addressing white men. I had often explained the meaning of the term and tried to get him to use my first name. One day, I broke his habit. After he had addressed me as master, I began to punch him on his arms. "Do not beat me, 'master,'" he said, partially in jest but surprised that I would hit him. "If I am your master," I replied, "then you are my slave and I may beat you." He and his friends roared with laughter, and after that we were better friends and used first names with each other.

I managed to get everyone into the car and we set off down the road to Lomo. The Mass was to be celebrated in a bower erected outside the partially completed church. Behind the bower, a large bonfire burned in a pit. The villagers, mostly Catholic, had gathered to warm themselves. It was the coldest night I could remember and, dressed in a light shirt and shorts, I was grateful for a chance to warm myself. When midnight came, the group assembled in the temporary chapel. The priest, a stooped old man with a white beard and white robes, stepped forward and began the Mass, assisted by village boys and the local church choir. Part of the Mass was in Latin, the rest in Kolongo. A good part of the congregation joined in a high whine characteristic of Kolongo and Abron singing. Sitting in the crowd was an effort for me, as I grew colder and colder, but the strange sound of this transplanted Roman ceremony was fascinating. Not only was the language African, but the whole tone, even the Latin, had been unconsciously translated by the singers into the local idiom. Yet the Mass was alien. The total effect must have been startling even to the non-believers present, for it was a performance set apart from the world known to any of us.

The Mass ended at two o'clock in the morning. The crowd broke up and reassembled around the still smoldering fire. Before leaving the village, we warmed ourselves once more. Riding back, I turned on the car heater. We were suddenly choking in a cloud of dust, which had gathered for weeks in the vents. In spite of the cold, we spent the rest of the trip shivering with the windows open.

My own fatigue drove me away from the village to someplace where I could get away from the constant noise of the animals and children. I parked behind the local schoolhouse and slept until well past noon, when the sun finally climbed over the roof and began to heat the car. Needing a break from the constant interaction with village life, I was determined not to return to Diassenpa that day, and as soon as I got up I drove out into the savanna along a road I had never traveled before. I headed west, toward Bouaké, but the scenery presented the usual monotony of green and red dust broken only by an occasional village. I passed from Abron country into the land of the Bini, but even there the landscape did not change much. The Bini are related to the Abron and their villages are impossible to distinguish from those of their cousins. They are dry, dusty, and no less red than the earth from which they are made. In the heat of the day, they appear deserted, for both animals and people are either indoors or on their farms. The only sign of life is an occasional chicken scratching in the bushes at the edge of the village.

Boredom had settled on me, and my attempted es-

cape from the tensions of field work had brought no relief. Just as I was about to head back to Diassenpa, I
noticed a smudge of smoke hanging above the trees
several miles off. I drove off to investigate. As I
approached the fire, the smoke grew quite thick. A
large area of the savanna was burning, a few hundred
yards from the road. The fire itself leaped up about
forty feet, almost high enough to scorch the palmetto
fronds which hang from the top of their thin trunks. A
large number of hawks circled over the fire, waiting for
rodents and other small game to emerge from the grass
in their flight to safety. Several of these large birds had
landed on the road in my path, and I was able to get a
good look at them. They are very large, almost the size
of eagles, black, with what appear to be very sharp
talons. They are handsome birds, very unlike the vultures, which are more commonly seen from so near. As
I drove my car toward the group of birds, they flew up,
scattered, and then, as they gained altitude, began their
slow circle of the fire once again. From time to time,
one would collapse in flight and drop like a bullet
through the smoke, to emerge seconds later with some
small animal tucked under its body. Sometimes an
antelope or a zebra will leap out and cross the road in
its flight from the heat and flames, but I saw no such
animals that day.

By midafternoon, it began to get so hot that the wind
through the car window, which had cooled me earlier,
merely added to my growing dryness. I turned the car
back and drove into the wind, thinking then only of the
relief I would find in the village. I arrived in Tabgne,
near Diassenpa, at four o'clock to find a carnival in full
progress. It was Christmas Day, and a time of celebration. The cooler winds of evening brought the people
out into the market place and some drummers were
performing. Men dressed in rags were dancing for the
growing crowd. They were moving rapidly, jerking their
bodies back and forth in a grotesque manner that
looked like a cross between sexual intercourse and epi-
lepsy. Occasionally, one of the dancers shouted an ob-

scenity at the crowd. This was greeted with much laughter. As the drumming grew more intense, one of the dancers jumped on the back of another and forced him into a crouching position. They then began to gyrate together, with the first man pressing his midsection against the buttocks of the other. Then a third dancer jumped on the first and soon there was a line of men front to back, all pulsating one against the other. This time there was no ambiguity in their movement. The audience went wild, screaming approval and encouragement. The dance had become one big sexual joke, enjoyed by the participants and the onlookers together. Then, from another part of the village, two dancers appeared on enormous stilts. They wore cloth masks covered with red beads. Each step they took on their ten-foot-high stilts covered a couple of yards. As soon as they got within range of the drums, their steps fell in with the rhythm. The crowd, which had been watching the other dancers, gathered around. The stilt dancers came forward, moved toward each other, and with a halting grace performed a circle dance on the inside of the crowd. Their steps became more daring and their bodies moved so fluidly that I was sure that one would topple over, but they had complete control over their movements. Finally, one and then the other did a complete backbend without losing his balance. Their bodies tipped backward until their heads touched the tops of the stilts behind them, and then, with a rapid jerk of their bodies, both men righted themselves. The other dancers joined the circle, and the men on stilts, who strode in and out among them like cranes dancing with a group of sparrows, continued their acrobatic display.

These men were Fon, from Dahomey. Most of the time, they ply less spectacular professions. Many of them were itinerant masons and housebuilders who traveled throughout the ex-French territories in search of work. On holidays, they became entertainers and were known far and wide. They performed in public hoping for gifts of money from the audience, but also out of the enjoyment that came with an unmatched skill. Fon dancers start their training when they are children. Beginning with short stilts, they graduate slowly upward until the master stilt dancers can top fifteen feet. They then exaggerate their own prowess and boast of experts who can top twenty-five feet and step over the roofs of houses. They also believe that they are protected from falling by a special magic. Their Christmas celebration was the finale of two days in which the influence of Western culture mingled with the mosaic of local custom.

12
Abron Medicine

My major informant on Abron medicine was Afua Morofyé. She had successfully raised nine children into adulthood and was skilled in herbal medicine. She knew which diseases could be treated by a secular curer and which required the professional services of a priest. I also had many chances to discuss medical theory with several kparesogo and when possible questioned sick individuals about their own cases. In addition, I constructed a questionnaire, during the final phase of my field work, which was administered to almost every resident of Diassenpa. This more formal approach provided me with data on cause of illness, what kind of treatment was appropriate to particular conditions, and what measures could be taken to prevent disease.

I observed health care on a day-to-day basis. Because the Abron have no concept of preventive medicine, except certain magical practices believed to ward off disease, I had to use what I had learned about prevalent disease organisms during my studies at Yale. This knowledge provided me with a framework for the observation of secular practices that would promote or inhibit the transmission of disease organisms.

Considering their harsh environment and simple technology, the Abron have evolved a successful system of personal and village hygiene. Those practices that we call public health and preventive medicine are not so grouped within the Abron behavioral system. They are part of the culture because they are part of accepted tradition. Frequently, when I asked Abron why they did something, the standard reply would be, "That's the way our grandfathers did it." On the surface, such a reply blocked my attempt to probe for the causes and function of particular behavioral traits. I am convinced, however, that what I call the "grandfather response" suggests several things about the behavior in question. First, it suggests that such behavior lies outside of some native theory, a theory that would link it to a set of causes and perhaps to other behaviors. In these cases, the behaviors cannot be explained in reference to something else. In addition, although I admit that this is more tenuous, I think that the "grandfather response" suggests that the trait in question falls into one or both of two domains. First, such behavior might represent the playing out of subconscious wishes. It might be a ritualized substitution, in the Freudian sense, for something more serious, a ritual action, for example, instead of overt, aggressive acts. Freud, in his collected essays, refers to the case of a woman who developed a severe and persistent tic. In the course of analysis, Freud discovered that, during the illness of her daughter, she had been warned by her doctor to watch over, but not to disturb, the seriously ill child. Fatigued after several hours of watchfulness, the mother began to express subconscious ambivalent feelings. She loved her daughter and wished to see her get well, but, at the same time, she felt aggressive toward the child, whose illness had pushed her to the extremes of fatigue. The aggressive feelings, which could have led her to seriously disturb her daughter, were translated into the relatively harmless tic. The tic had become a personal ritual substitution for aggression toward her daughter.

Second, such behaviors might be elements imbedded in a semantic domain that operates on a non-conscious level. Ordinary syntax is of this order. We speak language more or less correctly, according to a set of inherent rules, but we are unaware of these rules unless they are taught to us. In this case, the reason for the behavior is not repressed, as in the first case, but, rather, exists on a mental level that is not conscious for the ordinary informant.

Many of those behaviors which are explained by recourse to the "grandfather response," because they are not part of some native theory, might enter a behavioral system through direct rewards from the en-

vironment that remain unconscious, or at least unnoticed. Behaviors of this type might become part of the
culture through a process similar to pure conditioning,
the experimental practice used by so many behavioral
psychologists to train animals. The psychological school
closest to this approach is that of B. F. Skinner, which,
through operant conditioning, trains rats to run complicated mazes and, perhaps more striking for the layman,
teaches pigeons to play ping-pong! Skinnerians reward
naturally occurring behaviors that approach the desired
response and ignore those movements that do not fit
the emerging pattern. In this way, the animal's behavior
is gradually shaped to conform to a stereotype chosen
by the experimenter. If we substitute the environment
for the experimenter, we can arrive at a theoretical position in which behaviors that produce rewards, even if
these rewards are unconscious, could be reinforced,
while behaviors bearing a neutral or negative load
might be extinguished. Since everything we do has
some consequences, a good deal of human behavior
could be shaped in this way.

I do not wish to leave the matter here, however, because very few of our behaviors are shaped in this
way.

Human beings differ significantly from all other animals because of their symbol-making abilities, which
are developed far beyond the communication capacities
of other species. Symbol systems on the order of complexity of human language consist not only of discrete
units, but of rules that control the relationship among
these units. These sets of rules are called grammar.
These rules set constraints on the whole system and its
operation so that simple conditioning will have little or
no effect on the system as a whole. In addition, human
language is highly fluid. We can change the meaning of
symbols through extension and diminution of the
semantic context. We can create new relationships
among concepts through the process of metaphoriza-
tion and other, like mechanisms. Finally, we can use

these systems to imagine events that have not yet occurred or might never occur.

Recently, several anthropologists, particularly Claude Lévi-Strauss in France, have suggested that much of human culture other than language is made up of symbolic systems that have their own grammatical rules and can change only in orderly fashion according to these rules. Lévi-Strauss himself has examined such diverse cultural systems as cooking, kinship, and myth. These domains follow rules that link units into what he calls structures. Transformation rules can be extracted by comparing sets of related structures. In addition, Lévi-Strauss has suggested that each separate domain (myth, cooking, kinship, etc.) can be related to other domains within a particular culture. They are, according to this theory, different means of expressing the same symbolic messages.

Lévi-Strauss's theories touch very little upon pragmatic day-to-day activity, although, in one article,* he does deal with possible relationships between ecological adaptation and structuralism, suggesting that selection and internal grammar exert mutual constraints on each other. Lévi-Strauss is nonetheless concerned with those structures which underlie apparent reality—cultural systems buried in the unconscious.

Between fully conscious behavior, of which there are many examples from societies all over the world, and those systems which function on a totally unconscious level, there is a range of behaviors that deal with reality in a more or less overtly symbolic way. The analysis of these behaviors does not require systematic probing by the anthropologist, for if they operate on the level of metaphor, the metaphor is often direct and clear. Nonetheless, such behaviors may interfere with the kind of simple conditioning described above, for such behaviors constitute a system based on native theory. Such theory may deal with one set of cultural realities

* "Structuralism and Ecology," *Barnard Alumnae*, spring 1972, pp. 6–14.

while ignoring others. This is the case with Abron medicine.

I found that Abron theories of medicine were woefully inadequate for the treatment of disease, although they worked very well to focus attention upon social rifts within the society. Native therapists used disease as the raw material for curing social disorder. Illness was used as a metaphor for social pathology. As far as disease is concerned, the Abron have a theory that is largely wrong. Because it works in the area of social life, and also because most patients get well regardless of treatment, the theory continues to operate in the behavioral system. As far as medicine is concerned, it inhibits adaptive change.

As among so many preliterate peoples, there is no place for natural death in the Abron conceptual system. People become sick and die because some power, good or evil, has acted against them. The forces that cause sickness and death vary in power, motivation, and technique. Some can kill without warning, making it impossible to act against the threatening agent; others kill slowly, allowing the affected individual or his family to seek help. There are also forces that produce illness but do not kill. Disease symptoms are a sign that something must be done to return the individual to a state of well-being. Although in some cases specific symptoms are treated medically, the major aspect of treatment, at least for serious illness, consists of a social process in which the patient is restored to a state of balance with the social system. The cause of the disease, which is always social, must be treated along with the symptoms. If the cause is not discovered and attended to, the initial symptoms might go away, but the disease will linger in another form. Such a theory is not far away from our own concept of psychosomatic medicine, although the Abron are *perhaps* a bit less clear than we about where to draw the line between physical and mental illness.

There is an array of powers that may act as agents of disease in the Abron conceptual world. These cut across the natural and supernatural as we structure them. Ordinary people, supernatural entities, or God may all cause illness.

Even the high god of the Abron, Nyame, who rarely interferes in the unfolding of daily life, can cause disease. Very few Abron believe, however, that God makes people ill to punish them. He does so, rather, to prove that, as God, he can do with man as he wishes. When God causes illness, it is to remind man of his own limitations and his finite condition. Such a belief is congruent with Abron social structure, in which unquestioning respect for individuals of higher rank or age is a major feature of orderly social life.

Those diseases attributed to God are those that strike many individuals at the same time. Thus, epidemics are usually said to be caused by God.

Lesser deities within the Abron pantheon, including Tano, the high god for all the Akan people, can produce illness in those who do not fulfill contractual obligations that have been duly entered into by way of an appropriate ceremony. These may be social ceremonies such as the yam festival (Tano is the protector of the yam) or individual transactions in which someone has asked a deity for a personal favor.

I visited the temple of Tano at Assuifri. It is just outside the village, in a grove of trees. The structure consists of an enclosed room, which I was not allowed to enter, and an open, porchlike area. The wall of this porch is decorated with mud bas-reliefs. The major theme is women's breasts, pairs of which are scattered over the entire surface. In addition, there are several handprints. Hundreds of egg shells dangle on short strings from the roof. Clearly Tano is associated by the Abron with fertility. Tchina Kofi told me that the enclosed room contained a large jug full of water from the river Tano, in Ghana. This water, which represents the river god, is renewed each year.

The death of an individual does not mean that his or her social relations are cut off. Therefore, if a ghost to whom others are indebted makes legitimate demands that are not fulfilled, the ghost may punish the offending individuals. In addition, any person who dies may kill a younger member of his family in order to bring him or her into service. The age ranking that pervades Abron society continues between the living and the dead. During my stay in Diassenpa, two out of seven deaths in the neighboring village of Amamvi were caused by recently deceased individuals who killed their relatives for no other reason than to bring them into service. In one case, a man who was lonely in heaven killed his younger brother. Two months later, a sister of both men died. During the ritual questioning of the corpse, she revealed that she had been killed by her brothers so that she could cook for them.

The earth itself, as a personalized entity, can deal out punishment to those who violate social rules associated with cultivation. People who farm on rest days can be driven insane by *bonzam* (bush devils) acting as agents for the land. Other violations may be punished directly by the power of the earth. Two deaths that occurred in Amamvi during my field work were attributed to the earth. In one case, a man who found that some yams had been stolen from his garden prayed to the earth to punish the thief. He promised that if his request were granted, he would sacrifice a goat to the land. Next day, a young man died suddenly, and, when his corpse was questioned, it admitted the thefts. This fact was announced to the funeral gathering, and the next day the man whose yams had been stolen made the promised sacrifice. The other case was that of a woman who had started an argument with her husband in one of their gardens. The earth took offense at this and killed her the next day.

Sogo (Moslems) are said to have the power to cure illness or to inflict it on others. Their powers are usually limited to love magic, impotence, and Guinea-worm infection (dracuntiasis, a very noxious parasite transmitted by infected water). Sogo make people sick because they themselves have been offended in some way or because they have been hired to cause illness in others.

The fact that Sogo may kill as well as cure puts them in an ambiguous position. Many Abron told me that they would fear to go to a Sogo for treatment, and some said that Moslems indulged only in black magic. My own family did not share this view, since Tchina Kofi's brother, Azumana, was a Sogo. He was fully accepted by the family and was a great favorite of the children. In addition, the oldest man in Diassenpa was Moslem. He was respected by everyone as an elder and senior member of the village council. He did not, however, practice medicine. At any rate, I got the impression that those Moslems who were not trusted were outsiders to the village, particularly Dioula traders.

Witches (deresogo) are frequently blamed for causing illness or death. They do so out of envy and have power only over members of their own family. If a witch wishes to harm a non-relative, he or she must establish a contract with a witch in that person's family. A witch's power is completely supernatural; while a Sogo kills with magic agents learned as a craftsman learns skills, the witch is born with powers that produce supernatural results.

The Abron believe that an ordinary individual may cause illness in another person through *hareje*. This is a technique—a means of inflicting illness on others. Hareje is object intrusion in which a specially treated, pointed stick, bone, or nail may be projected magically into the body of a victim. Hareje is learned in the bush from bonzam. The basic symptoms of this illness are pains in the chest and back. Since these are common complaints and may be linked to malaria and some bronchial diseases, as well as various forms of rheumatic conditions, hareje is widespread. Tchina Kofi told me that someone had once practiced hareje on him.

All those individuals, whether they be deresogo, Sogo, or ordinary persons who use their powers to inflict illness on others, run the risk that their efforts may be turned against them. Priests, Sogo themselves, and some of the lesser secular curers known as *sise,* sell magic medicine that can be used to protect a person against the attacks of others. If magic is used against someone who possesses countermagic, the latter will act against the initiator.

A kparesé in Diassenpa told me that a deresé had once tried to kill her. Her own magic was ineffective against this particular witch, but another kparesé promised to help her. She was told to leave her village and use the medicine given to her—that the deresé would die in its next attempt on her life. One week after she moved to Diassenpa, her uncle died in her native village. When the corpse was questioned, it revealed that it had been killed by the countermagic of the second priest.

A schizophrenic woman of Amamvi is said to have become insane when her attempt to kill her brother failed. Her condition was related to her brother's use of countermagic.

Priests do not usually make people sick, but they may kill deresogo in professional service for clients. If a person wishes to harm another, he or she may attempt to enlist the services of a kparesé. If the cause is just, a case of adultery for example, the kparesé may agree to help. But if the priest is convinced that the request is unjust, he may punish the individual, instead of performing the requested service. In this case, the client may be stricken by the very illness he had wished on his victim. People known to perform hareje are subject to the power of the kparesé, who, through divination, can determine the cause of illness. For this reason, people other than Sogo, who are said to fear kparesogo, hesitate to employ black magic except through the offices of an outsider.

Illness requires treatment. The Abron have several sources to which they may appeal in time of sickness. Which source they will tap depends upon the perceived seriousness of the case and previous attempts to cure it. If a person is only mildly ill and familiar with the treatment for a condition, he will usually treat himself. Most Abron are familiar with medication for diarrhea and are particularly fond of applying self-therapy with potassium permanganate. Superficial scratches are covered with a leaf and sometimes forgotten until they develop into a serious infection, as they are wont to do. Mild fevers are treated with a variety of widely known herbs. When sickness occurs, the person will usually wait some days before seeking help from a specialist, but if the condition persists, such aid will eventually be sought. A persistent condition suggests that there are more than symptoms involved and that the cause must be discovered and treated.

When a sick person has not been able to obtain relief after several days of a mildly annoying illness, he will seek out a villager known to be familiar with various medicinal herbs. These people do not charge for their services, although they will receive a gift if a cure results from the treatment. Such curers are symptom-oriented and know several alternate treatments for specific conditions. Medical knowledge of this type is picked up casually from a wide range of individuals both Abron and non-Abron. An Abron who has been cured with European medication might recommend the same medication to a sick friend with an entirely different ailment. European medicine is particularly susceptible to use of this sort, for it is seen as generally good and powerful.

Some of the medicines used by Abron contain active agents of one type or another and do have a real effect on symptoms. Others are magical and cannot, by any stretch of the imagination, have other than psychological therapeutic value. In addition, Kolongo makes no distinction between medicine and amelioratory magic of all types. Thus, potions that produce protection against gunshot wounds, success in love, or business, and those which cure disease are all referred to as *siño*.

If a person is very ill, or is sick for a prolonged period, or is convinced that someone or something is trying to kill him, he will seek the aid of a kparesé. Ideally, kparesogo are supposed to be consulted for any condition, but this is rarely the case in practice. Most

Abron feel little anxiety over illnesses thought to be mild and non-fatal. These are in fact attributed to natural causes.

Conditions with severe internal symptoms such as violent headache, stomach ache, high fever, or extreme weakness, will usually lead a person to the kparesé.

While most kparesogo are familiar with a large selection of medicinal plants, their major concern is with disease agents. Their main professional task is to find the cause of the illness. In order to do this, they must consult their personal deity, or gbawkaw. It is the gbawkaw which determines the cause of illness and prescribes treatment. If the kparesé discovers that a person is the victim of a witch, the kparesé will combat the witch on behalf of the patient. In all cases of illness, the kparesé will deal with the cause but, at the same time, either prescribe medication or, in some cases, refer his patient to a sise for medicines.

Since kparesogo are familiar with a wide range of drug plants, one would suppose their treatment of symptoms to differ little from the treatment offered by sisogo and non-professional curers. This is not always so, however. A kparesé will rely on his or her gbawkaw for diagnosis to such an extent that the patient will not be questioned as thoroughly as he or she might be by some other type of curer. In fact, some patients go to kparesogo demanding treatment without having an examination and without revealing all their symptoms. Actually, if a kparesé were to ask a patient too many questions, it would bring the power of the gbawkaw into question, for the latter is supposed to be able to determine the reasons for illness through its own supernatural powers. The situation is very much like that joke in our own culture in which a patient refuses to describe his symptoms to the doctor because it is the latter's job to find out what is wrong. In many cases, therefore, kparesogo do not offer their patients direct treatment for a specific set of symptoms, even though they do prescribe medicines. This is not as strange as it might seem, however, for most conditions brought to the kparesé involve what, for the Abron, are ambiguous, internal symptoms, which are difficult to diagnose with certainty.

Western medicine has been known to the Abron for at least fifty years. For the past twenty years, they have had hospital service at Bondoukou as well as clinics staffed by trained paramedical personnel at Tabgne and Tanda. In addition, they are able to buy a wide range of European manufactured drugs in the market place. I have seen people buying penicillin by the pill from large jugs, as well as other antibiotics, including certain quite dangerous preparations. Because medicine and treatment are separated in their conceptual system, most Abron believe that if they can obtain good, powerful Western drugs in the market place, they do not have to consult a doctor. Recently, clinics have become more popular for persistent conditions, but most people hesitate to go to the hospital if this will require a stay of more than one day. On the other hand, because they treat cause more than symptoms, kparesogo are not reluctant to send their patients to the doctor for treatment. A symbiotic relationship has developed between kparesogo and Western medical practitioners. European medicine has been incorporated into existing theories of disease and treatment. Like siño, European medication is just one other possible means of dealing with symptoms. The doctor cannot replace the kparesé, since Western medical knowledge cannot deal with the root cause of illness: social tension.

Few Abron express much anxiety over the power of the dead, and, while some deaths are explained in terms of family obligations, most sickness and death are attributed to other causes, primarily witches. Illness attributed to witchcraft causes much more anxiety than illness due to social infractions. This might be linked to the fact that, in the case of social obligation, the cause can be easily rooted out and ameliorated, while in the case of witchcraft, the cause is malign and difficult to combat. In one situation, illness is caused by the individual himself; in the other, it is caused by the actions of someone else who has evil power. In any case, I was struck by the frequent preoccupation with witchcraft, which contrasted with the rather secular approach most Abron had to other aspects of life. The major anxiety displayed by the average adult Abron probably concerns the attacks of witches. The only witches who can harm an individual are those within one's own family. Thus, although Abron have close and affectionate family relations, there is an obvious underlying ambiguity in the social system. As my field work progressed, this ambiguity became more and more apparent to me, and I began to wonder what could produce such a striking pattern.

13
Becoming an Abron

Abron children are ubiquitous. Much of the time, they occupy the background, silently watching the flow of daily life. When they play, it is in groups of boys or girls of the same age. When they work, it is in the context of their own families. They work, play, learn, and are punished in public. Strangers to a village provide them with an entertaining diversion. Their eyes become fixed on every activity and they are not inhibited by the rules of etiquette which apply to adults. One can chase them away with a shout of *"Gu bo, gu bo"* (Go away) or punish a particularly severe breach of privacy by asking, "Who brought you up?" but they are quick to return. I was, of course, particularly fascinating. Sometimes, in the evening, when I wished to escape attention, I would retire to my camper, pull all the curtains shut, and try to read. If a single crack was left between the curtains, it would soon be occupied by an eye peering in at me from the dark.

Although I found this behavior unnerving, it did facilitate my own observations of Abron culture as it concerns children. As my notes grew, I began to see a clear pattern emerging which could be used to explain many aspects of Abron social life.

Any observer can see that the Abron love children, for they show them great affection. A newborn baby is the focus of attention for all the female members of the mother's household. I noticed immediately the amount of touching that takes place as the baby is washed and fed. Crying babies are swung onto the breast of the nearest female. Until the age of one, this is likely to be the mother. Later, if the mother is not present, any adult female member of the household, with milk or not, will offer her breast in comfort. In addition, babies are not confined to a female world, even though they spend most of their time on their mother's back. Fathers and older male relatives frequently visit women's courtyards, especially when there are babies to play with. I often saw men bouncing their children on their knees or carrying them around the village. When a boy baby begins to cry and there are no women present, a man often plays with its genitals, sometimes kissing its penis several times. If this does not quiet the infant, a woman is sought to feed it.

Except when ill, infants rarely suffer obvious discomfort. They are seen nestled on their mother's back or in a soft bed, and if they soil themselves, they are cleaned immediately. If a baby is hurt while playing, it is comforted by whatever older person is around, including older siblings. It is allowed to play with almost anything it can get its hands on. The only event in the daily life of an infant or young baby that might be unpleasant to some, is the bath. The naked child is held on the lap of the mother or some other woman, with its head away from her body. The woman scrubs it vigorously with a cloth, using ample amounts of soap and water taken from a pan at her feet.

Sick babies are often heard squalling from the discomfort inflicted by strong enemas, generally laced with cayenne pepper. Since dysentery is common, no child avoids this experience entirely.

Mothers take their babies with them to the farm or to fetch water, so their social experience develops rapidly. In addition to the attention of male relatives, babies are often carried on the backs of their older siblings. In fact, female children as young as five years of age are involved in infant care and must take this responsibility seriously. They learn this aspect of their future role through actual practice rather than play fantasy.

After a child has learned to walk, it begins the painful process of separation from close personal contact with the mother. The youngest child in the household is always the center of attraction and attention. As a child grows older, new babies replace it. In this way, growing children move farther and farther from the center of the family stage. The last child in the family is "babied" for a longer period, but eventual separation from the comforts of infanthood is an expected part of the maturation process.

This growing separation leads to frustration. For the first time, immediate needs are not satisfied. The child's frustrations are compounded by a lack of sympathy from adults and other children. There is a sudden transformation from all-loved, with its concomitant total indulgence, to partial displacement in favor of a still younger child. In addition, this change is aggravated by a radical change in social status. With the exception of infants, young people are disfavored in Abron society. The child finds that he is at the bottom of the ladder of privilege. He or she is now obliged to perform services for all Abron who are even slightly older. Possessions, few as they may be, are no longer private objects. An elder may, without asking, borrow them, so the child soon learns that none of its belongings are safe from the demands of others.

This sudden shift of fortune often leads the child to strike out against those who deprive it. Intolerant of anger in children, parents punish aggressive acts with a fury rarely seen in Abron society. In addition to having no one to turn to, the Abron child has no one to turn against. He or she must be good to babies and obey older siblings as well as other older children in the village. The one possible outlet for aggression against humans, the peer group, is blocked by an over-all taboo on fighting, and in any case, aggression within this group brings little satisfaction, since peers as equals rarely frustrate each other. Serious fights between Abron children are rare. The kind of aggressive play that so often breaks out into overt fighting in our own society rarely develops into anger among the Abron, and when it does, some adult puts a stop to it immediately.

A child who has been fighting, for any reason, is not only beaten by its parents but is also humiliated before its peers and subordinates. One evening, when half the village was gathered on the stoop of my house enjoying the strong light of my lantern, the mother of a ten-year-old girl came raging after her daughter. She had been told by a woman of another house that her child had been seen fighting that day. The mother made no attempt to find the cause of the argument or the reason for her daughter's involvement. She began to beat the child and to yell at her in a staccato voice. The child's cries only increased her fury. She became so angry that she picked up a discarded, half-eaten orange, and threw it at her cowering child. The orange thudded off the girl's back and rolled into the dirt. The mother picked it up again and again until her anger finally abated. The assembled group of adults made no attempt to intervene, and when at last the mother left, they ignored the girl, who crouched on the ground sobbing for some time. The violence of the mother's actions was not out of keeping with the usual punishment for one of the three serious infractions of accepted behavior in children, the others being lack of respect for elders and not bathing.

Children learn a great deal from each other. Parents ignore children once they begin to walk. They are cared for by their elder siblings, and join them in learning the daily round. As soon as a child is old enough, it begins to perform some of the simpler household tasks. The youngest children are more likely to assist a brother or sister in these jobs than a parent, who reserves his or her attention for more serious business. Groups of children often fetch water. Beginning with a small pot, children graduate to larger and larger receptacles as they grow stronger and learn to balance things on their heads. Some mistakes are gently corrected by older siblings, but errors interpreted as foolishness by the frequently intolerant teachers may bring ridicule down on the head of an offender.

Once, an eight-year-old boy slipped and fell into a deep and muddy water hole. One of the children helped him out, but when he emerged, wet and covered with sticky mud, he began to cry. This amused the other children, and they began to make fun of him. He responded to their jeers by louder crying and finally ran away to sulk for the rest of the day.

The education of children by their elder siblings even includes toilet training: The Abron use deep pit latrines located some distance outside the village. Such facilities make early toilet training hazardous, for, in addition to the possibility of falling in, dangerous snakes sometimes congregate around them. Children are taken outside the house when a parent thinks they are about to eliminate. If an accident occurs, the child and the soiled area— sometimes the floor, sometimes a woman's back—are cleaned up gracefully and without complaint. No one is put out by these frequent mishaps. When a child reaches the age of five or six, he or she is taken to the latrine by an elder sibling. By this time, it is not hard to teach the child that there is only one appropriate place for defecation, and no issue is made of it.

Contact between parents and children for the purpose of training is confined to gardening. Even here, the child is not taught what to do, but learns by watching and helping. Boys and girls from about the age of five accompany their parents to the fields. In the summer, both sexes help their mothers weed, and, in the winter, boys help the men with the coffee and cacao harvest. Although immature boys help women with their garden tasks, young girls never do men's work. One of the few social signs of a boy's growing up before marriage and full adult status is his relinquishment of feminine tasks (pounding, weeding, and fetching water). These activities are replaced by the planting of his own yam garden. The techniques associated with successful gardening are learned from the father. At first, this involves passive watching. Very early, the child helps his father carry tools to the garden but does not participate in either planting or harvesting. Around the age of eight, boys begin to harvest alongside their fathers; and by the time they are ten, they know how to plant and tie up the yam vines.

Girls begin to weed when they are seven or eight and to plant such lesser crops as maize, tomatoes, squash, onions, and eggplants by the time they are ten. They also help in the house; as we have seen, many a five-year-old girl bears some responsibility for the care of a baby not much younger than herself.

In the winter months of the dry season, children who do not go to school have a great deal of time to themselves. Lacking toys, they find amusement in imitative play or in watching adults work and talk. Because children are of potential service to adults and because they remain quietly in the background, their presence is tolerated even during serious discussions.

In the heat of the day, no one is very active, but, in the cool of the evening, children find each other and explode into energetic play. The little girls dance and sing, led by some of the unmarried older girls; the boys run around the village playing tag or engaging in mock fights. At the approach of the rainy reason, when the afternoon sky is overcast and the air somewhat cooler, the boys make crude two-wheeled wagons from the large nuts and spines of palmetto trees and race them around the village. The nuts which serve as wheels are joined by a stick and the palm spine which becomes the chassis is placed over them. Although no toys are bought, a child will sometimes rescue a sardine can from the garbage dump, make a hole in one end, attach a string to it, and pull it around. Some children also make crude toys out of palm fiber or grass stems. These usually take the form of pinwheels or airplanes but are not common.

Children are never overtly rewarded for good behavior; it is expected of them. The emphasis placed on behavioral rules reinforces the heavy Abron commitment to social control. Discipline, which is harsh in relation to aggression and rules of conduct, is, in spite of older children's intolerance, mild in the matter of skill training. Children are rarely punished for the way they perform tasks, but they are punished for refusing to do them. Once they try, they learn quite quickly.

Thus, task and achievement and, in general, the training for most young people are mild.

The culture does not make excessive demands upon either children or adults to rise in social status. This is a standard feature of what anthropologists refer to as tribal society, in which too much status-striving would produce serious social dislocations. In the past, every Abron was a member of an equal lineage. Lineages were cemented together by marriages and economic exchanges in which neither side attempted to gain economic advantage. Village chiefs were arbiters in disputes but could not impose their will on the group. The king held the only true political power. As in many African states, kingship was stuck onto a kinship base in a society that was non-hierarchical in its wider structure.

With the breakdown of the lineage system, and the introduction of private property, there has been a slight shift in attitudes toward work. At the present time, the one factor in Abron society that leads to striving on the part of some individuals is the search for, or the maintenance of, the status that comes with a large family and a substantial house. Among the Ghana Brong, this position comes more or less automatically to lineage heads, but, in the Ivory Coast, Abron society is now much more fluid and status may be raised or lowered according to wealth and the way in which it is used. Many of the men who try to accumulate property are Moslems or Christians, who count among the most acculturated to Western values. Moslem and Christian parents teach their children the value of wealth and include some schooling in their training. Their children are the most likely to succeed economically, but they are also the most likely to leave the village.

Economic striving among the more tradition-oriented Abron is limited to the sons of rich fathers who have a close relationship with their male parent and who stand to gain from hard work and loyalty, for, although a father may not leave possessions to his sons, he can make substantial gifts of property to them in his lifetime.

Thus, in spite of continued matrilineal inheritance, having a rich father can lead to a rich future. The Ivory Coast Government has banned matrilineal inheritance, because of the feeling in government circles that it encourages laziness. Any movement away from this practice is, therefore, sanctioned by official policy.

One of the rising stars in Diassenpa, perhaps the hardest worker in the village, is the first son of the richest man. He has been inspired by his father with the need to maintain the high status established for the family. Because Abron ideology still holds that a man cannot inherit from his father, he must work hard on his own to maintain family position. If he is shiftless, his father will not endow him with gifts, and the riches of the older generation will in fact pass to the father's sister's eldest son. This orientation toward maintaining the status of a patriline (a group of men related through male links) is an example of the imbalance between matrilineal inheritance and patrilineal sentiment in Abron society.

The assumption of proper sex roles is highly dependent upon residence. All children spend their early years in the mother's house, and many of their first tasks are within the sphere of woman's work. Normally, as soon as a male child can walk, he begins to take his meals in a men's house. Ideally, this is the house of his father, but sometimes a youth will go to eat with his maternal uncle, the man from whom he will inherit. This change is the first shift toward assuming the male role. The second shift comes a bit later, when he moves into a men's house permanently. The third step, which signals full integration into the community of adult men, comes only with marriage. This may be delayed several years for a poor young man whose family cannot afford the high bride price.

Sexual identification comes through work as well as through residence. Young men participate in housebuilding, planting, and hunting. During a hunt, boys armed with clubs and slingshots accompany their older brothers and fathers. They often serve as beaters and fire starters. A few, privileged boys may also become drummers, performing first at secular occasions and later, if they show talent, at the various ceremonies. Girls learn to help their mothers clean the houses, fetch wood and water, weed the garden, plant lesser crops, and cook. Since the sexes are isolated, at least in the house, both girls and boys form strong ties with their own sex. After the age of five or six, play groups become exclusively male or female. The young boy first plays with the boys of his male household, the girl with the girls of her female household. Later they join their respective peer groups in the village. Children of both sexes will, however, work together at the various tasks open to them, and, of course, there is a great deal of sexual bantering, which begins early and involves playful, but aggressive, encounters between boys and girls.

Eating and, later, sleeping in a men's house are important factors in cementing the bond between a boy and his half brothers. Because half brothers are in different matrilines (remember, inheritance is through a line of females, and half brothers in the same house share the same father), boys have wider social spheres than girls, who are restricted in their households to a group of females who are all in the same matrilineage.

By the time full adult status has been achieved, men have had wide contact with both sexes in their own and other villages. They have listened to discussions of village affairs, both in their male households and at village councils, and they have participated in village activities (hunting and ceremonials). They are familiar with female tasks, but have also mastered those of men, and have learned that a man's role requires that he be outspoken in village affairs.

The difference between men and women in respect to social participation is qualitative rather than quantitative. Girls grow up in the friendly and confident atmosphere of the women's house. While their social contact within this house is restricted to a narrower set of relatives than in a men's house, they do interact with men from an early age. At first, their contact with men is limited either to visits of close relatives to the women's compound or to their carrying of food to the men's house. Since eating is a major time for free socialization and discussion, girls and women both miss the conversations that go on during meals in the men's house. They are, however, privileged within their own household, and men are equally excluded from the social interaction that takes place around the women's table. Later, girls may visit men's compounds during the day and may often be seen sitting quietly, listening to adult talk.

The major difference between the world of men and that of women comes from differences in work patterns. Woman's work is more demanding and time-consuming than man's work. Consequently, women spend less time outside their own household. Since girls do not have to learn a new role identification, because, unlike boys, they do not have to shift either their tasks or their residence even at marriage, their identification with their close relatives is probably more intense and rewarding. The perpetual contact with close female relatives reinforces their identification within a limited core group.

A woman's status as a full adult does nothing to change her restricted role in village affairs, and most women are content to run things in the microcosm of their own households, where they may dominate if and when they become senior females.

The one woman who is not restricted in this way is the queen mother, whose voice in village affairs is sometimes stronger than the king's. In preparation for this future role, girls of the royal lineage have much more contact with the world of politics than do other females. Their position within the house of the queen mother is analogous to that of their brothers in the male-centered household. They witness the daily political dramas and learn how decisions are made.

The granddaughter of the Queen Mother of Diassenpa had a personality that set her apart from the

My sister, Ajoa Badu, 1962

Fon dancers; a Christmas celebration in Tabgne, 1961

Decorated wall in the temple of Tano, in Assuifri, 1962

Kparesé with her gbawkaw, 1962

other girls her age. She joked freely with boys of her own age group, but also managed to maintain a special bearing even when she descended to the adolescent horseplay common to her peers. By the time she was twelve, she had learned to be regal, but also to be proficient at female tasks, for which she would be responsible even if she were to become queen mother in her turn. She is trained as a woman, but also as a leader, a role that usually falls to men.

Women in their later years, after menopause, may sit in village councils and exercise the privileges that come with senior status; but only a minority do this. Most are content to dominate their own household, planning the marriages of the young women, supervising the daily tasks, and raising the younger generation of children.

Most Abron, for all their love of visiting, feel most at home in their own houses or those of their relatives. But it is in the household also that specific tensions provoked by the hazards of unequal status and authority develop. These tensions lead to ambiguous feelings among kin, which in turn give rise to expression in witchcraft beliefs. It is the close tie between fathers and sons, for example, that helps to create tensions around matrilineal inheritance, though the opposing tie to the mother and her kin group probably influences the maintenance of such rules in the face of severe social change. The patterns established in childhood among kin become effective as structural models for adult behavior.

So far, I have discussed patterns of interaction in relation to kingroup membership, residential units, and domicile. A picture of interaction patterns on the basis of average individuals in relation to each member of a set of important relatives becomes important if we are to understand the pattern of witchcraft, to be discussed later. These data were collected after I came to know the villagers well enough to recognize specific members of the various family groups. Once I had these relationships established, I concentrated on the systematic observation of interaction patterns between sets of relatives. While the following material is abstracted from many individual observations, these patterns are so regular that they can be applied to a high percentage of real individual interactions.

MALE: FATHER

Early contact between father and son is minimal, because infants are limited to the mother's house. During infancy, the male parent will spend little more than one hour a day with his child. The Abron, however, enjoy physical contact with their young children, and the short time spent with an infant son may involve intense physical contact. The baby may be caressed, fondled, and carried around the village. Thus the male parent becomes an important if limited source of affection during early life. More important, a child is less likely to be aware of a difference in affect between him and his father coming with the birth of another child, for it is in the context of the women's house that the rejection first occurs. Furthermore, because a male child begins to eat in his father's house after weaning, he does not lose place as severely as does a female child. It might be that this difference is responsible for the greater confidence shown in social affairs by men, and conversely, for the continued dependence as well as jealousy shown by women toward the members of their own group. Unfortunately, these are only suspicions on my part, since I did not realize this possible effect until I began to examine my notes after leaving the field.

Even though the female household prepares food, the father gives food favors (usually meat) from his own plate to his sons. In this way, the male takes the role of provider, although he does not completely replace the mother, since children do snack from time to time at their mother's house. When a younger sibling joins a men's house, the father's attention may shift to it. A child who has been enjoying the privilege of special food may quickly lose it to another. In any case, as the child matures, the father disciplines him and, at the same time, begins to withdraw much of his overt affection. This is not caused by a loss of love on the part of the parent but because the Abron do not openly express positive emotion toward children past the infant stage.

While all adults can punish children, the father has the most contact with his sons. Also, he is responsible for their behavior. He becomes the behavioral model for male children, teaching them through example and restraining them when necessary. The eldest son occupies a special position, because he works most closely with his father and helps him in the training of other children. Father and eldest son are extremely close, and when the son reaches the stage of young adulthood, he becomes his father's trusted adviser and assistant in the male household.

MALE: FULL BROTHERS

From birth to death, full brothers spend a great deal of time together, in work and play. They are ranked by age and, although an elder brother suffers replacement by his mother's next child, he soon learns that his position on the scale of authority puts him above his younger siblings and gives him certain advantages. He can commandeer the personal property of his younger brothers and demand simple tasks from them. Eventually, he becomes one of their teachers, passing on skills to the younger members of his own generation. Brothers soon learn to work in harmony, and in adult life the ties between them strengthen. There is no conflict between this relationship and Abron social structure. As children of the same mother and father, these men belong to identical patrilineal and matrilineal groups. Although inheritance is matrilineal (from a man to his sister's eldest son), once a nephew has inherited, his gain is also a gain for all his full brothers. Inheritance from one generation to another must wait until a line of full brothers have all held property. When the last brother dies, the eldest son of the eldest sister stands to inherit.

MALE: FULL SISTER

The relationship between brothers and full sisters is the closest male-female tie, for siblings of opposite sex are the cement that bonds male and female households. If a sister is older than her brother, she is likely to be one of his most important surrogate mothers. If she is younger, the male becomes her protector. As members of the same matriline, they have common interests which persist throughout life.

MALE: HALF BROTHERS

Half brothers enjoy much less contact with each other than do full brothers, since they are born into different female households. They do, however, share the important primary group centered in the father's household, where they live and are members of the same eating group. During the father's lifetime, they work and play together as members of a house and economic unit. When their father dies, they eventually turn to their mothers' families. As members of different matrilines, their interests separate, and therefore half brothers grow apart in later life. The distance between grown-up half brothers compared to the closeness of full brothers is apparent in the daily course of village life. It is a full brother who will later be invited to share the house of an elder sibling and who will become one of the trusted assistants of the houseowner.

MALE: HALF SISTER

This relationship is even more distant than the one between half brothers. While half brothers spend a good deal of time together, at least during youth, in their father's household, half siblings of opposite sex share no common residence or domicile. Contact between half brothers and sisters is no more frequent or intense than contact between unrelated children of the village, but, of course, incest regulations apply to them, so they may not marry each other. As members of different matrilines and different households, they have no economic interests in common.

MALE: MOTHER

The relationship between a man and his mother is warm and intimate throughout life. The mother is the first source of comfort for the child, and while she may transfer a good deal of her affection to younger children, she never completely cuts herself off from her older children. That is to say, the cutting-off process is real but social. The child feels rejection by all adults, including father and mother, but the rejection by the parents is less severe than the rejection by others. Until the age of seven or eight, a boy will sleep in his mother's house, and when he is not occupied by his male group, will help her in the daily round. As he grows older, he will spend more and more time with his father, but he never cuts his maternal ties. In later life, a "good" son will build a house for his mother, and it is with her that his wife may live if she comes from another village.

MALE: FATHER'S BROTHER'S MALE CHILDREN

Patrilineal male cousins living in the same male household will interact in much the same way as brothers. They are equal members of the temporary economic unit, which is male-based, and, as children, share the same table. When they grow up, however, they will separate, since their mature social ties are with different formal groups. Cousins who do not live together in the same house interact like other, unrelated children in the village.

MALE: MOTHER'S BROTHER'S CHILDREN

Male cousins on the mother's side normally reside and domicile in different households and have no more social contact than do non-kin in the village. They share no membership in any temporary or permanent formal group. The relationship between cousins of this type is special only in a negative sense, because it is between them that jealousy over inheritance is likely to occur.

MALE: FATHER'S BROTHER

The relationship between a male and his father's brother is close, especially, as is usually the case, if they live under the same roof. Since all brothers of a houseowner are themselves potential houseowners, all males in the generation below them stand in the relationship of son to father, and more generally, male to household head. Since an uncle is less affectionate with his nephews than with his own sons, the relationship between uncles and nephews of this type may be somewhat less well balanced between affection and discipline than the relationship between a son and his father. The pattern of respect and dominance will be the same, however. When the paternal uncle does not reside in the house of a brother, the relationship between him and his nephews will be more distant, because they will have less daily contact, but the formal pattern will still exist.

MALE: MOTHER'S BROTHER

Except in those few cases in which a man is in domicile with his matrilineal uncle, social contact will be slight and take place primarily in the mother's house. The uncle may discipline his nephew, as may all adults, but there is no special formal relationship between them. When a boy does take domicile with his mother's brother, the relationship is similar to that between father and son in the normal male household, except that tension over inheritance between the boy and the household head will not exist, for it is from the uncle that the boy will eventually inherit.

The Abron are very different from many matrilineal societies, because of their peculiar residence rules. Often, in matrilineal societies, men will reside with both parents until marriage, but with their mother's brother (avunculocal) or the bride's family (matrilocal) at marriage. Since residence is either matrilocal or avunculocal in these normal cases, a boy will have intense contact with both his father and his maternal uncle, who may play two different roles in his upbringing. Often, the father is affectionate and the uncle, from whom the boy will inherit, demanding, serving as the disciplinary force in the boy's life. On the other hand, the Abron usually know their fathers well and their uncles much less well. Furthermore, in the most common situations, the boy will live with his father rather than his uncle or mother. This creates real tensions between the residence unit as a social group and the group of matrilineally related relatives who constitute the official or formal social unit which has generational depth and legal authority.

FEMALE: MOTHER AND STEPMOTHER

From birth to adulthood, a girl remains in her mother's household and is a basic part of it. Her early experience with the mother parallels that of her brothers. Her experience outside the female-centered family group is more limited than that of boys, and, after adolescence, she spends most of her time around the mother's hearth. An Abron woman's contact with male houses is limited to those of her father, her matrilateral uncles, and her husband. In each, her major task concerns the preparation and transportation of food. Of course, married women spend several nights a week with their husbands when they are not pregnant or nursing, but wives come to their husbands after dark and in private.

A girl is therefore trained almost exclusively by her mother, her mother's sisters, and her own elder sisters. Her schooling is centered on household and farming tasks, with little attention to wider village affairs. As an elder sister, she soon becomes familiar with the duties of motherhood, and at an early age may herself take on a maternal role with her younger sisters. At the same time, she is responsible to and may be disciplined by her elder siblings.

A tremendous loyalty builds up between a girl and her own mother. If a dispute arises between wives of the same man, a woman will take her mother's part. A girl's attitude toward her stepmothers (the other wives of her father) is usually hostile, and she has very little to do with the other female households in her own set of kin. Unlike her brothers, who domicile with their full and half brothers in their father's house, a girl lives only with her full sisters. Her half sisters will be in their own mothers' households with their own full sisters. Thus, for a girl, there is no conflict between domicile and household, between affectionate ties and the dominant social group, between living arrangements and rules of inheritance. All her structural groups are the same. The female household is also the close part of her matriline. The conflicts of divided loyalty that beset Abron men do not occur for Abron women.

FEMALE: FATHER

A warm relationship exists between a woman and her father throughout life, but she has less contact with him than do his sons. Daughters help their fathers and brothers even after marriage, but their allegiance to these is partially split because of responsibilities to their husbands. Males are almost totally excluded from the training of their daughters.

FEMALE: MOTHER'S SISTER'S FEMALE
    CHILDREN

Terminologically, structurally, and emotionally, these women are sisters and members of the same household. They share the ties of kinship, residence, and generation. They remain close throughout life in their loyalty to each other and to their respective mothers.

FEMALE: FATHER'S SISTER'S AND
    MOTHER'S BROTHER'S SONS

The relationship between what are known in anthropology as cross-cousins is reciprocal. Marriage is allowed (but rarely occurs) with cousins of this type, and forbidden between parallel cousins (offspring of either mother's sister or father's brother). Social contact with such kin (and here I refer to all cousins of either type) is not significantly different from contact with age-mates of other kin and non-kin categories around the village. Age-mates in general form an in-group, especially in play and in such common tasks as water bearing for girls and hunting for boys.

There are no taboos on contact with either female or male relatives for either boys or girls. The same type of play may be observed among related and unrelated children, among those whom a person can marry and among those who are excluded from the marriageable group.

We can see that men have a wide range of relatives with whom they interact intensely, if in different degrees. For a woman, there is really only one primary group, the mother's household, while for a man there are two, the mother's and the father's households. Within the web of kinship relationships, men have a wider set of contacts on various levels. The significant relatives for a woman are her mother, her sisters, her mother's sisters and their daughters, and her full brothers. A man's significant relatives are his mother and her sisters, his own sisters, his half brothers, his full brothers, his father and his father's brothers, his father's brother's sons (his male parallel cousins), his mother's brother, and his mother's brother's sons (the latter a relationship of tension). Abron men are outgoing and readily involve themselves in village and extravillage affairs. In comparison with men, women are shy and withdrawn (although there are exceptions). This difference can be explained by two features of the socialization process: Men have early contact with, and are socialized by, a wider range of people of both sexes than women, and men are trained to tasks that require participation in village affairs.

Abron village life is centered on family relations, and political decisions, which must be made in common, are made by the village elders, who are the heads of individual households. In former times, these decisions were made by the heads of the matrilineages in the village. In both cases, political authority is in the hands of people whose power is legitimized by their place with a kinship segment of the village. Every Abron is born into a system in which kinship plays the major role in defining relationships. Each Abron, as a member of a specific household, learns the rules of his or her society from that household outward, as he or she comes to know a wider range of relatives. The peculiar form of residence which involves the separation of men and women into sexually segregated houses, immediately creates differences in the future social relations of the newborn. The fact that this residence pattern is congruent with other aspects of the social structure for women and incongruent for men creates strains within the society, particularly among men, that are specifically Abron in character. At the same time, the pattern of socialization that develops out of the facts of residence and rules of inheritance provides each member of the society with a base of personal strength and support. The strength of a woman's personality, and I was impressed over and over with the fact that Abron women are, within their own domain, confident of their abilities and their roles in social relations, comes from the usually harmonious and reinforcing nature of her residence and kinship. For a woman, even though jealousy occurs in her closely knit group, the household is a good place to start building character. Men have a more difficult time, for they are subject to a wider range of social interaction, some of which involves tensions that are built into the system. It is perhaps this very difficulty that helps them to accept compromise in the building of consensus in village affairs.

In spite of the supportive aspects of Abron culture, it was my impression that most Abron, both men and women, did indeed have aggressive feelings, though they were expressed in roundabout ways. First, they overpunish their children. Ironically, this occurs as the parental response to aggressive acts *by* their children.

Second, Abron enjoy mildly sadistic jokes and often respond to simple requests with petty refusals. Overt aggression in the form of physical violence never occurred among adults during my stay in Abron country, but occasional arguments, usually between women of different households, were often harsh and noisy. At times it looked as if these disputes were about to escalate into overt fighting, but the final step was never taken. Arguments between men, although rarer, share this quality. Now and then during such encounters, threatening gestures are made, but there is always someone present to prevent physical contact. Things work out this way too often for such restraint to be accidental.

Finally, there is the question of witchcraft. During my second trip, witchcraft anxiety became quite severe in Amamvi and Gumeré. This fear was related, understandably, to an elevated number of deaths in these two villages. Such deaths had to be explained, and many were finally blamed on witches. Diassenpa was exempt from this fear, because medical services provided by me and the doctor at Bondoukou, where I often brought sick individuals, kept the deaths in the village down to one person, a baby that died of septicemia before adequate medical care could be administered.

Witches occupy an interesting position in the Abron belief system and in Abron society. They are mortals who nonetheless have supernatural powers. Like European witches, Abron witches fly, change themselves into animals or inanimate objects, and kill their victims at a distance. They inherit these powers from other witches, through family lines. Not everyone in a witch's family is destined to be a witch, however.

As far as real life is concerned, there are no witches; that is, no one sees him- or herself as a witch. It is an empty category. Deresogo exist only in belief, but are made palpable by the confessions of those who, after death, admit to having been witches in their lifetime. In addition, they can be caught alive through the office of the Gban, performed, the reader will remember, by outsiders.

Witches aggress against Abron but are not directly attacked by Abron. Their identity can be discovered only after death, when they are no longer dangerous, and it is when they are no longer dangerous that they are punished. Living witches are caught by non-Abron outsiders hired for that purpose.

After considering all these facts, it seemed to me that witches served as perfect vehicles for the projection of repressed aggressive feelings in Abron society. Remember that children, who from birth to weaning are the center of affectionate attention, are suddenly replaced when a younger sibling is born. Remember, too, that angry and aggressive feelings that emerge in response to this first rejection are severely punished. Under such conditions, aggressive feelings may be suppressed. The Abron ethic is strongly opposed to aggression. The idea that normal people can display such feelings, is unthinkable. At the same time, social tensions do not disappear. In such cases, it would be likely for aggression to be projected away from the individual toward others. Such feelings can, however, be projected into the supernatural realm. Witches, then, become the embodiment of aggression: an essence of evil that purges the normal Abron of evil feelings. They are defined as a set of abnormal people who through *no fault of their own* inherit the power of supernatural evil.

After I had discovered that there was a connection between fear of witches and Abron socialization, I was led to test a related hypothesis; i.e., that strains in the social system were responsible for the particular pattern witchcraft took in Abron society. The reader will remember that there is a disharmony between inheritance and residence for men, but not for women, in Abron society. I therefore expected to find differences in attitudes toward witchcraft among men and women. I asked many men and women why witches kill. In all cases, both sexes replied that witchcraft is the result of jealousy, but men related this jealousy directly to disputes over property, while women related it to the number of children born to females. Abron women like to have large families and treasure children of both sexes. If a woman is blessed with many children, and one of her relatives who is a witch is barren or has few children, the witch may attack her out of spite. The jealousy of men over property is amplified by the fact that during his lifetime a man can give substantial gifts to his sons and thus partially abrogate the matrilineal rule of inheritance. A man may wish to kill his uncle before such gifts can be made and thus insure title to his uncle's property.

Although all Abron grow up in the context of a tightly knit family structure and although each village is like a large family, Abron social life does not automatically produce a paradise. Witchcraft beliefs appear to be one negative outcome of a series of strains that cut across both the social system and the manner in which children are reared.

I must add, however, that most Abron are socially confident and their children appear happy. As an outsider, I was particularly struck by the ability of almost all the people I knew well in Amamvi and Diassenpa to assume their social roles with a minimum of discomfort and to lead what I think are relatively happy lives. The virtues inherent in the pattern of interaction with a large number of kin and even non-kin from an early age is that children do not have to depend upon a single set of parents set within the structure of the nuclear family, as do our own children. Reciprocally, parents are freer to pursue their own interests fully confident that their children will be brought up correctly by a whole set of individuals including themselves. This aspect of child rearing has great value for both parents and children.

At the other end of the scale, but for the same reasons, old age is secure in Abron society. An individual is always a part of a family circle. Old age never involves rejection, as it might in our own society. Age brings wisdom and authority. Even when it is accompanied by infirmity, respect continues to be exercised toward the elderly. Thus, in comparison to our own system, the Abron do not waste human life. Children and the elderly are not subject to the whims of individual relatives, and parents are not slaves for years to growing babies. Within each widely extended family, a circle of love and confidence is created.

My wife and I have already raised our children into adolescence. We have enjoyed the process and often wonder at their development both physically and intellectually. Nonetheless, if we could repeat the process, we would probably raise them in the context of a communal experience. Our ideal group would include a collection of individuals who, while guarding their personal privacy and professional lives, would contribute to the socialization of the children as a group. This would allow the children a wide range of early and intense contact with adults and children with different personalities and interests. In addition, a proper distribution of responsibility and freedom within the group would allow the adults to participate more freely and with less conflict in the process. Men would spend more time with the children, women less than is usual. Both sexes would be free to pursue their professional and intellectual interests without neglecting the community's children. Loss of time by professional women who want to have children would be avoided. The rules of such a community of individuals would have to be formed on an *ad hoc* basis, according to experience. Its continuation after the maturation of a generation of children would be doubtful, however. Experiences with communes, including those in Europe among groups of middle-class people, suggest that they could be stable enough to successfully carry through the raising of a generation of children but not stable enough to continue into the old age of their founding members. Thus, modern communes appear not to have coped with the problems of elderly people in our society.

The system of nursery education practiced on the Israeli kibbutz and, in a different fashion, in China, are interesting attempts to overcome the problem of social fragmentation that has come with the dominance of the nuclear family. The Chinese system requires a complete change in society at large; the kibbutz involves a commonality of work which might not prove convenient in an urban context. Both systems are geared, however, to care for all members regardless of generation. In both cases, the rejection of the elderly is avoided.

The Abron pattern of social care for children and the elderly is a common feature of preliterate societies. Such societies are maintained on the basis of kinship relations that are concretized and reinforced through daily interaction. As Abron children grow up, they learn their social roles and mutual responsibilities from elders and peers and come to see themselves as members of a wide set of linked households. As long as the economic standing of these units remains relatively equal, little rivalry develops among them. As inequality of distribution becomes a feature of Abron social relationships, the tensions created within the family group begin to manifest themselves with increasing frequency.

A new feature of the educational process is the local school in Amamvi, which was established in 1960. Most of the male children and a few girls from Amamvi and Diassenpa attend this school, which was directed, during my first two visits, by a teacher from another region of the Ivory Coast.

I attended a day of classes at Amamvi in the winter of 1961. The students, dressed in tattered uniforms (khaki shorts and shirts for the boys, blue dresses for the girls), arrived at school early in the morning. It was a long, two-room building with louvered windows along both lengths. Only one room was used for the single class of children, ranging in age from about six to fifteen. The teacher, housed in the village at local expense but paid by the government, sat at a table at the head of the classroom. The students sat on benches in front of low, narrow tables. Although simply furnished, it looked like what one might expect to see in any rural, one-room school. The teacher moved rapidly from subject to subject, calling on the children to repeat the lesson they had learned for that day. Although some eager students raised their hands, most seemed afraid and unanxious to be called upon. Those who were chosen stood up and repeated the lesson by rote in a monotone voice. The courses covered that morning included arithmetic, geography, history of the Ivory Coast, and "observation." The latter was clearly planned to allow for a bit of spontaneity in the classroom. The children were asked to describe the preparation of palm oil. One young man got up and told how his mother went through the process. The teacher flew into a rage. This was not the method he had in his notes. It appeared that even "observation" was to follow a textbook example.

The teacher had the nasty habit of ridiculing the students whenever they made even a slight mistake. Since this technique is far from anything they experienced at home, most of the children appeared to loathe school. In addition, I noticed that the teacher clung almost desperately to a set of tattered notes that apparently served as the basis of his lessons. I had the notion that if they were to blow off the table and become disordered, he would panic and be unable to continue. In spite of these terroristic methods, several of the children had begun to learn French, and a few spoke quite well.

During my last visit, in 1973, the teacher had been replaced by an Agni from Agniblikourou. He was an intelligent and well-trained man who treated his students with respect and apparently enjoyed his job. Although firm, he did not bully the children, and they responded quite well to him. I expect that, in the years to come, many Abron children will be moving on from their now excellent village school to the next stage in the educational process. Many will go to the lycée in Abidjan and some to the university. In this way, they will join the main stream of national life.

14
Leaving

Sonia's arrival in the field came toward the end of my stay. Concern for the health of our two small children had precluded taking them to Africa, so we had agreed that she would join me for one month at the end of field work. By that time, my research had progressed considerably, but I would have preferred to stay on longer. The understanding of another culture comes slowly, and I had just begun to feel comfortable with the more easily accessible aspects of Abron life. The time had come, however, to return. I needed to write up the material and submit it for approval as a doctoral thesis. Work with the Abron was, in the context of my academic training, an exercise to prove that I could do field research and analyze it professionally. The next step would be university teaching. The Abron experience and my other training would help to form me as an anthropologist, but my theoretical stance would develop only after many years of teaching, reading, and thinking. The meaning of my field work was to undergo a long process of change as I reflected upon it in the context of my personal and professional development.

The day before our departure we arranged our belongings. Notes and clothes were gathered together on the bed with the cameras and film. The rest of our equipment was piled up on the floor and the table. Finally, we divided everything into two piles: things to be taken home and things to be distributed to friends. Oppong and I had already decided that he would take the refrigerator and its contents instead of his last month's pay. My lantern was to go to Tchina Kofi, the dishes to the men of the house and their women relatives. Certain items of clothing would also be given to the men and boys of our compound. A spare tape recorder was given to the local lineage chief. He accepted the gift with great pleasure and hurried off to his house. He planned to record and re-record in solitude until his speeches were fine enough to please everyone in the village. He was a master of metaphor, with a deep rolling voice, who could talk for hours without hesitation—a real titan of words. But even he felt the need to rehearse. The recorder could be used as a real tool. For the first time, he would be able to hear himself talk. He would correct his language, polishing his speech until it glowed like the gilded swords used by kings as a symbol of office.

Our less spectacular gifts were received with apparent pleasure, and by spreading things as far as we could we managed to fulfill all the obligations that had accumulated during the field-work period. The immediate household came first, as these were our closest male relatives, then the women of related houses, and finally those who had been particularly helpful during our incessant prying.

After the division was complete we set about packing the rest into our suitcases. When this was done the room, which, along with the camper, had served as a home for so many months, looked drab and bare. The table and shelves were empty. The bed, set against the wall away from the door, was covered with an old gray army blanket and sagged in the middle like so many French beds, but a bit more. It looked as if the heat had melted it in the middle.

The room was not pleasant. It had never been decorated with magazine cutouts by the men of the house, and I had done nothing to diminish its cell-like atmosphere. Perhaps the next tenant would be kinder to it. The shelves, which had held my few books, our clothes, and a growing pile of notes, could be used to exhibit a collection of tropical bric-a-brac. The table, on which I had typed most afternoons, could be covered with a bright cloth; flowers could be placed on it, at least during the rainy season.

But all this was a silly fantasy. These were things I

could have done myself, not something any Abron
would do. Rooms were for sleeping and for the storage
of goods. They were neither haven nor refuge. The
Abron are not "private" people. They live outdoors,
constantly in the company of others. The outside of
houses and their courtyards are important; rooms are
neglected. They are often drab and even messy.
Belongings are heaped on the floor, against the wall or
under beds. Only those parts of the village that are
public are decorated. Women's kitchens, always three-
sided and open to view, are carefully cleaned and maintained. The kitchen of a fastidious woman is better
cared for than any of the local shrines, which are kept
in closed rooms. The village is swept clean at least
twice a day.

The private room is part of one's interior life but the
interior life is minimized in Abron culture. The person,
above all, is on constant display. Frequent bathing
makes the skin glow; hair styling adds beauty. Fine
clothes draped over thin, muscular bodies are for all to
see and enjoy. Although a large well-built house is a
desired sign of success, most Abron carry their pride on
their backs.

We had nothing more to do that afternoon. The heat
of midday had already penetrated the courtyard and
was beginning to invade the room. The village was
quiet; people were either asleep or talking quietly in the
shadows. We succumbed with the rest and fell asleep
on the sagging bed. In the early evening, as the heat
began to recede, we were awakened by excited voices
and the scurry of people back and forth across the
courtyard. We got up to look outside. The courtyard
was full of villagers. Most of the activity centered on
the entrance to Oppong's room, but, because of the
crowd, we could not tell exactly what was going on.
Rather than push through, we decided to wait until the
excitement was over. The activity remained intense for
several minutes. The voices of the children rose to high
squeals as they peered under the legs of the adults and
tried to squeeze in between them. Some gave up and

ran around the courtyard yelling rapidly in an abso-
lutely unintelligible Kolongo. Certainly nothing serious
had happened; no one seemed upset. In fact, a joyous
atmosphere pervaded the scene.

Finally, one by one, the adults disentangled themselves from the crowd and crossed the courtyard toward the exit. Each was carrying a dish with some food
on it or some ice. With the food we had given him
along with the refrigerator, Oppong, too, had been set-
tling his debts. For the moment, we were forgotten and
he was the center of attention. This suited him very
well, for it gave him a chance to display his overbearing
personality once more before departing. He proved
again that he was a man of importance and standing in
the world of Diassenpa.

That evening, we sat in the courtyard for the last
time. The lantern already given to Tchina Kofi was lit
in our honor, and the men of the house were grouped
around it. The talk was low-pitched and intermittent.
Two hours after dark, around eight o'clock, Salaman
and two other Mossi, accompanied by several of the
village children, came into the courtyard.

Shortly after my arrival in Diassenpa, Salaman had
come to see me with a medical problem. At the time,
he walked slowly into the courtyard in apparent pain. I
asked Oppong what was wrong with him, and he said
that the problem was constipation. There was no
reason to doubt the diagnosis at the time, and I gave
Salaman some pills to take. I did not see him for several days after that. Then, one day, I was called to the
house of his employer. Salaman was very ill, I was told.
I looked in on him in his room. He was writhing on the
bed with a look of pain mingled with fright on his face.
He was seriously ill. In this case, there was no chance
that I could or would treat him. I told his employer
that I wanted to take him to the hospital at Bondoukou
immediately. Fortunately, both he and Salaman agreed.
We helped Salaman into the car and set off for the hospital. We arrived during the morning consultations. In
general, the long line of patients was seen only by a

nurse, who prescribed mild medication for what were diagnosed as minor illnesses and shots of penicillin for more severe cases. Chills and fever were a sure sign of malaria and the appropriate pills were given out freely. Because I was white, I had direct access to the doctor. I willingly exploited this particular vestige of colonialism, which allowed me to get my own villagers faster and better medical care than was available to the average local African.

The doctor was French, doing his military service in the Ivory Coast, which had contracted with the French Government for a range of aid programs. Although quite brusque with his African patients, he seemed very competent. Later, when Sonia was ill with a stomach upset, he treated her efficiently. His brusqueness was due partially to his tremendous case load. As the only doctor for miles around, he was responsible for all types of general medicine as well as obstetrics and surgery. His operating room was well equipped and was served by the only air conditioner in the entire region. Although his nurses provided a buffer between himself and the average sick person, he still managed to see at least fifty patients a day and performed several operations a week.

I helped Salaman into the doctor's office. Oppong and I acted as interpreters. It did not take the doctor long to find out what was wrong. Salaman had an inguinal hernia and required an immediate operation. Although somewhat fearful of being left alone in the hospital and also afraid of being cut, Salaman was in enough misery to convince himself that he had better accept the treatment. Oppong assured him that we would send a village woman to the hospital to cook for him and that his employer would supply enough food for his stay. This was necessary, because bush hospitals provide medical care and beds only. Relatives of each patient must come to the hospital to prepare their food. This is not a bad system, because it provides a link for the patient with normal life and the kind of food he or she is used to eating.

When I went back to Bondoukou about two weeks later to get Salaman, I had a chance to look over the hospital. It was a large, barracks-like building made of cement blocks painted white. Instead of windows, it had the usual louvered walls. Inside, rows of beds lined both sides of the room with a corridor running down the middle. The beds were old army cots. The linen, such as it was, was personally owned and therefore varied from patient to patient. On one side, a porch stretched out across the width of the building. On the other side, the two male nurses in attendance had their small offices. The hospital was built next to the clinic with its examination room, a small laboratory, the doctor's own private office, and the operating room. Between the two buildings, as well as on the open side of the hospital, the relatives of the sick were camped. In most cases, they were women: wives, mothers, and in some cases, sisters. Many of the women had young children with them. Each had her own cooking fire and a store of food. Since they were near the market, it was not difficult for them to replenish their stock.

In principle, each patient got free medical care and free medicines. In some cases, the doctor asked the patient if he could afford his own drugs, because some of the required medication was very expensive and the hospital budget was low. Some nurses attempted to convince the patients that none of the free medicine was very good and operated a business on the side selling drugs that should have been given free. Thus many patients ended up paying for their medication, although the amounts varied according to their ability to pay and the nurses' ability to extort funds from them.

Before I took Salaman home, the doctor examined him for the last time and told him not to work for three months, so that his scar could heal correctly. He also instructed me in the techniques necessary for changing Salaman's bandages. This I had to do for several weeks after our return to Diassenpa. The first week, the wound was still quite fresh, causing me to fear infection; but I was careful, and eventually the wound closed without complication.

Our last day in Diassenpa marked the end of Salaman's recuperation. The next day, he was to resume work on the coffee plantation of his employer. He came to our house to tell us of this and to give thanks for the care he had received. Salaman and his two Mossi friends came in fact to dance their thanks for us in our courtyard.

The village boys who arrived with them had a collection of coffee cans and gourds, which were to serve as drums. The boys settled themselves on the terrace in front of our room and began to beat out a rhythm. The three men threw their togas off their shoulders, and, winding them around their waists, began to dance.

As I have mentioned before, the Mossi are taller than the Abron and their faces are scarred with clan markings. In the bright light of the Petromax lantern, these scars looked like the deep grooves cut into theater masks to give them expressive force. The light also flattened perspective and projected strong shadows on the cement floor of the compound. As the men danced, these shadows shortened and lengthened with their distance from the light. Two complementary patterns of movement played against each other: one formed by the three perpendicular bodies, their sizes never changing; the other by the constantly decreasing and increasing flat black shadows. All three men danced well, but Salaman was extraordinary. In the first set of dances, his movements were mimetic. Like a sorcerer, he transformed himself into animal and human forms from one moment to the next. First he was an antelope grazing warily on the plain, then a hunter approaching, again an antelope tasting danger, again the hunter, and finally the fleeing animal. Then the dance changed and Salaman went through another metamorphosis. He dropped to the ground, pushed himself up and forward with his arms; his legs followed his body forward across the dance space. He was a crocodile. The other dancers joined him in this transformation. As three beasts, they

moved slowly back and forth across the dancing space,
perfect in their animal movements.

A final change. Led by Salaman, they got to their
feet and began an abstract dance. They were men once
more, doing what only humans can do, taking movement and translating it into art. Surprisingly, many of
their movements were balletic. Their virtuoso leaps and
turns could have been part of certain modern-dance
performances I had seen in New York. All three could
spot-turn well, a trick professional dancers use to keep
themselves from getting dizzy as they spin around.
Their bodies were supple and capable of moving with
exceptional fluidity. This kind of movement requires
great effort, control, and practice.

I don't think that there is a dancer anywhere in the
world more talented than Salaman. He is a member of
that small class of great dancers who grace only a few
of the world's better dance companies. Undoubtedly
Salaman is still in Africa, perhaps in Diassenpa, perhaps home in Upper Volta. If he dances, it is for his
own pleasure and the pleasure of his friends and relatives. He does not know that professional dance exists.
Salaman is a farmer. But he is also one of the gifted
few who are the unconscious guardians of a fragile culture too easily broken.

Colonialism involves more than economic and political exploitation. In its new forms, it is the great cultural
leveler of independent countries everywhere in the
world. Even where isolated ethnic groups have not
been drawn into the web of consumerism, even where
they are not part of the international labor force, they
are subject to ethnocide (the destruction of a particular
way of life) through a new kind of exotic tourism.

Western man has had his senses dulled through
overexposure to his own affluence. Material goods are
no longer enough to satisfy his need to seek out new
forms of stimulation. Consumerism has been extended
to all parts of the world by tourist agencies, which offer
economy voyages to exotic cultures. The uninitiated are
titillated by the chance to be the first to visit this or that

tribe whose rites are advertised with the same techniques used in the past to sell soap and deodorant. These voyages are cheap and safe. Many Third World countries have responded by building high-class hotels with swimming pools and air conditioning. The danger of tropical diseases and the discomforts of primitive living arrangements and long travel have disappeared. One can now take Christmas in the Sahara Desert or in the highlands of New Guinea. Tourists can travel to the Amazon Valley to "witness" primitive rites. The spirit of adventurism has been translated into a magic carpet guaranteed to take one "away from it all," if only for a few days or weeks. These are always round-trip voyages, which leave the traveler with his Super 8 memories of superficial contact with Rousseau's "natural man." These travelers participate in a holiday pageant that features the destruction of a way of life. They go in groups, as school classes go to zoos or museums, and they leave souvenirs of their own culture that break the fabric of the societies they touch. The men and women members of distant ethnic groups rarely benefit from the money spent to get tourists in and out of their exotic regions. They are merely exhibits, which make it profitable for others to run agencies and hotels. Their youth are touched by Western culture without real access to it and without understanding. They frequently abandon their old culture, but have nothing to replace it with. Elders become disillusioned with the young and refuse to initiate them. Another way of life, another philosophy dies, and the leftover people join the mass of migrants to urban slums and routine work or, more usually, unemployment.

Those who participate in this tragic farce are wasting the variety of the human experience the same way we have wasted and destroyed thousands of wild species. But they are doing it to human beings. Real culture and its derivative arts are being transformed into plastic conceptions of the primitive. The losses that result from this accelerating process are unrecoverable. A dead culture can never be resurrected. The remnant human beings are absorbed only with great suffering and a loss of human values.

Here I am not preaching neoromanticism, which teaches us to love and respect primitives because they are primitive. Nor am I saying that all change is bad. Culture is always in a state of change and there are no societies untouched by world commerce. But the direct or indirect imposition of the meanest aspects of our way of life on others without respect for local values is a clear evil which must be vigorously protested. Cultures, if they are to change, must do so on their own terms and in their own time. Individuals and collectivities must be free to choose what is to be retained from the old system, what is to be borrowed from the new, and how these new elements are to be integrated. This freedom is impossible when power and affluence rest solely with a dominant culture. As long as non-Western societies are seen only as resources open to exploitation and spoliation, they will remain endangered. Thus, tourism to exotic "tribes" is a new obscenity for our times.

Salaman danced his thanks to me for his cure. True, he was cured with Western medicine; true, he rode to the hospital in an automobile produced in Western Germany. And he danced for me, a stranger to his culture. But all of this happened in a context far removed from the tourism described above. I lived with the Abron, as much as I could, on their own terms. I was there to learn from them and to interfere as little as possible with their own culture. The few belongings I left behind were familiar objects. Furthermore, the Abron and the Mossi have strong cultures. Their people have not been decimated by our diseases or by malnutrition. Both societies were coming into the modern world gradually, and in 1962, at least, were making it on their own terms.

Salaman and his friends danced late into the night. By the middle of the evening, over half the village had crowded into our courtyard to watch. We were as enthusiastic an audience as you could find anywhere.

Salaman had captured us all. When the dancing finally stopped and the music had ended, everyone sent up a cheer. For once, the Abron had seen what kind of a man a Mossi could be. They, too, were touched profoundly by Salaman's dancing.

After all had gone back to their own houses, we got in the car and set off for our last night behind the schoolhouse at Amamvi; as soon as we had parked the car and arranged the bed, we fell fast asleep.

At dawn, about five-thirty, a voice somewhere outside awoke us: "Alex—Alex—Alex." Someone was calling out. As I shook myself out of my sleep, I realized that it was Kwasi—the Kwasi who had so often kept me awake at Amamvi my first trip out. I was determined not to answer. "Alex—Alex—Alex," he kept calling out. Sonia awoke. "Shh," I whispered, "maybe he'll go away." We tried to go back to sleep. The voyage would be long and hard; we needed to sleep more. "Alex—Alex—Alex"—Kwasi would not stop. After several minutes, I shouted from within the car. *"Kere bo"* (Quiet there) as I had so often shouted at Kwasi the year before at Amamvi. Still he would not stop. Finally I opened the door. There, several paces from the car, squatting on the ground, smiling softly, was Kwasi holding four eggs out to us. I almost cried from shame. He had been sitting there since dawn, waiting for us to wake at what he considered the normal hour, so that he could be the first to give us a parting gift. We had slept beyond all reasonable time. He felt it would be polite to disturb us and had called out. I had most certainly insulted him. But if I had, he did not show it. As soon as we saw him there, we accepted the eggs as gracefully as we could and thanked him as one only thanks a grandfather or chief for the most considerate of gifts. We arranged the car, and Kwasi headed back to Amamvi and we to Diassenpa.

Everything was packed. The suitcases were carried out of our room by Kwamé and Kofi, the two boys who had helped us so much during our stay in Diassenpa, and we set off around the village to thank everyone and to say good-by.

After the circuit of the village was complete, we returned to our house. There we found the whole family gathered, much as it had been several months before, at my arrival. This time, there was no joking about Badu and me. She was now my sister, my wife was at my side, and no one appeared to be in the mood for humor. Tchina Kofi came forward and, with tears in his eyes, kissed us, in the French fashion, on both cheeks. We piled into the car and tried to hide our own tears. As we drove off, raising the usual clouds of dust, we saw Kwamé, dressed as usual in his tunic, which hid his umbilical hernia, running after the car waving and crying profusely.

15

Final Return

On March 26, 1973, eleven years after my last previous visit, I returned to Diassenpa with two students, for a ten-day visit. Physically, the village had changed little. Although there had been no new construction, two houses had shed their thatch and were roofed with corrugated iron, and the two picturesque Kolongo-style round houses were no longer there. The population had grown from 112 to 127, and there had been seven adult deaths, including one very old woman (the Queen Mother). The royal family was particularly hard hit. The Queen Mother's two granddaughters had died, leaving her young but married great-granddaughter, who had been a teen-ager in 1962, as the current Queen Mother of the village.

Death had also touched my own family, although not where I expected it. Both Afua Morofyé and Tchina Kofi were alive, but my handsome and still young brother, who was the head of his household, Kwasi (Tan) Daté, died suddenly in 1967 while on a visit to another village.

Driving with a broken fan belt, we came to a fork in the road near Herebo about five in the evening. Although I had made it that far in a Renault 4L rented in Abidjan, I was worried about the overheating car and was not sure of the road on the last part of the journey. It was imperative that we reach Diassenpa before dark. I pulled up alongside two women returning from the fields carrying pans of yams on their heads. *"Nna o mane,"* I said, wondering if my feeble Kolongo would still work. *"Mnin nda,"* they replied in unison. *"Mia Diassenpa"* (I am going to Diassenpa), I said, pointing to a fork in the road. They answered my gesture with a rush of words I did not understand, but finally it became clear that we were at the entrance to Herebo. I thanked the women and drove on through Herebo to Tabgne. The latter had grown tremendously since my last visit. Wide streets newly cut by a still-present bulldozer scarred the main axis of the town. An unfinished mosque rose above rows of old mud and many new cement buildings. It was made of cement blocks that had not yet been stuccoed, and its baroque tower leaned slightly, but in several directions at the same time. I later learned that Tabgne had reached the stature of a new subprefecture and that electricity was to arrive in two years from Bondoukou, which itself had a new, air-conditioned hotel. In addition, the paved road, which had already been extended from Abengourou to Agniblikourou was to reach Bondoukou in three to four years. Abron country was certainly perched on the edge of accelerated change.

In Tabgne we picked up a hitchhiker bound for Amamvi, and he, speaking good French, directed us onto the still-minor road to Diassenpa. Our passenger, dressed neatly in a pressed shirt and pants, informed us that he was a "planter" and then, taking another look at me, asked if I was Alex. "Yes," I said, "I have come back to pay a visit to the Abron." He uttered a high pitched *"Eh"* of surprise and said that he remembered me from my last visit. *"Alors, M. Alex, c'est bien que tu es arrivé! Tu vas rester combien de temps?" "Je peux rester que dix jours." "Eh bien, c'est bien de te voir. Est-ce que tu me reconnais? J'habite près de Pong Kofi, ton premier hôte." "Non. Excusez-moi, je ne vous reconnais pas, mais ça fait longtemps depuis que je suis venu."*

I was afraid that perhaps I would have trouble remembering people in Diassenpa. Not recognizing this man, however, represented a quite different situation. Amamvi was, after all, a bigger village than Diassenpa, and even during my first stay I had had trouble keeping people straight.

We passed through Bracodi, the Kolongo village less than a mile from Diassenpa, and finally arrived in Diassenpa itself at about six o'clock, just before sundown.

As we got out of the car, a group of children rushed toward us. This was normal curiosity, and, of course, none of them recognized me. Then Kofi Apo came out of his house, next to which I had parked. We recognized each other instantly. He looked just the same as he had during my last visit. We threw our arms around each other as more adults came out of their houses to see what was going on. A flood of familiar faces surged toward us. *"M. Alex," "brouni"* (white man), *"mi ase"* (friend) came through the choruses of *"Eh."* In the general confusion that followed, people began asking me questions in Kolongo and French. Was I really there? How long was I going to stay? Was this woman my wife? (Those who recognized that Marilyn, one of the students accompanying me, was not my wife Sonia wanted to know if I had taken another wife, if I had divorced, or if Sonia were dead.) They were surprised that Sonia was not with me. I told everyone that she was in Paris with the children, that they had school, and that it was too expensive for all of us to have come. Then I carefully explained that Marilyn and Steve were students. They had come with me to meet the people of Diassenpa. Marilyn wanted to stay in a women's house, and Steve, a linguist, had come to learn the language. It was hard to convince people that Marilyn was not my wife, but when our residential arrangements were straightened out, with Steve and myself in a men's house and Marilyn with the women of my family, people began to realize that she was in fact a student.

Steve and Marilyn, as young single people, fit into a social category that had been closed to me, and it was very interesting to watch their interaction patterns develop with the young unmarrieds of the village during our short stay.

I was remembered by everyone, welcomed by the whole village. It was an experience I will treasure always. "How long since you were last here?" *"Nunu lesita"* (Eleven years); *"Nunu lesita"* was repeated over and over, passed from person to person. The num-

ber rippled through the crowd of villagers who had
gathered around us. "How long are you going to stay?"
"We can stay only ten days; we are here for a visit, to
see old friends, to see how Diassenpa has changed, to
see the children grown up."

There were faces missing from the crowd. Where
was Atta, Tan Daté's son? Where were young Tchina
Kofi and Kwamé, the boys who had been so helpful to
me, so intelligent and so kind? Atta was at school in
Tanda, Kwamé at the lycée in Abidjan, Kofi in the
army, already becoming a cadre. These boys, so full of
potential in 1962, were on their way into the national
system, to make their mark in the country at large.
Where was Tchina Kofi, my father? Our hitchhiker had
told me that he was still alive and well. "Oh, Tchina
Kofi, he is visiting Assuifré. He still likes to travel, you
know," Apo told me. "And where is Afua Morofyé,
my mother?" "She is in her house; she will come; she is
very old."

We went into our house, into the courtyard, the children and adults trailing after us. The questions continued in the courtyard. More people came in, many I did
not recognize. These were the children of 1962 grown
up, the girls among them already married. My brothers,
who had been young single men during my last trip,
were now also all married. Their wives filtered in and
we were introduced to them one by one.

And then Afua Morofyé came through the doorway
into the courtyard. She was more lined, older, but still
stately, still beautiful. She took one look at me, said
"Tan Daté," and began to cry. I put my arms around
her, calling her *"mi nna,"* my mother. She shook with
sobs. My arrival had reminded her of the death of her
favorite son, Tan Daté, whose name had been given to
me. Seeing me brought back all the pain of his death
mingled with the remembrance of my stay at Diassenpa
so many years before. Finally, she composed herself
and asked us if we were hungry. Had we eaten? Apo,
who was now the senior son, and his brothers asked us
if we would eat with the men, at the same table. But

would we like to bathe first? "Yes," we replied gratefully. Women were sent out to get water for us, a
chicken was brought and presented as a welcoming gift.
We gave it to Apo and told him to add it to the evening's meal. We asked that not too much cayenne be
put in the futu. It had begun to get dark. We took our
baths, set up our lantern, and joined the men in the
courtyard, who had already arranged themselves
around the low eating table. A bowl of water was
passed around. Each person washed his right hand.
The futu had already come in. Bowl after bowl had
been brought by the women of the household. They
placed them by the table and silently walked out. Everything was ready for the meal. Apo took a bottle of
commercial steak sauce out of his room and placed it
on the table. When the futu was divided, he poured
some of it on each of his portions. Forks and spoons
were brought out for us, but we refused them and
dipped into the futu with our hands. Taking our first
meal with the family, we were beginning the integration
into village life.

The welcome was overwhelming, but the heat was
oppressive. We had arrived just after the first rain. It
was the transition period between the long dry season
and the coming of the rains. The cemented house and
courtyard, the iron roof, were projecting the accumulated heat of the day at us from all directions. It was
more humid than I had remembered.

After dinner, the young people of the village came in
and began to play the drums, which were standing in
the corner of a roofed but open part of the courtyard.
This was the place where I had given first aid during
my previous stay. Everyone began to dance. Older men
and women joined and asked us to dance with them.
Marilyn, who is a very good dancer, created a sensation
with her spectacular and instant integration into the
basics of Abron movement. Soon the sweat was pour-
ing off us. The excitement generated by the music was
amplified by our presence.

I took out my tape recorder and began to record the

music. Immediately, some of the older men, including the royal lineage chief and his brother, came over to me and said that they would take out the old drums, that a proper welcome could not be played by the boys. He said that we should go to their house to dance. We moved across the village to the courtyard of the royal lineage chief, where the traditional drums were kept. These were brought out and tuned. Soon the village was resounding to Abron traditional music. The master drummer, using long sticks, beat complex polyrhythms against the background patterns provided by three lesser drums. One after another, the older men sang a lead and were followed in the singing by the women. Other men danced into the center of the courtyard, while the spectators, in a shifting mass, held their right arms out as a sign of respect of one or another good dancer. Once, during the music, the master musician stopped and asked me to record the talking drums. Everyone quieted down as he beat out the names of the past chiefs on the same two drums he had used for the music. The pattern was staccato, with rapid bursts of sound interrupted by uneven breaks. His two drums, one smaller than the other, echoed the tones of Kolongo, forming words: the names of the chiefs and their place in the royal genealogies. After he had finished, I played the recording, to the satisfaction of everyone, and the dancing commenced again.

Finally, about ten o'clock, people began drifting off to bed. Noting that we were very tired from the trip and the heat, we retired to our respective houses, where Steve took Tchina Kofi's room, Marilyn bedded down in Apo's room in his mother's house (he had moved there to be near her, because she was now very old and might need his help in the night), and I set my air mattress and sheet up in the roofed portion of the courtyard, where, I hoped, it would be cooler.

The sounds of the village had not yet died down. The younger boys of the house, now quite numerous, slept in another roofed open area across from me, but, like children everywhere, they kept up a conversation for some time after everyone else in the house had gone to sleep. Outside, some of the pre-teen and teen-age girls assembled under the tree in the center of the village, where they sang in beautiful harmony and danced alone in the dark.

I was completely drained. Hot and very tired, an emotional letdown began to set in. The heat came at me in waves, almost suffocating. In spite of the welcome, in spite of the happiness I had felt only several minutes before, I began to wonder why I had returned. The heat and broken silence awakened a depression in me and a foreboding I could not explain. It was, I thought, going to be a hard ten days.

I now suspect that the heat and the emotional strain were responsible for a physiological response that may have been partially due to salt loss. At any rate, although I continued to find the nights painful, each succeeding one was less so, and the days were full of surprises, hard work, and the joy of finding myself once again in the heart of my African family.

In the morning, the first order of business was to find Tchina Kofi. Marilyn, Steve, Apo, and I set off for Assuifré in the morning, stopping in Gumeré to get the fan belt repaired. By the time the work was done, it was early afternoon. Assuifré is about twenty miles from Gumeré, almost on the Ghana border. It is a large Abron town with its own market and many sprawling streets. In comparison to Diassenpa, it is positively urban. We drove up to the house of Tchina Kofi's host and parked. Upon entering, we were greeted, as is the custom, by the houseowner and went through the usual formal speeches one makes when arriving from another village. It finally became clear that Tchina Kofi was no longer there but had moved on to still another village, Karabingue, which was closer to Gumeré but off the main road. As we were getting up to leave, a familiar face appeared in the doorway. It was Kwamé Kosinu, one of my brothers from Diassenpa. We greeted each other as long-lost brothers do, and he chided me for not having replied to his last letter, which it appears he

had sent in 1962 or 1963. He showed me the address
he had sent it to and I explained that the letter had not
gotten to me because I had moved. We agreed to
recommence our long-broken correspondence.

Kwamé was now married and, being a member of
the first generation of literate Abron, of whom there
were very few, was working as a petty functionary. He
traveled around Abron country for the national census,
moving his household from time to time, as he worked,
from one local region to another. He was about to
move from Assuifré and asked us if we could take his
heavy iron manioc press back to Diassenpa for him.
We lifted it into the trunk of the car and set off again in
search of Tchina Kofi.

We arrived in Karabingue about four in the afternoon. Apo took us straight to the house in which he
now expected to find the old man, only to be told that
Tchina Kofi was out working in the yam gardens. Apo
asked if we wanted to go out and find him, saying that
it was quite far from the village. We agreed and, in
spite of the heavy afternoon heat, set out on a path that
wound away from the village toward the broken forest
that surrounded it. After about twenty minutes of walking, we came to the first yam gardens. A woman was
helping her husband plant the tubers in newly formed
hills. We asked her where Tchina Kofi was and she motioned that he was farther along the trail. We set out
again, this time for another march of about ten minutes, which led us to another garden patch in newly
cleared forest. Tchina Kofi was nowhere to be seen. A
man working in this field said that he had gone to another part of the cleared area to drink palm wine. We
set off again. As usual, we were one step behind this
eighty-seven-year-old man. The palm wine was drunk
up and he, we were told, had returned to the village.
We traipsed back, by now hot and tired, only to find
that Tchina Kofi had passed through the village and
gone down the road to another source of palm wine.
Again, both the wine and Tchina Kofi were gone. Sure
that we would not find him, we returned to the house at

which our search had begun. There, sitting calmly on a chair in the shade of a tree, was Tchina Kofi, dressed in a fine cloth. He had a look of great satisfaction on his face, which had aged well. He had lost a few teeth and his cheeks were a bit hollow, but his eyes still burned with the intelligence and animation I had come to respect, and love. *"Mi nda omane* [How are you, my father]," I said. *"Mi tugun* [I am well]," he replied. And as we hugged, tears came to our eyes, and he began to kiss my cheek with rapid little pecks, repeating *"Eh," "Eh," "Eh,"* over and over. My arrival was now complete.

After the formalities were over, we gathered up Tchina Kofi's things and left for the return trip to Diassenpa. We arrived in the late afternoon, just before the evening baths. Since Steve had been occupying Tchina Kofi's room and because all of us had been using it as a kind of base, I asked the old man if he would like his room back. He laughed and said that he would stay with one of his wives and that it would be his pleasure if we stayed where we were. He did, however, ask our permission to go into the room to recover a few of his possessions and take them to his wife's house. He entered and, looking around at our things, he set about collecting his blankets and some old clothes from various pegs set in the wall. Finally, he began to rummage around in a small box that had been under a pile of things in the corner. He pulled an assortment of objects out of it, mumbling all the time to himself. Then he found what he had been looking for. It was a large beetle, with a geometric design in black and white on the carapace, and long antennae. It was dry and in perfect condition. Tchina Kofi handed it to me, saying nothing. I admired it, holding it gingerly. Then he said, "Do you like it?" "Yes," I replied, "it is very beautiful." "Take it," he replied; "I have been saving it for your return for ten years."

Attawa, my "wife," had grown into a beautiful woman. The night of our arrival, she had come shyly into the courtyard. Obviously still aware of our fictive relationship, and now really married, she greeted us with averted eyes and quickly returned to her own house. Later, I asked if I could take her picture and, after much preparation, she came back into the court-yard with her baby daughter, dressed in her finest clothes. Like all Abron, she set her jaw as tightly as possible and posed so stiffly that I thought she would break. I tried to get her to smile, and after a great deal of prompting, she cracked only a bit. Finally, I took the pictures as she wanted them, but then caught her in a series of candid photos with my telephoto lens.

The last day of our stay, during the final dance which was our send-off from the village, Attawa came up to me and, in what was a very un-Abron gesture, particularly for a woman in her age category, said that she hoped that God would protect me and that I would have a good and happy life.

Among the young grownups were Yawa, Badu's daughter, who had been a toddler in 1962. Yawa at thirteen was a pretty girl, wistful, and a bit lost living in the house of her grandmother, Afua Morofyé. Badu had married a taxi driver and resided with him, many miles away. Three of her seven children still lived with her mother, in Diassenpa; the others, with her and her husband. Yawa, who had been somewhat mistreated by her selfish and immature mother, had grown up, as might be expected, lacking emotional stability. While she loved her grandmother and had the usual contacts in Diassenpa with her family and the girls in her age group, she missed her mother very much and had difficulty expressing her needs. She became very at-tached to Marilyn, but the night before our departure could only act silly and manic. She rushed around her house repeating all the French verb conjugations she knew. Badu was supposed to visit Diassenpa the Sun-day of our stay. When Yawa's stepfather's taxi rolled into the village, she rushed out to it expectantly. Badu was not there, however, and Yawa, without showing any of the pain she must have felt, went back to her house, acting as if it did not matter. Yawa did her share of work around the house, but she approached life with an indolence uncharacteristic of most Abron girls and women. She was more shy and slower even to move than her age-mates, and, although obviously intelligent, often acted silly.

I had told Apo that we would need two people who spoke good French to act as our informants and interpreters. On our second evening, a young man from Amamvi who turned out to be Pong Kofi's son came over to the house and asked if he could help us. At the same time, Steve made the acquaintance of two young men in the village, Étienne and Célestin. Both of them seemed intelligent and both spoke good French. Célestin was a relative of the royal lineage chief, and Étienne lived in our house. His father had died several years before and he was now domiciled with his maternal uncles. As a nephew in their care, he was being sent to school in Amamvi. Étienne turned out to be a good friend, an intelligent informant, and a taskmaster who, in his own desire to learn, kept us up late many a night giving him English lessons. He was one of those perfect people who exhibit talent, confidence, and a physical presence. Étienne was only thirteen, although he looked at least seventeen. He was an excellent soccer player, who in spite of his deftness with the ball, played a team game. He liked school and did well, working late in the night on his homework in the weak light of a hurricane lantern. In addition, he had his own yam garden, of which he was very proud.

Apo told us that Étienne was available for a few days and could work for us, because his schoolteacher was sick. He would miss school anyway during a good part of our stay. The same afternoon, Apo came into Tchina Kofi's room trailed by another youth, who, he said, could help us. This was Pascal, the son of the village secretary. He was a rather ungainly youth whose French did not impress us very much, but because he was the son of an official we thought that we would, at least, have to try him out. That evening, when I began to gather myths, one of the major goals of my trip, Pascal and Étienne were both there to act as interpreters, as well as Pong Kofi's son. Tchina Kofi was the story-teller that evening, and, as usual, his style brought a hushed appreciation from the audience. During the tell-ing of the first myth, Pascal responded to each phrase with a grunt, which is the traditional way of punctuat-ing a story and informing the teller that his audience is attentive. At the end, Pong Kofi's son translated, telling the story in French with almost as much verve as Tchina Kofi had told it in Kolongo. The next set of myths and stories was translated by Étienne, who dis-played a good memory and a sense of drama as well. At the very end, I asked Pascal to translate the last myth, since he had done nothing all evening and I had not been able to determine how good his French was. He replied that he was too tired, excused himself, and padded off to bed.

The next day, Apo made it clear that the villagers did not want us to hire Pong Kofi's son. The reasons for this were kept vague, but the displeasure was real. Steve thought this stemmed from Pong Kofi's son hav-ing come from Amamvi and that Apo wanted to keep our money in Diassenpa. This might indeed have been the case, but I had had no trouble eleven years before with Oppong, who had not only come from farther away, but was not even an Abron. Then, however, it had been clear that I needed an English speaker and, when I arrived in Diassenpa, he was already a part of my household. It was take us both or lose us both. None of us was thrilled with the thought of hiring Pas-cal, since his French appeared rudimentary and he seemed a bit indolent as well. But we were faced with a real problem, which represented perhaps one of the most important changes in the life of Diassenpa since my first visit. This was the existence of the village sec-retary.

For the past several years, every village in the Ivory Coast, even the smallest, has had a village secretary who is appointed by the Parti Démocratique de la Côte d'Ivoire. His job is to keep a census of the village and to punish minor infractions of the law. He also keeps a general eye on things for the government and has the power to put people in the local jail (there is one in Diassenpa). As my Abron friends and informants put it, *"Il est bien respecté."* While I was not sure how far the secretaries' powers extended and I had no idea how the Diassenpa village secretary would respond to us (he was, after all, a local man whom I knew well and who had been very helpful to me during my first stay), I thought it prudent to hire his son as an informant in spite of his obvious shortcomings.

Pascal turned out to be a mixed blessing. He washed our clothes and dishes for us and was very helpful with information on farming and technology, which I wanted to recheck. He was well informed as far as social relationships within the village were concerned and he helped me unscramble a genealogical problem that had bothered me since my first trip. He tried to add to our store of myths and riddles by mechanically reciting some of the proverbs he had learned in school, and for this I indulged him with my tape recorder.

His negative side became clear the third day of our stay, when I was to run a group of sick people up to Tabgne, to the infirmary. As the car was very small, I asked that only Apo accompany those in need of medical attention. Among these was his stepmother, the younger wife of Tchina Kofi, who was suffering from a very bad case of malaria, a woman with severe diarrhea, and a sick baby who had to be accompanied by its mother. That morning, Pascal told me that he also felt very sick and that he needed to see the nurse. On this basis, I squeezed him in the car and left without finding if there were other sick people in the village who needed the attention of the clinic. As soon as we got to the market in Tabgne, however, Pascal asked me to stop, got out of the car, and disappeared into a store. He never did get to the clinic that day and apparently felt fine.

After all the patients had been taken care of, I went to the market to do a little shopping and Pascal appeared, a bit contrite, but smiling. I bawled him out roundly and he silently brought our things back to the car. When we returned to the village, I went off to the fields, leaving my morning's purchases in the room with Steve, who was looking over some notes on the language. A few minutes later, Pascal came in and asked Steve to give him "the can of pineapple juice Alex bought for me this morning." Steve, knowing that I was angry with Pascal, asked him if I had really bought him a can of pineapple juice, and Pascal assured him that I had. Steve handed over the juice and Pascal disappeared for the day. When I returned to the village and heard about this, I exploded. I dressed Pascal down, particularly for taking the place of a sick person in the car, but also for stealing the juice. However I did not fire him, for fear that his father might take measures against us. As it turned out, Pascal did feel sorry about what he had done and tried quite hard for the rest of our short stay to be helpful. He even spent some time at home working on a genealogy of the royal line, something that interested me and which I had no success in getting from the older men, who refused to talk about anything that seemed in the remotest way to be political. Their standard answer was that these questions must be asked of the King.

Our first days passed without incident. One way or another, I was forced to go to Tabgne every morning, either to get something we needed or to take sick people to the infirmary. At first I thought that the villagers were extraordinarily healthy. There were many fewer sores than I had come to expect from my previous visits, but as the news of our arrival reached Bracodi and Amamvi, people who had various complaints began to drift in to take advantage of my morning first-aid sessions. There was a great deal of malarial fever, and some of the children had bad cases of fungus. In addition, many peoople were suffering from various kinds of stomach trouble as well as vague aches and pains. For this I had a new weapon with me: Alka-Seltzer, which became the instant hit of our medical practice. The Abron had never seen effervescent medicine before, and when the tablet was dropped into water it was pure magic for them. I used Alka-Seltzer for a range of complaints and took people to the infirmary only if their symptoms did not respond to this treatment. It turned out to be a miracle drug second only to injections in prestige. Its taste was exotic enough for most to be accepted as medicine, and although I told people that it was *"ho dun"* (good-tasting), most Abron found it satisfyingly *"ha dui"* (bad-tasting).

I had raved to Steve and Marilyn about the good fruit we were going to have in Diassenpa. We had arrived in what should have been the season of pineapples and mangos. Instead we found that oranges were just coming due and that there was little fruit other than bananas. Although far south of the great drought that had killed thousands of humans and more than half the animals in the fringe countries of the Sahara, Abron land had also suffered, if to a lesser degree, from a lack of rain. Small vegetable gardens producing greens and such vegetables as tomatoes and eggplants had failed that winter. These gardens require watering from nearby streams and had failed early. More serious, from the economic point of view, was the fact that the coffee crop had been very poor that year as well.

Noting these problems, I was worried about the food supply in general and the ability of our hosts to feed three more mouths, if only for ten days. The yam harvest, however, had been good, producing enough of a surplus for those who had worked hard to sell yams both in the local market and to buyers from Abidjan. The price of meat and dried fish was still low, there were plenty of lentils for the children, and the pots of futu were never skimpy. On the other hand, Apo seemed particularly anxious to get as much out of us as he could. When we arrived, I told him that all our camping equipment would be left behind for the use of the house, and that we would pay two informants for ten days' work. In addition, during our stay I made al-

most daily trips to the infirmary and bought a good
deal of medicine for those seriously ill. The infirmary
no longer gave many drugs free (even tetanus shots
had to be paid for), and worse, there was no pharmacy
in Tabgne, obliging the sick or their families to go all
the way to Bondoukou for medicine. My provision of
medicine took a considerable burden off those people
who were treated during our visit.

To add to this, I found myself buying small items
every day. These ranged from bottles of cooking oil
and kerosene to shotgun shells for Apo's gun. Whenever the occasion arose in which it might be appropriate to drink, I was asked to buy palm wine or gin.
This included the finishing of a genealogy, afternoon
dancing, trips to other villages, the visits of outsiders to
our house, and the end of storytelling sessions.

On the last day of our stay, during the dancing which
lasted from afternoon well into the night, Apo took me
aside looking very grave and said that there was a serious crisis brewing for the afternoon. Here, he said, we
were having a fine fete, but there was no tanga for the
old people. This was poor hospitality. He suggested
that I take the car to Tabgne and buy enough whisky
for the whole village. Knowing that this was an absurd
request, I refused, and that ended the matter.

Tourism, although still in its infancy, had begun to
touch the Abron's relations with the outside world as
well. I was admitted to the tomb of an Abron queen in
Herebo only upon payment of two hundred African
francs, and a weaver of Bracodi wanted one hundred
francs' payment to let me take his picture. Although I
paid on these two occasions, I avoided offering money
to people except for services rendered directly. Just to
the south, in Agni territory, easily reachable by paved
road, the King had already become something of a
tourist attraction. A half day's drive from Abidjan
brought sightseers to the air-conditioned Hotel Indeiné,
near Abengourou, from which various side trips could
be made. A tourist brochure describes these excursions:

After a visit to the mosque, you will call on the high chief of the Agni people. Perhaps you knew that the Agnis, descendants of the Akans, or Ashantis, live in accordance with a rigorous organization. . . .

2nd day: After breakfast, leave for Zaranou village 30 miles from Abengourou. The village chief welcomes you and first of all shows you his own house: a rectangular court with the dwelling at the rear end, and, to the right, on entering, the area for public meetings known as the adanzie. . . .

The chief will then relate to you the history of Zaranou, former capital of the Ndenye, a people who gave their name to the kingdom as a whole, Indeiné, where the district headquarters existed from 1893 to 1916. It was here that King Boa Kouassi the First welcomed Binger, who stayed three years in Zaranou.

After the presentation to the notables, you will sit next to the chief and watch the ceremonies organized in your honor. Men, women and children have left the fields to give you a welcome in a fantastic frenzy of dancing, singing and gaiety to the sound of tom-toms and balafons. Turn and turn about the dancers leave their lines—men and women—and will hail you. They will stop dancing only to ask you for news of your own land. . . .

The chief will finally offer you some refreshment, and the moment to leave Zaranou, a proud and hospitable village, will have come. It will be hard to forget Zaranou.

On the afternoon of the second day you return to Abidjan and to the hotel.

The escalation of demands by the Abron, but particularly by Apo, could have been due to growing notions about tourists in the Ivory Coast, by the tightness of the economic situation, or by Apo's natural talents for squeezing favors out of others. Already in 1962, it was Apo who had bothered me for small favors, and now, as head of the household, he had responsibilities to his brothers and their sons, to his mother and his sisters and their daughters, and to his wife and child. It was his new function to see that all went smoothly and that the high economic standing of the family was maintained.

I do not mean to suggest that we were in some way overexploited. We were, after all, the guests of the entire village. Apo provided us with antelope meat and wild mushrooms, as well as the more mundane items of daily food. His wives and sisters brought us water twice a day for baths, and drinking water whenever we needed it. The only thing that had changed from my first visit was the escalation of the demands upon the visitor in playing his part of the game of reciprocity. If I had shown up in the village without even a car, as I had in Amamvi, I would have been welcome for some time.

The Abron are not fools. They will give willingly, but they also take willingly. They will take everything a visitor offers and ask for what he does not offer. If he is fool enough to give it, so much the better. That is all part of the game.

This habit of making outlandish requests, however, is softened by another Abron custom which I, or to be more correct, Steve did not discover until this last trip. Steve had rapidly become adopted by some of the young men of the village. Both Célestin and Étienne told me that they were very fond of him. As age-mates of his, they could interact with him much more easily than they could with me, and they were fascinated to meet an outsider who fit more or less into their age category. At the same time, they were also curious about Steve's belongings and would have been happy if he had left them his things, ranging from his Swiss army knife and lantern to his camera and watch. On several occasions, he was asked for each of these items. The lantern was duly promised to Célestin and the knife given to Étienne, who really had also wanted the lantern. The watch, Steve said, was a gift from his father and not giveable, and talk of the camera was stopped by flat refusals to part with it. Steve, who had never ex-

perienced the game of *Give me; O.K., don't give me,*
played by most Abron, was naturally quite put off at
first by all these requests. Finally, in discussing his feelings about this with Célestin, he was told that a polite
Abron will ask for something only one time. If it is refused, he will say thank you anyway, and the subject
will be permanently dropped. After we discovered this
(previously I had been only vaguely aware that requests were never pursued very long), we began to
actively test it. It turned out that, in every case, a flat
refusal to a direct request ended the matter immediately.

There were, however, ways of prolonging conversations concerning the desire for one of our belongings
or for some service. This was to talk about the desired
object but not to request it directly. Such conversation
was unlikely to elicit a direct refusal, and so one could
talk around the subject for a considerable time, making
obvious a particular desire but never fully broaching
the question. My second day in Diassenpa, for example, the Queen Mother approached me and asked
where I was going the next day in the car. I replied that
I was going to Tabgne. She seemed not to hear and said,
"You are going to Gumeré." "No," I repeated, "I'm
going to Tabgne." She walked away. A few hours later,
she reappeared at my door. *"Owo ya brouni caso
dechego?* [Where are you going tomorrow, white
man?]" *"Mi ya Tabgne.* [I'm going to Tabgne.]"
Then she volunteered, *"Mi ya Gumeré caso dechego.*
[I'm going to Gumeré tomorrow morning.]" And
then "Aren't you going to Gumeré?" "No," I said,
"I'm going to Tabgne," but, catching on to what she
was asking, I said that I was going to Gumeré two days
later. But this did not help. Two days later! Why was I
not going to Gumeré tomorrow morning? It was, she
almost implied, the natural thing to do. Finally, after
more hemming and hawing, she asked me straight out
to take her to Gumeré. I told her that I could not. Immediately, she thanked me politely and walked away.
The next morning, she set off by herself for Gumeré.

Marilyn had a tremendous social advantage in Diassenpa. She was young and single. Although she had had
some pretrip anxieties, she fit herself immediately into
village life. Living in the women's house, she was able
to observe and participate in the daily round of the
women, something about which I knew very little. But
because she bathed and took dinners at our house, she
became friendly with the men and boys who lived
there. Her natural ability to dance also contributed to
the positive impression she created in the village.

Marilyn loved heat, and except for one or two days
when the sun exaggerated its presence and the humidity
mounted to its prestorm intensity, she reveled in the
high temperatures. In addition to working in the fields
with the women of her house, she was appreciated for
the English lessons she began with a group of about
five young people. While both Steve and I participated
to some extent in these lessons, Marilyn devoted most
of her evenings to the group. Her star pupil was
Étienne, whose ear for language was marvelous. He
rapidly learned several key phrases, starting as we had
done in Kolongo with greetings, and soon adding a
large vocabulary list. He also mastered several verb
conjugations, writing everything down in his school
notebook in his own form of phonetic script, which
reflected a mixture of French and Kolongo pronun-
ciation. At one point we suggested to Étienne that he
would make a fine ambassador to the United States. He
took this suggestion seriously, and we promised to send
him an English book from Abidjan on our return to
that city. This we did, and no doubt Étienne is busy
every evening teaching himself English.

Marilyn's house was short of adult women. Of Afua
Morofyé's three daughters, all had married men of
other villages and were living away from Diassenpa.
Badu was the last to leave. In her own generation,
Afua Morofyé was alone. Her house had been built for
her by her husband, Yao Fram. The only adult women
there were Apo's young wife and the young wife of
Kwamé Kosinu. Yawa, wrapped up in her own long-

ings for Badu, paid little attention to the crowd of very young boys and the few daughters of the third generation who ate and slept in her grandmother's house. Apo's daughter Afua and another younger girl, a neighbor, also named Afua, both attached themselves to Marilyn. This affection was reciprocal, and both children spent hours on Marilyn's lap or playing in the dirt around her legs. Afua Apo's strange beauty—large, oriental eyes and a wide, sensuous mouth—was immediately appealing, and her quick response to affectionate attention from adults, particularly women, forged a link between her and Marilyn that the latter was reluctant to break at the end of our visit.

It was Afua, at most six years old, who came to her father's house every morning at dawn to sweep the courtyard. Like the other children, she was treated very much as an adult and had her required tasks to perform automatically without a glimmer of appreciation from the adults of the village. With Marilyn, Afua had found her lost babyhood and was once more, if only in this limited way, the center of adult attention. Her response showed how readily Abron children will return to a position of complete dependence on adult affection when given the chance. Since Marilyn did not speak Kolongo and Afua did not speak French, the relationship was based entirely on physical contact and mutual tenderness, which cut through the barriers of language.

Steve is a talented linguistics student from the University of Pennsylvania who had previously worked on American Indian languages. Introspective and self-contained, he had admired the calm and closed affect of his Indian informants. He had enjoyed and shared their orientation toward personal solitude. Steve's personality was totally at odds with that of the average Abron. The excitement that greeted our arrival appeared false and strange to him. At first he was convinced that the villagers had put on a show and interpreted the affection that greeted us as unreal. This feeling was reinforced by what seemed to him to be a too-easy offer of friendship, particularly by his close age-mates and the young un-

married men of the village. His suspicions were increased by the early requests for gifts that were made
as his personal belongings were scrutinized and evalu-
ated. I had told Steve that this would happen and that
his equals in the village would ask for everything he
had of even the most remote interest to them. I had
also told him that a refusal would be greeted with nothing more than a shrug of acceptance. Still the suspicion
that one's belongings count more than one's self, a natural feeling to have under these circumstances, cannot
be easily overcome even if one is warned in advance. It
is difficult to disengage this pattern from one of genuine
acceptance. Nonetheless, three of the young men of
Diassenpa who spoke good French attached themselves
to Steve very early in our stay and he repaid their attention with concern and interest. One of them came
up to me on our third day and said, "I like Steve so
very much," a statement which, although apparently
true, was very un-Abron. This was testimony to the
fact that, although shy, Steve was able to establish good
rapport with his age-mates in the village.

Steve's relationship with the single men of the village
was immediately better than mine had ever been, for
this was his real place in the group. The fact that I was
married, even newly so in 1961, created a barrier between myself and those who were socially a generation
below me.

After the first day, spent chasing Tchina Kofi, Steve
began to participate with village youth in soccer, threw
himself into Étienne's English lessons, and began to
work with informants in Kolongo. His shyness rapidly
submerged in the rhythm of daily life, but he was never
comfortable with the crowd of Abron that tended to
surround us everywhere. The heat added to his
uneasiness too. Worn out by daily activities and the
noise of incessant conversation, Steve usually went to
sleep early, got up late (by Abron standards), and frequently took solitary walks away from the village.

Steve, Marilyn, and even I to a lesser extent were
also annoyed by a new element in the background noise

of Diassenpa. This was the transistor radio. Five already existed in the village, and in the early evening they were all at top volume, their noise obliterating the more pleasant sounds of women pounding futu and the low pitch of household conversations as people drifted back into the village after a day's work. It was possible to get at least five stations in Diassenpa, two from the Ivory Coast, two from Ghana, and one from Liberia. Most played a mixture of good and bad rock-and-roll music and highlife as well as news broadcasts in French, English, Twi, and other African languages. It did not seem terribly important what was broadcast. Frequently, this or that radio would drone on for hours in a language certainly unknown to the listeners. All but one of these radios were cheap Japanese models that emitted poor sound, punctuated with whines and whistles. When played at top volume, whatever proper sound they were capable of producing was distorted beyond the capabilities of our ears to endure.

Steve had a deep sense of honesty and moral commitment. Pascal's escapades, particularly his taking the place of a sick person in the car, disturbed us all, but Steve could not accept this behavior in the context of other, more positive things Pascal did during our stay. He could not accept the degree of excitement associated by an Abron with a ride in a car. His dislike for Pascal smoldered all during our stay and afterward. Yet, this dislike had its opposite, and it amplified his developing alliance with intelligent, open, and thoroughly honest Étienne. Steve's reaction to individual Abron increased my awareness of personality differences among people in the village as well as highlighting those features that are more or less typically Abron. My own sociability, which was closer than Steve's to the Abron pattern, blinded me somewhat to this. By observing Steve, I was able to learn a great deal about the Abron and myself at the same time. This is, perhaps, a major advantage of field work with others, who, as individuals with different personalities, provide one another with a means of reflection.

On Sunday morning, Steve, Marilyn, and I, accompanied by Étienne, Pascal, and Célestin, went to Catholic services in Amamvi. The church is at the far end of the village, away from Diassenpa, in a small grove of trees that tend to shade its corrugated-iron roof. We traversed Amamvi, followed by the usual crowd of children, and arrived before the service. The awaiting crowd were mostly young, reflecting the parallel between school attendance and conversion. The service was to be conducted by a deacon, a man of Amamvi, in the absence of the French priest, who serves, as he told us, forty-two villages in a wide circuit embracing much of Abron territory. At the arrival of the deacon, an iron bar that hung in front of the church was hit several times, announcing the service, and the awaiting crowd began to file into the church. The one-room structure was equipped with two rows of benches divided down the middle by an aisle. Women and girls took their places on the left, boys and men on the right. At the far end of the church, away from the door, was a table that served as an altar. On it were placed a wooden cross and two candles.

The service, in French and Kolongo, began with the lighting of the candles. Hymns and prayers were recited in one or another of the two languages. Unlike the Mass, at which only a priest can officiate, scriptural reading and interpretation provided most of the service. This was punctuated by singing as well as by responses by the congregation to the reading of certain passages. Almost everyone seemed familiar with the established order. The deacon read the Kolongo rather well and the French more haltingly. There seemed to be a bit more enthusiasm for the Kolongo parts of the service. Few of the women present spoke any French. Toward the end of the service, which lasted for about one hour, a boy about fourteen years of age went down the aisle taking a collection. Members of the congregation dropped small coins, ranging in value from five to one hundred francs CFA, into a wooden plate attached to a long handle with which the boy was able to reach along the full length of the benches. A Mossi youth, marked by his scars and poor dress, put a ten-franc coin into the plate and then took change for his offering amounting to at least fifty francs. Steve, standing behind him, saw the whole performance and was scandalized. No one else in the near vicinity appeared to notice. After the service, Steve told me that he had almost reached out to stop the thief. He was quite disturbed that anyone could steal from so poor a church. I reminded Steve that the Mossi were themselves victims of Abron exploitation and suggested that he consider the theft as a means not only of profiting in a small way from the Abron but also as a form of vengeance for treatment that was often far short of kind. I had in fact been startled by the presence of a Mossi in church. Most of them are either Moslems or practice their own religion, and Christianity has made little headway among them. It was only when he took the money that I realized his motive in attending. Undoubtedly, he augmented his meager income each week through pious observance of the Mass.

Before we left on our field trip, Steve was undecided as to whether or not he might stay on alone for a few months to work on the language. Although he rapidly changed his view of the Abron, the extreme heat, the difficult and cramped nature of our accommodations, his own preference for a more quiet setting, and, most important, the difficulty of finding an adequate informant for rapid and intense linguistic work, convinced him to leave with Marilyn and me at the end of our own brief visit. Since I had told the villagers upon our arrival that Steve might wish to stay on and because our household was prepared to accept him for a longer period, I had to explain the reason for his decision to quit the village. Feeling that the extreme climate provided the excuse that would cause the least ill feeling, I told Apo and his brothers that Steve could not take the heat. This was accepted as reasonable, and nothing more was said about it in our house. Afua Morofyé, however, was not satisfied to hear of Steve's departure from her sons, and she therefore asked me if it was true. "Yes," I said, repeating the story about the heat. "That's a shame," she sighed. "He is too thin, and if he would only stay on for two or three months, that would give me enough time to fatten him up."

Tchina Kofi's room had a window facing outward toward the space between two men's houses. To the right and slightly beyond the corner of our house wall was a women's living area with two mud-walled houses and an open courtyard in which food was prepared and cooked. We did our own cooking on the terrace, which was walled off from the rest of the courtyard by a cement railing. Although we lived largely out of cans when we did not eat with the men of the household, Apo and other villagers supplied us with fruit, mainly bananas, as well as eggs, yams, and, much to our joy, on two occasions antelope meat and wild mushrooms. Since the village was carefully swept twice a day, and because I had seen villagers throwing their garbage on the ground around their houses, I began to throw all our peelings out the window to avoid dirtying the courtyard. We kept our cans, however, so that the children would not collect them and cut their hands on the sharp edges. After three or four days of this, Apo came to me quite disturbed. "This is my concession," he told me; "outside belongs to someone else. If you have garbage, throw it right in the courtyard, where the women will clean it up." Not wanting to dirty the premises further, we began to collect everything in a plastic bag and transported the garbage ourselves to the dump at the end of the village. Although this behavior met with amusement by the men of our house, it seemed better to us than dirtying the courtyard. Our mistake was to have considered the immediate environs of the house as part of the family territory. Like so many other mistakes, this one taught us something about Abron customs that we might not have thought to ask about.

Each afternoon and evening, when I was not otherwise occupied, I worked with Pascal and a group of other young Abron (often in the company of older men and women) on a family genealogy, on the collection of data on various customs, and on farming practices. Wishing to recheck some data on marriages which I had collected in 1961, I touched on kinship and the possible existence of a minor form of patrilineal inheritance which I knew existed among the Ashanti. This is the Ntoro group, which recognizes the role of the male in procreation and creates a minor alliance between groups of lineally related men for a small number of generations. Among the Ashanti, the Ntoro is also totemic, in the sense at least that members of each Ntoro are associated with an animal they are forbidden to eat. Not wishing to put words into my informants' heads, I asked about the existence of men's groups in a roundabout way and, finally, getting no response at all, I posed the question directly. Again the response was negative. Finally, knowing that most Abron spoke Twi, I introduced the Ashanti word *Ntoro* into the conversation. The immediate response was quite unexpected. The girls and women who had gathered at the fringes of our group immediately ran away giggling. The boys and men tittered and looked very embarrassed. I asked Pascal what had happened. "You used a bad word," he said. Evidently the only meaning *Ntoro* had for the Abron, at least in Diassenpa, was semen! This was not a subject for conversation even among men. To utter the word in the presence of women was a social *faux pas*. I could elicit no further information on the possible existence of the Ntoro group.

Later that afternoon, during the telling of a folk tale, I stumbled on the fact that traditionally the Abron had initiation ceremonies. In the middle of a story, Étienne mentioned that the principal character had the scars of initiation on his forehead. I stopped the tape recorder and said, "Ah, then the Abron do have initiation ceremonies!" Étienne looked embarrassed, and the others in the circle around us looked equally uncomfortable. One of the older men said, "We used to, but it's not done much any more." Because the story concerned a young man, I purposely asked if they had ini-

tiation ceremonies for women. Again, I got a reluctant
affirmative answer. "What about men?" I said. "No, we
do not initiate the men" was the immediate reply from
the assembled group. "But in this story," I reminded
them, "it is a young *man* who bears the scars on his
head." Étienne then had to admit that men's initiation
was, or as he put it, had been, a part of Abron custom.
I tried to press this matter further, but it was clearly a
highly sensitive issue, as it is in many societies. Although many Abron had some confidence in me, this
was an area that I was unable to penetrate. As in the
case of witchcraft, however, the break came with the
discovery of the phenomenon. I suspect that if I had
been able to stay in Diassenpa longer, the whole process of initiation might have unfolded for me. Anthropologists are often frustrated by the need to leave the
field before all their questions have been answered.

The evening before our last day, Badu's husband returned to the village to visit his friends and mother-in-
law. Just before bedtime, he came into our courtyard to
sit and talk with the men of his age group, Badu's
brothers. Under his arm he carried what I thought was
a transistor radio. After a few minutes, he put it on the
table and said to me, "This time I am going to record
you." I looked at the machine again. It was a radio and
cassette recorder. "Since you cannot see Badu, you can
send her a message," he said. I picked up the micro-
phone. *"Mi eyeko* [My sister]," I said, "I am sorry
that I missed you here in Diassenpa. I had hoped to see
you very much. At any rate I am glad I was able to
meet your fine, handsome husband and to see Yawa
grown up and beautiful. I hope that your life is good
and that you will be happy in the years to come." The
tape was then rewound and immediately played back.
Badu's husband was satisfied. The machine was put
away once more and the talk continued. Two days
later, on the paved road beyond Agniblikourou, a truck
that we had just passed on the way to Abidjan flashed
its lights at us. I pulled over to the side of the road. I
was quite puzzled until the truck stopped and Badu's

husband got out with a big smile. "How are you?" he said in French. "I am taking this truck to Abidjan and saw you as you passed. I wanted to tell you that Badu was very happy with your message and that she sends you her best."

The day before our departure started off just like any other. But, by midafternoon, most of the men were quite drunk. The chief of Bracodi had come to visit, and all the adult men went to the house of his host to drink tanga. I was asked to come over and take pictures of everyone and, of course, to drink tanga as well. This tanga was particularly strong. The sweetness had gone out of it: the sugar had all been converted into alcohol. I am not fond of tanga in this form and remembered how drunk it could make one, but to be polite I drank a large, full calabash. This, plus the heat of the day, sent my head spinning, and as I stumbled back to our house I wondered if the pictures I had just taken would come out. Tchina Kofi was sitting in the shade. As I entered, he grinned at me and, pointing to the house from whence I had just come, said, *"Bo tanga ha dui* [Their tanga is not sweet]." He grimaced and pulled a clay pot toward him. *"Mi tanga ho dun* [My tanga is sweet]," he said, offering me a large glassful. I could not refuse, and so, taking the glass, drank it down rapidly. It was in fact sweet, but combined with what I had just drunk, it immediately made me feel weak and sick. I reeled into our room and fell asleep.

About four in the afternoon, the younger people began to gather in the courtyard. We had asked everyone to come and dance in the daytime so that I could take movies. The music began and, as the afternoon waned and the air cooled, more and more people began to dance. A mask that was used to amuse the children was brought out, and one of the older men danced with it held over his face. He moved his body from side to side, swaying his head and shoulders and wagging the mask. He kicked his feet, which were spread wide apart, and moved back and forth in front of the delighted children. After a while he put the mask down,

and one of the little boys picked it up and began to imitate his movements. Then the mask was put away and
the girls began to dance in a line, singing as they
moved, gracefully swaying their hips in a gentle rolling
movement. Their hands were held up in front of them,
almost as a boxer might protect himself, and moved
forward and back with a countermovement of the
shoulders against the hips. People kept coming in and
out of the courtyard, the men appearing more and
more drunk. Tchina Kofi got up to dance for the camera, mugging and swaying, not quite staggering, with a
silly smile of contentment on his face. The two Apos
put their arms around each other and danced in a circle
with a look of complete abandon on their faces. More
palm wine was brought in and distributed to the men.
It was a happy, drunken time. About five-thirty, the
young men stopped playing the drums and went out to
the soccer field to play the evening game. Before doing
so, however, they paraded around the field in military
style as they had been taught to do at school. Led by a
teen-ager with a referee's whistle, they marched in single file around the four sides of the playing area. Every
so often, they would jump up in the air, almost in
unison, and give a yell. Then they were ready to play.
Sides were chosen, and with the teen-age girls and
those few older men who were not drunk as their spectators, the usual afternoon game was played.

After dinner, the dancing resumed, and the adult
women performed a dance I had never seen before.
This was done to the accompaniment of an hourglass-
shaped talking drum. It was held under the arm of one
man, who altered the tone by squeezing with different
pressures on the strings connecting the two heads. He
beat on the top of the drum with a stick, while another
man beat out a counterrhythm on the bottom. The
women formed a tight circle. One of them hit a gong
with a stick to provide the final counterrhythm. The
signal to dance began when another woman in the circle struck up a refrain. Her voice was soon joined by
the chorus of women's voices, and some of the group

began to move around a core of stationary singers. The foot movement was not unlike what I had seen before: little mincing steps, two with the right foot, two with the left foot. They moved around the circle with a swaying at the hips. One or two women would suddenly move out faster than the others and sweep around the group repeating *"Ya—Ya—Ya—Ya"* over and over again. Then they would rejoin the slower-moving group.

At nine-thirty the dancing broke up, and although the courtyard remained full for some time, there was a general drift homeward by the crowd, which had come from other houses and from Amamvi and Bracodi. Chairs were brought for those who remained, and we sat in the middle of the courtyard under the stars. Speeches were made about our leaving. People thanked us for the help we had given in taking care of the sick, and statements were made about the affection we all had toward one another. On our arrival, I had made the mistake of telling everyone that our belongings would be given to the house for the use of its members. Apo was quite angry at this and told me that it was his wife and mother who had done all the work for us. In addition, he did not want to see any of our belongings fall into the hands of his half brothers, who were not members of his own matriline. That final evening, one of his full brothers asked me publicly, before all the other household members, who was to get our camping equipment. I said that I had agreed with Apo that everything was to go into his charge because it was his women who had helped us the most. The brother replied that what we gave to Apo we also gave to him, because they were full brothers, and so it was good. This repaired a mistake in which I had favored a whole men's house instead of the more viable social group, a matriline. The tension that had built up around our potential distribution of gifts was the same that builds up around property questions in any residential unit out of harmony with the social system.

Finally, Tchina Kofi asked me what I would like to

do the rest of the evening. I was very anxious to collect more stories from him, but realized that the work was over for that trip. I searched for something appropriate and finally said, "I would be content this evening, which is our last, to sit beside Tchina Kofi. That is enough." The old man nodded his head gravely at this and, with dignity, he pulled himself straight in his chair and said, "That is well." So we sat for some time, until Tchina Kofi said, *"Mi ya fye* [I am going to bathe]," which was the signal for everyone to go to bed. The children disappeared into the night and we settled down to our last sleep in Diassenpa.

Early in the morning, after washing and having our morning coffee, we went around the village saying good-by. Apo's wife came into the courtyard and assembled all the things we were to leave behind. We paid our informants, gave Tchina Kofi a gift for the use of his room, and distributed a few small gifts to friends. After making sure that we had paid everyone, Apo said, "That is enough; you have taken care of everyone." Then we said our final good-bys to the household and got into the car with Tchina Kofi, who was going back to Karabingue, where we had picked him up so few days before. There was not a dry eye in the village or in the car as we pulled out onto the road. No one was in a mood to talk, and the ride to Gumeré was silent. When we got there, I got out, went around the car, and opened the door for Tchina Kofi. Steve and Marilyn helped him get his things out of the car, and we three accompanied him to a chair under a tree, where a taxi would pick him up for the rest of his trip. I threw my arms around him and we both began to cry. We both knew that this was probably the last time we would see each other. Tchina Kofi was very old. Each day of his life was a gift, and no one could say how many more he had coming to him. I did not know how to break away. This old man had crept deep into my heart. Finally, he pulled away and, almost angrily, said, as one says to a child, *"Gu bo! Gu bo! Gu bo!* [Get away! Get away! Get away!]" He pushed me toward the car, his face set in a grimace of pain, with tears streaming down his cheeks. He then sat back on the chair, still saying *"Gu bo,"* as we got into the car and drove off not looking back.

16
Epilogue

I have walked on the surface of Abron culture. I have learned much; I have much to learn. At times, I feel that I understand the world as an Abron might; at other times, I realize that my field experience has shaped my perceptions but that they remain my own. In some senses, I now stand between two cultures.

I have experienced the warmth and kindness expressed toward strangers, as well as the curiosity that renders them objects. I have felt the sense of community that pervades every aspect of Abron life. I have experienced the mistrust and tension that overflow when sickness and death touch the life of the village.

I went to Africa with certain expectations; I came away with some of them confirmed and others modified or destroyed. I was, for example, prepared for the disintegration of an indigenous system under the pressures of Western technology and saw the beginning effect of neocolonialism in action. I had expected to find, and did find, a society based largely on kinship relations, but was surprised by the degree of erosion this system had undergone with the development of private property. I was not surprised to find an increase in social tensions, but did not discover until several months had passed how new economic patterns and the traditional social system combined to produce increased anxiety and hostility, expressed in witchcraft. Yet I was surprised to see how eclectic Abron culture was, borrowing not only from European models but from a wide range of neighboring peoples. This was a feature of the pragmatic and open approach of the Abron to everyday problems.

In addition to the many Abron, I came to know the Protestant missionaries in Gumeré, and, less well, the Catholics in Tanda. I also had a casual friendship with

Dupont, a French trader in Gumeré. Like these people,
I was a stranger to the Abron. Each had his or her own
ideas of the Abron and their country, and the Abron
reacted to each in different ways.

Dupont had been installed in Gumeré about ten
years. Originally from the north of France, he had
come to Africa shortly after the Second World War.
His shop was a one-story affair with an apartment in
the back made up of a living room, dining room, and
bedroom. The store itself occupied the entire front of
the building, running about thirty feet across and about
fifteen feet deep. It was divided along its length by a
narrow counter. Most of the wares, which ranged from
lanterns to bicycle tires, were arranged on shelves running along the wall behind the counter. Dupont's place
was dingy and did not look as if it could support its
owner. Part of this appearance, however, was the result
of planning. Dupont, who kept meticulous personal rec-
ords of every purchase and sale, wanted to present himself as a sloppy, inefficient *commerçant* who barely
scraped a living out of his meager set of wares. Every
year, when the tax collector came to discuss the year's
business, Dupont put on a dumb show that made him
look dim-witted and poor. Meanwhile his money accumulated in a bank in France, and his escape back to
Europe and early retirement was planned well in advance.

Dupont lived with an African mistress. She was an
Ashanti and spoke good Twi, English, and French. She
was a woman of considerable charm and talent, and
conversations with her were always a pleasure. When
Dupont invited one of his European friends to dinner,
however, she never appeared. After cooking the meal
in the kitchen shed behind the house, she would
discreetly vanish. When Dupont returned to France, in
1965, she was left behind.

One evening while Dupont and I were drinking wine
and talking about the changes that had occurred in the
region, we heard a noise by the side of the house under
his window. Careful listening suggested that someone

was urinating against Dupont's wall. He grabbed his shotgun and flew out the door, shouting into the dark, *"Qui pisse contre mon mur?"* In the dark, a figure barely discernible in the shadows wheeled away from the wall and came face to face with Dupont. It was the chief of a local village. *"Excusez-moi,"* he said, embarrassed. *"Non, excusez-moi,"* replied Dupont, who realized that, as a chief, the man had certain prerogatives. The chief wandered off into the dark, and Dupont and I returned to his house. Once inside, he began to laugh and laugh until he could hardly control himself. The idea of surprising a chief in such a position appealed to Dupont, and I am sure that he repeats this story over a pastis many an afternoon.

Dupont loved Africa, but he did not love Africans. He was very cynical about the Abron king, and took nothing very seriously that happened in the Ivory Coast except a rumor that passed around the country in 1962 that the government was going to force French businessmen to reinvest at least 50 per cent of their profits in the country. He enjoyed the freedom to love as he wished, and whom he wished, and to hunt the small game, particularly guinea fowl and small antelopes, which were still fairly common in the region. He worked very little: his hired man took care of sales, and his mistress took care of his other needs. Dupont loved the peace and color of the African sunset, the heat during the dry season, the cool mornings when the harmattan blew. When commerce in the area began in earnest and more traffic began to use the road north, he took to complaining about modernization. The introduction of transistor radios were, I think, the last straw for him, and he decided to go home. The old Africa, a simple place to live and work, was dying, and he had no interest in the developments that would follow independence.

When Dupont was conscious of Africans, it was to sell something from his store or to project himself large, a Frenchman, against the *"petit nègre"* officials or local peasants, who were, to his mind, superstitious and primitive. He spoke a little Dioula and no Kolongo; he was aware that some Abron and other Africans spoke French, and with them he would often enter into inconsequential conversations, dealing with the weather, the price of coffee, or the design of some car. Consciously, his position on black Africa was totally neutral: he was not there to teach, to bring French culture; he was not there to change anything.

My Abron friends liked him well enough. He lived unostentatiously, and his economic wealth did not seem to be much above their own. There were Abron who were clearly richer than he. He dressed simply, in shorts and open shirts; he never beat his mistress. While he did not sell on credit, he did not cheat anyone locally and his prices compared to those in African- and Lebanese-owned stores. For the Abron, Dupont was there as part of the scenery, and they were more or less in the same position in his eyes. He knew nothing of their life or customs.

His was a privileged life, on a modest scale. Intentionally or not, he made it appear that he took almost nothing from the people among whom he lived. Of course, hundreds of Duponts around the country, providing some service but taking what were really high profits, were all contributing not only to their own wealth but the wealth of the mother country. Their profits went home to accumulate interest in French banks, and it was in France that most of their money would be spent.

The missionaries were by no means neutral. The Catholics operated a maternity clinic and had been implanted, at least in Tanda, for many years. The priest spoke excellent Kolongo; he was interested in local customs to some extent, but spent most of his time around the dispensary and the church. He enjoyed his wine, preached civilization, and frowned upon polygamy. The good medical care available in the dispensary no doubt accounted for the saving of many lives. Because the Catholics were French and because the official language of the Ivory Coast is French, and finally because

many of the government officials were both French-
speaking and Catholic, the Church, since 1962, has
made a good deal of headway among the Abron. More
than half of all the school children go to church, and
some of them have managed to attract their older siblings and parents as well.

The Protestant missionaries are American. Although
they freely give first aid to anyone who comes to their
door, they are not equipped or trained to give real medical assistance. Nor do they teach. They are there to
convert. They believe that paganism is wrong and that
the devil is active both among Catholic Abron (they
detest the Catholic Church perhaps more than any
other religious group) and among the witch-ridden pagans. Since they frown on drinking and polygamy and
even the wearing of rings (many types of rings in the
area are worn for magical purposes), and because they
live away from the village and are a type of Christian
little known in the area, they have made few converts.
When they do convert, they demand obedience to a
wide set of rules which touch not only upon religious
matters but on such customs as residence, dress, etc.
These are all considered to be a part of local versus
Christian living. Most Abron whom I know find them
peculiar.

As for myself, the Abron finally began to accept me
when they realized that I had come to learn and not to
teach. They were also pleased that I could serve them
in simple medicine and provide occasional transportation. For some, I was certainly more than just a
source of help. Among the members of my own family,
I am sure that genuine affection developed on both
sides. My behavior was surprising, however, to everyone. I was unpredictable. I attempted, in some ways, to
live as Abron live, but I used a Coleman stove and had
a car; I took occasional trips to Abidjan. I asked incessant questions; I said that I had come to learn the language, yet my progress was not impressive.

I think that, for the majority of the Abron, I became
their white man: someone who, for some strange

reason, was not like the others, who took a real interest in village affairs, who could be trusted at least partway with what Abron believed. I think that most Abron were amused by my attempts to become Abron. My wearing of Abron dress was, at first, tolerated as a whim. Later, the chief and some of the other notables enjoyed having themselves photographed with me in my toga. In this role, I was the village mascot. My presence broke the boredom of daily existence: I was interesting, just as I found even the most mundane Abron tasks interesting.

For me, the Abron were, above all, a widening set of individuals, each with his or her own personality, who nonetheless shared a set of customs I had come to learn about. They represented a puzzle I wanted to crack. In order to do this, I lived in their midst, and by so living, became involved not only in my search, but in the lives of real people on a daily basis. I hated being a social chameleon who on the surface had to like everyone, but I came to enjoy my stay as I developed affectionate relations with some Abron. I disliked certain aspects of Abron culture to the day I left the village, but I came to respect other aspects more and more. I could never get used to the constant attention and company, which grated on my need for occasional privacy and reflection. I was often maddened by the constant requests for services, some of which were outlandish. However, I enjoyed the humor and kindness of Afua Morofyé and Tchina Kofi, as well as the latter's enormous gifts as an actor. I shared the Abron's general affection for their children, and their respect for others. I came to admire their life rhythm, which involved physical labor set to a human pace, although I was constantly shocked by the inequalities between men and women in work patterns. No Abron works too hard, but Abron women certainly do much more than men, and it is only women, except in very rare cases, who will work beyond a state of simple fatigue. Nonetheless, as I came to understand the culture better, I began to see how much power a woman has over the running of her own life. A senior woman is mistress of her house. She has a say in the running of the associated men's houses, and if she is a member of the royal family, she can have a genuine role in the determination of village affairs.

Above all, I was deeply impressed by the sense of community which pervaded everyday existence. Although this could be broken by arguments, or more seriously by occasional outbreaks of witchcraft, the social unity and communal spirit of the Abron village is a living example of what so many of our current generation of young people are themselves looking for. In our own culture, I have experienced this kind of unity only during crises. Once was during the rebellion at Columbia University in 1968, when I spent one night in Fayerweather Hall listening to the intense conversation of the occupants. Whatever we feel about this type of protest, and I was sympathetic to the students at Columbia in 1968, those of us who have experienced it know how exhilarating and unifying it can be, for revolution in its active phase is a social contract that generates an intense co-operative spirit.

My understanding of this feeling of unity grew by means of contrast with another experience, which occurred in the fall of 1970. A young AWOL soldier was hidden in the university chapel by a group of pacifist and radical students. The students had decided that they would not only provide sanctuary but resist any attempts by the government to arrest the young man on their territory. The action was bound to fail, but few present were ready to admit it. The talk was incessant. A great deal of what was said was immature and romantic; some was dangerously out of touch with reality. A former Columbia student and neighborhood mental case played his fantasies off on students all too willing to listen to his tales of spying and foul play. Points of view that conflicted with the spontaneous leadership of the movement were shouted down with cries of "Cop." By 1970, it was painfully obvious that the movement had degenerated into an attempt to relive something that had, in its time, been real and

spontaneous. What most of the participants appeared
to long for was a commune in the heart of the university. However, this longing resulted from real feelings
of alienation and loss of social cohesion, which are
characteristic of our society.

The one other time I have felt a sense of total community is in S., a small French village in which I have a
summer home. S. has about 250 permanent inhabitants
divided politically among old-style radical socialists,
Communists, and Catholics who tend to vote Gaullist.
To some extent, this division is between the men and
the women of the village. The former are anti-Church,
while the latter are regular participants at Mass, at least
on Sundays. There are, of course, other political divisions in the village, ranging from far left to extreme
right, and while everyone is polite to everyone else,
there is a good deal of quiet grumbling about this or
that neighbor. Such complaints are more likely than not
to be shared with vacationers, particularly foreigners
such as ourselves, for, as strangers, we are a safe audience, one that can be confided in without much risk.

Unity comes to the village when the *glas* sounds.
This is the ringing of the church bell announcing death.
It is a somber peal, slow and deep. With the ringing of
the *glas,* a hush falls over the village, and, until the funeral is over, the community grieves as one family.

Abron funerals are also community affairs, but so
are political decisions, visits by friends and strangers,
annual feasts, marriages, and even the raising of children. The sense of community goes beyond village
boundaries, and all Abron feel part of a culture. When
they can, they travel, particularly the men, and visits to
the far corners of Abron territory are common. Even
the market is a place where Abron from different villages meet to exchange information and renew friendships. There is no alienation in Abron society, except
for those few who are accused of witchcraft. No one is
lonely. The sick and old are cared for by relatives, and,
if there is no family, by age-mates and village notables.
When Abron migrate to the city in search of work, they

go to live in Abron neighborhoods, where they feel at home and are fed and clothed by members of their own ethnic group. When they find work, they contribute money to their relatives and friends. Even in the city, the social network established from infancy continues until death and even beyond, under circumstances far removed from village life.

The Abron conception of man is closer to the views of modern biology than that which centuries of the Judaeo-Christian philosophy have imposed upon our own culture. The Abron see the human community in the context of a wider set of relationships. Human beings are part of a unified system that includes the entire natural (and supernatural) world. Of course, this conception is based on metaphysical concepts different from both Western science and Western religion, but because Abron cosmology does not separate human from nature, it provides the basis for good natural ecology. Through the centuries, the Abron have come to understand their environment and to exploit it without upsetting the delicate balance that exists among species. This knowledge translated into practice is bolstered by an ideology which, in its own way, sees nature as an ecosystem.

The Abron, however, are now perched on the edge of violent, perhaps catastrophic change. Since the introduction of cash crops forty years ago, they have decreased their fallow to ten years on the savanna and seven years in the forest. It is already too short for adequate regeneration of the land. The introduction of cash crops with a long growing cycle has made village settlement more permanent and probably forces people to go farther afield to farm (although they claim that farms are far from the village only to protect them from sheep and goats). The money economy has affected the Abron in other ways as well. Most significant has been the breakdown of the lineage system and the development of private property. There is evidence that this has increased social tensions and the frequency of witchcraft.

The Abron have already become consumer-oriented. The government has encouraged the construction of standard cement rectangular houses with corrugated-iron roofs. Motor bikes are becoming more and more common. Even automobiles have made their appearance, although not yet in Diassenpa. I have already mentioned the advent of the transistor radio. In addition to such basic but recently created needs for industrially produced goods (fuel, sugar, and salt), the Abron have become almost exclusively dependent upon manufactured cloth.

To date, the Abron are well off in terms of the local and the national economy. Their environment contains both savanna and forest land, and they are able to grow a wide variety of cash and subsistence crops. The harvest season of coffee and cacao comes during the winter, when the yams have already been set up in their storage racks. There is no conflict between subsistence labor and labor for profit. As yet, the Abron do not sell yams in large quantities, and those few that are sold, generally find their way into the local market and remain within the immediate system of distribution. There is pressure, however, to sell yams on a wider scale, and commerce with Abidjan has begun.

The Abron labor system, which in the past was dependent upon slavery, now relies upon hired labor. The richer men already hire many non-Abron to work their fields. Private property has rapidly produced an unequal distribution of wealth, which will, no doubt, widen the separation between those Abron who hire others and those who will continue to subsist on the basis of an increasing marginality or be forced to migrate to the city and become absorbed into the developing industrial proletariat.

When cash-cropping replaces subsistence-cropping, that is, when yams in large quantity are sold to the city, the Abron will become dependent upon the market for their own food. The wider adoption of manufactured goods, including foods, will lower the nutritional standards of the poorer members of the society. Already,

many Abron have replaced the vitamin A-rich palm oil,
which can be produced locally, with nutritionally inferior peanut oil bought in the trading stores.

Manioc, which is easy to grow and can be planted on
the same fields for many years without rapid soil deple-
tion, is beginning to make its appearance. Inferior to
yams in nutritional value, it can only contribute to the
degradation of the Abron diet and the general health of
the population.

In terms of national statistics, in the years to come
the Abron will make their contribution to a rising
standard of living in the nation as a whole. Some of
them will even become rich, but the future will convert
the majority into peasants and industrial workers. For
the latter, at least, the statistics of earned wages within
the cash economy will show an increase in income, but
with a loss of independence—above all, economic independence. The Abron will become detached from their
harmonious world and victims of the modern industrial
system. All of this will be fueled by consumerism.
Abidjan is full of attractive goods. Wage earners will be
able to buy some of the items and thus fulfill new
dreams and desires. A rise in buying power that is
bound to accompany the increasing industrialization of
the country will convince many that they, too, can
someday become rich and comfortable.

A new elite is developing in the Ivory Coast. Some
Abron will become part of that elite. Already, many
speak French; parents are sending successful sons on to
the lycée in Abidjan and even to the university. Abron
country is in an ecologically rich part of the Ivory
Coast, and early wealth is bound to be translated into
further capital accumulation. The new elite will divide
this wealth with the old colonists, who have discovered
that neocolonialism is cheaper than the previous form
of domination. The presence of the French and other
foreigners is very obvious in Abidjan. Many of the
larger businesses, including the rapidly expanding
building industry, are under the control of outside
investors. A new, African riviera is on the drawing

boards as a suburb of the city. When completed, it will have living space for 120,000, including 7,500 hotel beds. As in other parts of the world, a burgeoning tourist industry is making profits for foreign investors.

Anthropologists have long been accused by some of standing in the way of progress. We wish, it is said, to guard the old way of life in a world that is rapidly eliminating the very substance of our subject matter. We are said to thrive on quaint customs and superstitions, and to take unto ourselves the task of deciding what is good for people.

I am sensitive to these criticisms but must reply that tribal customs frozen in time for the tourist camera frighten me more than the development of national pride along with respect for diversity in ethnically varied countries. Customs preserved to maintain the outward appearance of "primitiveness" lose all vestige of meaning. Their only function is to verify for Europeans that they are the economic and intellectual masters of the world.

Besides, I do not see how anthropology could really stand in the way of change. Nonetheless, I am saddened by the rush into a world in which a viable system of human values will be sacrificed for profit. The only changes in Abron society that I can see as positive are the introduction of Western medicine, which (along with native practice) provides more-comprehensive therapy for prevalent diseases, and the ending of slavery, which has unfortunately been replaced by a form of exploitative wage labor. I doubt that any of the material items introduced into the local economy except the rather primitive mass-transportation system are going to be worth the dislocation they will cause the society and the local environment. I am not happy at the prospect of seeing the Abron become peasants and laborers in a national system that generates tremendous inequalities of distribution.

If the Ivory Coast were struggling toward a different kind of nationhood—a nationhood in which the old dignities would be maintained as the old inequalities were eliminated, in which the local African systems of respect and care in the communal context were preserved —then I would be for change. What worries me is the possibility that the Ivory Coast and many other African countries will become locked into the world economic system as the providers of raw materials and tourist attractions: countries in which the difference between rich and poor will widen and the sum total of human misery increase. This is not the future I want to see for the grandchildren of Afua Morofyé and Tchina Kofi.

Afterword 1990

As I write this it has been exactly thirty years since I first began fieldwork among the Abron. I have not been back to the Ivory Coast since 1973. In Diassenpa and Amamvi a whole new generation has reached maturity. I have, sadly, lost contact with my African "family" and friends. A few letters were passed between us, but correspondence over the years has waned to nothing. At present, the Ivory Coast is going through a political crisis caused largely by falling coffee and cocoa prices on the world market and the inflexibility of a government that has been in power ever since independence. No doubt this crisis has affected the lives of the Abron. They are part of a nation that is, itself, part of the world system. The Ivory Coast, one of the richest countries in Africa, remains nonetheless a part of the third world, dependent as it is upon world prices for its major exports, coffee, pineapple, and cocoa. The events of recent history, particularly the world economic crisis and the international debt it has caused, have had catastrophic effects on many countries in Africa, Latin America, and Asia.

Anthropology as a discipline has changed a great deal since the 1960s when this book was written. When I did my first fieldwork, ethnographies were written in what is known as the *ethnographic present* (a kind of timeless *now*) which suggested to the reader that the things, events, and lives described had always been and always will be as they were set down by the anthropologist. As Johannes Fabian put it in his book *Time and the Other* (Columbia University Press, 1983):

> Anthropology emerged and established itself as an allochronic discourse; it is a science of other men in another Time. It is a discourse whose referent has been removed from the present of the speaking/writing subject. This 'petrified' relation is a scandal. Anthropology's *other* is,

ultimately, other people who are our contemporaries (p. 143).

At the time I wrote *When the Spider Danced* yet another problem existed in a large segment of the discipline. This was the myth, fortunately already waning in the 1960s, that there existed somewhere in the world a pristine "primitive" society untouched by contact with other cultures. We now realize that such a society was part of our own mythology. Since the rise of civilization in different parts of the world, the world's cultures have always been in direct or indirect contact, with a few temporary exceptions.

Imperial expansion and trade have been the rule, not the exception. Some cultures have been dominant, others subservient, but the flow of ideas and materials has always been a two-way street. The elimination of the notion of the pristine society from anthropology has liberated us to work where we please with, of course, the informed consent of those among whom we live and study.

Since 1984, my wife Sonia and I have been working with a group of French farmers who successfully resisted the French government's attempt to take their land away for the expansion of a military base from 7000 acres to 35,000 acres. During their nonviolent struggle, which lasted from 1971 to 1981, the lives of these farmers changed forever. They have opened up to the world and have developed a strong sense of justice, particularly for the underdog. We have been careful in this project to avoid the built-in sense of timelessness Fabian mentioned by anchoring our research in local and national history and paying attention to events in their diachronic (through time) dimension. We own a house about 30 miles from our field site, the Larzac plateau in southwestern France about 30 miles from the Mediterranean, where we have spent summers and three sabbatical years since 1967. We have been involved in this research since 1984, spending each summer until 1987 in the field and then a twenty-six month period from June 1987 to September 1989 continuing the study.

Sonia and I speak French well, and we are both students of French culture. As they grew up, our children spent most of their summers in our village and we feel very much a part of French rural life as, at the same time, we remain Americans. This long term experience in a foreign culture we know well has been very different from the short time I spent in the Ivory Coast so many years ago. Now I know a great deal more about anthropology — how it is done and how to do it. The book to come from our French fieldwork will be less personal than this one, but better informed and more sophisticated than *The Spider*, written as it was by a young anthropologist just starting out in his professional career. I hope each book will end up serving a different purpose. *When the Spider Danced* is meant to introduce readers to the problems faced by a young and inexperienced anthropologist when he first undertakes fieldwork.

When I wrote this book the ethnographer was seen as a silent "other" always present — even participating — in the culture, but invisible in the pages of the published results. Of this Fabian says:

> Anthropological discourse often exhibits (or hides, which is the same) conflict between theoretical-methodological conventions and lived experience. Anthropological writing may be scientific; it is also inherently autobiographic (p. 87).

Here I am less guilty of following the mode criticized by Fabian, although I do not wish to exaggerate my consciousness in the 1960s of the problem he refers to. While the autobiographical nature of ethnography *is* something I was conscious of when I set out to write *When the Spider Danced* (this book was one of the early anthropological accounts in which the anthropologist, presenting data on a culture, also speaks of his or her personal experiences and, more importantly, how the process of fieldwork unfolds), Fabian is also referring to the heavy influence one's own culture and theoretical orientation have on what might seem to be the mere reporting of simple facts. Facts are not simple, particularly when they are drawn from a context foreign to the ethnographer. Anthropological writings are not collections of facts, but interpretations and explanations of data gathered (and in a real sense, data missed) in the course of fieldwork. My discipline is now quite conscious of this. While this problem clearly needs to be discussed, books written to analyze other anthropologist's fieldwork and results are now the mode in anthropology, sometimes, and ironically in my opinion, at the expense of new and original field research which, I believe, should remain the major focus of the discipline.

Before I leave the problems inherent in the presentation of anthropological data as ''fact'' I must refer to another important concept, *cultural relativism*. Since Franz Boas, the founder of American anthropology, the discipline has been dominated by this notion which demands objectivity in research. The anthropologist in the field and, later, when writing up his or her materials, must gather and record the ''facts'' through observation without imposing value judgments on the material. In this way, scientific objectivity is supposed to be achieved. But humans are a tricky species. They both do and think about what they do. This is equally true of the anthropologist at work and the people studied. The anthropologist, whose task is to explain the reasons behind the ''facts'' — their origin or cause and/or how one fact fit together with others making the ''whole'' of a culture — is forced to impose a set of *interpretations* on the data in order to make any sense out of them. Thus, for this reason also, there *are* no objective facts. What we see is colored by our conscious and unconscious interpretations, by our own personalities and cultures. In our search for objectivity it is, perhaps, we who have been the naive ''primitives''!

In recent years a large group of anthropologists have taken up these important methodological problems in an attempt to delimit what anthropology can and cannot do. Some believe that anthropology can only be interpretive in nature. For them, in different degrees, anthropology should be akin to literary analysis rather than a science of human behavior. Some in this school see ethnographies as nothing more than texts, to be interpreted the way critics interpret novels. Finally, a few members of this school even see cultures themselves as texts to be read by anthropologists *cum* literary analysts. Others, like myself, believe that anthropology can and should, while remaining acutely aware of the problems of objectivity, remain true to its scientific origins and attempt to explain as well as interpret the reasons behind human cultural behavior.

The specific work among the Abron, only partially described in *When the Spider Danced*, was an attempt to study their hygiene and medical problems. The theoretical orientation behind the study was borrowed from the notion of adaptation in evolutionary biology. I wanted to see if societies facing specific health problems would, through time, at least partially adapt to them by developing cultural practices that make sense in terms of what we, in our own culture, call "public health and preventive medicine." This idea was innovative at the time I did my research because, up to then, the subdiscipline of medical anthropology had concentrated on medical beliefs and treatment practices (often magical in nature) rather than what are rather mundane everyday behaviors. I assumed, on the basis of what I knew of public health in my own culture, that everyday behaviors—behaviors which, nonetheless, are the stuff of preventive medicine (diet choices, hygiene, and so on)—affect health and disease in rather spectacular ways. My hypothesis, put simply, was that when certain adaptive (disease-preventing) behaviors occur—even by chance, even unconsciously—they are "rewarded" by nature. Infection rates drop. Conversely, when behaviors are maladaptive, because they increase the risk of disease, nature "punishes" those who engage in them by making them sick. Infection rates go up.

But my notions about "native" public health were more complicated than this. I also assumed that some routes to disease were "straighter" than others, that is to say, the causes and prevention of certain diseases would be easier than others to work out in a culture without a germ theory of disease. For example, diseases spread directly from person to person with characteristic visible symptoms would be more likely to be prevented (or at least inhibited) than diseases with ambiguous symptoms spread by insects.

Although I was somewhat naive in not taking into account what the *social* costs of certain behaviors (avoiding friends, for example) might be, my data show that Abron daily behavior is indeed medically adaptive for the predicted kinds of disease conditions. Even though the Abron do not have an official western style public health system, they do have cultural practices unrelated in their own minds to health that serve to prevent disease.

In a course entitled "Culture and Biological Determinism," one I have been teaching over the years at Columbia University, I try to make students aware of two major problems. First, that while all human beings are shaped by both biology and culture too much simple-minded, popular, or "folk," biology has been accepted as fact by the public at large. It is this folk-biology that tempts some people to exaggerate or distort the way biology determines our contemporary behavior and gives rise to racism and sexism. Second, that it is common for humans to define people outside of one's own group as an "other" and to attribute false, usually negative, characteristics to that "other." Thus, in the Middle Ages, a mythical "wild man" was invented onto whom negative feelings created *within* society were projected.

The world has changed a great deal since I began my anthropological studies. The pace of change has increased in just the past two years (1989-1990) at a dizzying pace. We used to think that our profession was doomed to die out with the disappearance of those small-scale "pre-literate" societies typically studied by anthropologists in the past. We now know that the true anthropological task is the study of the human condition in all of its cultural forms whether this be in the third world, in our own culture, on the land, or in the cities. Anthropology remains, for me at least, an exciting field which I can recommend to anyone interested in the cultural behavior of our peculiar species.

Index